I0800123

IMAGES
of America

ETOWAH COUNTY

VOLUME II

IMAGES
of America

ETOWAH COUNTY

VOLUME II

Mike Goodson
and Bob Scarboro

ARCADIA
PUBLISHING

ISBN 978-0-7385-1625-7

Published by Arcadia Publishing
Charleston, South Carolina

Printed in the United States of America

Library of Congress Catalog Card Number: 98-86142

For all general information contact Arcadia Publishing at:
Telephone 843-853-2070
Fax 843-853-0044
E-mail sales@arcadiapublishing.com
For customer service and orders:
Toll-Free 1-888-313-2665

Visit us on the Internet at www.arcadiapublishing.com

CONTENTS

ACKNOWLEDGMENTS

To document a county's rich history is an undertaking that requires many people to complete. To the many people who have taken time to share a photograph or a story of the early days of our county's past a great deal of thanks is given. The writers of this book are also indebted to the staff of the Gadsden Public Library, whose help made this publication possible.

INTRODUCTION

Etowah County is nestled in the foothills of beautiful Lookout Mountain in Northeast Alabama. This county is one of the smallest in land area in the entire state, although its history is as interesting and colorful as any other in Alabama. The county's early history would revolve around the commerce and trade on the Coosa River and later the railroads through Attalla and Gadsden.

The early people living in the area known today as Gadsden were settlers around the stop on the stagecoach route known as Double Springs. The first house built in the Double Springs area was used as a stagecoach stop and is still standing near the intersection of Third Street and Tuscaloosa Avenue. Later, in 1846, the first riverboat to navigate and clear the Coosa River for riverboat traffic landed in the area. The *Coosa*, captained by James Lafferty, stopped in the Double Springs area, and shortly after, a town began to grow. The early settlers attempted to name the town Lafferty's Landing, but the town was eventually named Gadsden in honor of James Gadsden.

Several enterprising individuals were among the early settlers in Gadsden, and the town began to grow at a rapid rate. Among these individuals were Col. R.B. Kyle, Capt. James Elliott Jr., Gen. Daniel Turrentine, and Judge John H. Disque. Colonel Kyle and Captain Elliott founded and operated many of the early industries and businesses while General Turrentine was a wealthy businessman and land owner who felt the need for many strong churches in the city. Judge John H. Disque was a local attorney who served as a judge and later the first president of the Gadsden City Board of Education. Judge Disque worked his entire life to bring a strong public education to the Gadsden area.

Etowah County was originally formed from lands from six surrounding counties—Blount, Cherokee, Dekalb, Calhoun, Marshall, and St. Clair. Known originally as Baine County, it was abolished less than a year later and reformed with the name changed to Etowah. Gadsden was chosen as the county seat, although on two separate occasions Attalla has attempted to lure the seat of the government away to the "Junction." On one occasion, a single vote kept the county seat in Gadsden. The county has had three beautiful courthouse buildings during the last 130 years, the first two of which were located between Fourth Street, Broad Street, Court Street, and Locust Street in downtown Gadsden. The present site of the Etowah County Courthouse is located on Forrest Avenue between Eighth and Ninth Streets, the original site of the Kyle and Elliott homes. These were two of the most recognizable mansions in Etowah County, in a time when Forrest Avenue was lined with beautiful homes from Twelfth Street to Seventh Street. This is primarily a business district today.

Life in Etowah County is both fast-paced and lazy at times. Residents of this county met the call when their country needed them the most. Over the years, men and woman have served in all branches of military service. During World War I, the Rainbow Division, formed in part by local National Guard units, won worldwide fame in combat in Europe. During World War II, citizens of Etowah County worked at the Gadsden Ordnance Plant as well as several other industries that were necessary for the war effort. Camp Sibert, which was located in Etowah County, was important in training troops in chemical warfare and was also a Prisoner of War Camp. When Camp Sibert closed following the war, the city of Gadsden acquired some of the land, including the Gadsden Airport.

Following World War II, life returned to normal in the county with new businesses opening throughout the area. The late 1940s and the 1950s saw movie theatres again becoming popular places to go for the young people. Gadsden's beautiful Pitman Theatre and Attalla's Etowah Theatre opened shortly following the end of the war. These theatres became instant competition for the Princess and Gadsden Theatres. In all, there have been over 40 movie theatres located in Etowah County over the years. In 1946, the first drive-in theatre in the county would open to bring new dimensions to movie-going in the area. The Tower Drive-In and later the Grove Drive-In opened to pave the way for the Rainbow, Rebel, Ranch W, and Lake Rhea Drive-In Theatres in Etowah County.

Etowah Countians have always enjoyed local sporting events. The Gadsden Pilots were a local baseball team whose games were well-attended and enjoyed by many. The local high schools have brought home several state championships in football, basketball, and baseball over the years. Several local athletes have gone on to play professional sports following outstanding college careers, while others have played professional baseball following graduation from high school.

Etowah County Volume II also features the businesses that have shaped the community. Fond memories can be recalled in the local drive-ins and fast food restaurants of the 1960s and 1970s where baby-boomers spent Friday and Saturday nights. The ever-changing downtown business districts are pictured during a time when going to "town" was a monumental event for many, and when every building contained a shop or retail establishment of some sort. Also contained in these pages are photographs of some of the many schools and churches that are found in the Etowah County area, and the faces of the many "ordinary" people who play an integral part in the community's growth. Many of these people have stepped up when called upon to make Etowah County a memorable place to live.

The photographs contained in these pages are derived largely from the Scarboro collection. Bob Scarboro has spent much of his life assembling an extensive collection of vintage photographs, which numbers several thousand. Although this volume contains primarily photographs from the Etowah County area, Scarboro's collection has also expanded to cover many cities in Alabama. Through his lifelong profession as a photographer, he has compiled an impressive array of images that bring the history of Etowah County to life. All photographs are from the Scarboro Collection unless otherwise noted.

Another local photographer who has contributed to these pages is Hugh Hall. Hall photographed much of the downtown Gadsden and Attalla areas during the 1950s. The quality of the Hall photographs are exceptional, and his choice of subject matter has helped in preserving Etowah County's local history.

The text that accompanies these images was written by local writer Mike Goodson. A love for local history has prompted Goodson to do in-depth research into several areas of Etowah County's rich history.

One

Street Scenes

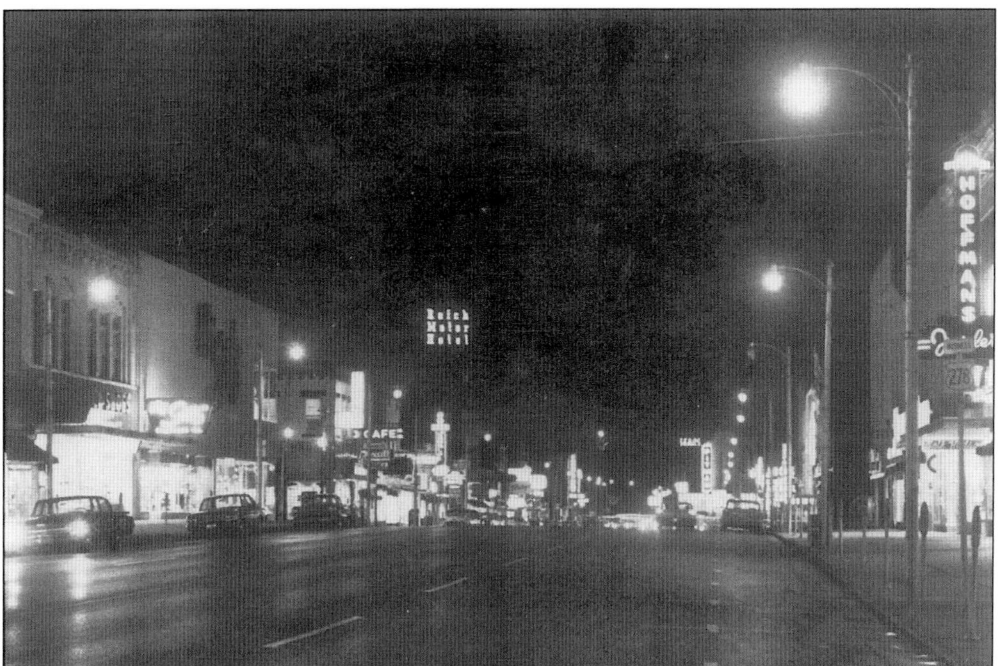

A photo taken in 1964 reveals Gadsden's Broad Street at night. Ike Saks, located on the 400 block, was one of Gadsden's finest clothing stores. Hoffman Jewelers, located across the street, was owned and operated by the Hoffman family for many years. The sign from the Reich Motor Hotel can be seen near the center of the photo.

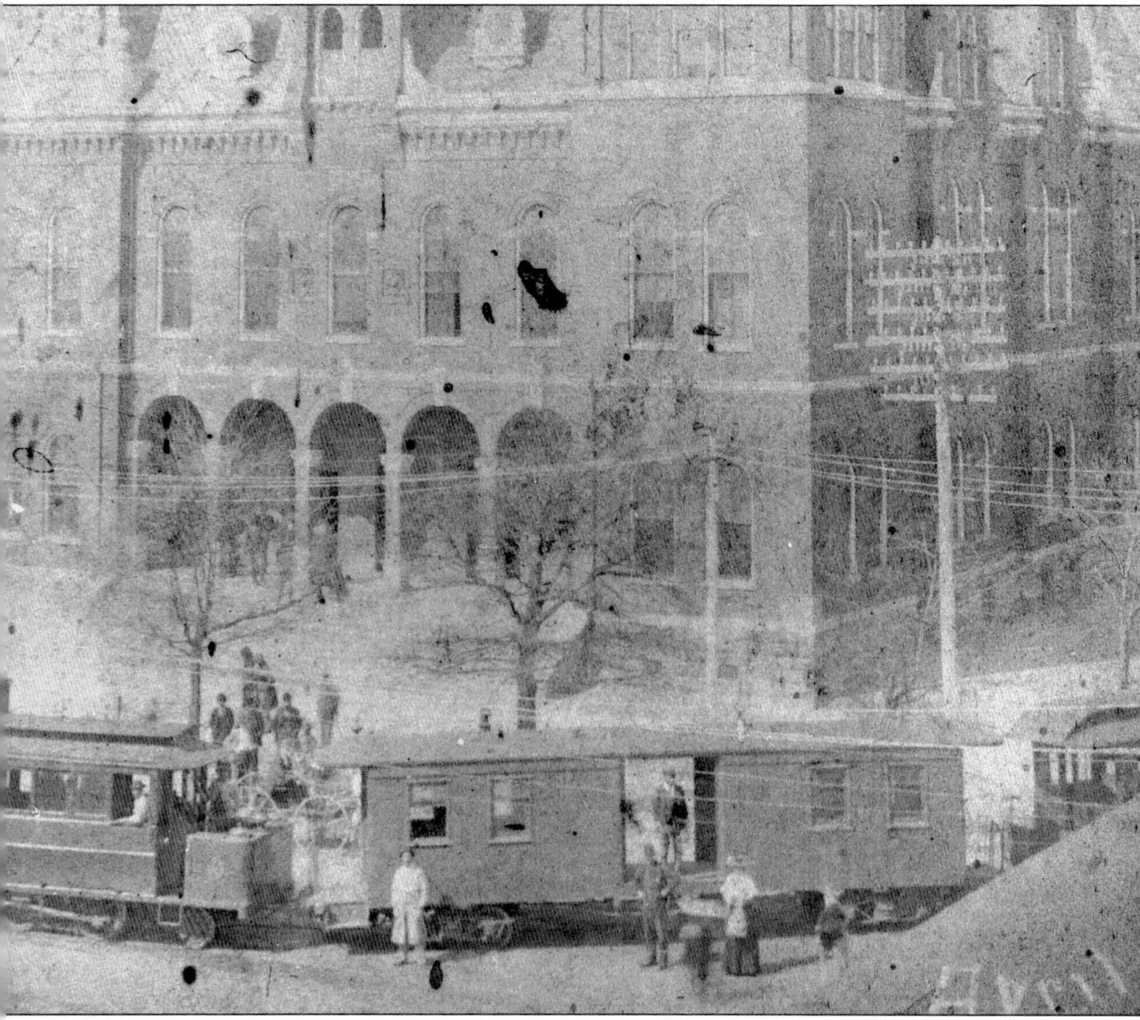

A rare photograph from April 1, 1894, shows the dummy engine that pulled the streetcars from the downtown Gadsden area to Alabama City and Attalla. The dummy line was a small steam locomotive that pulled passenger cars; these engines were later replaced when the streetcar line was powered by electricity. Taken on the corner of Broad and Fourth Streets in front of the Etowah County Courthouse, this image depicts the present site of Railroad Furniture. (Courtesy of Ed Smith.)

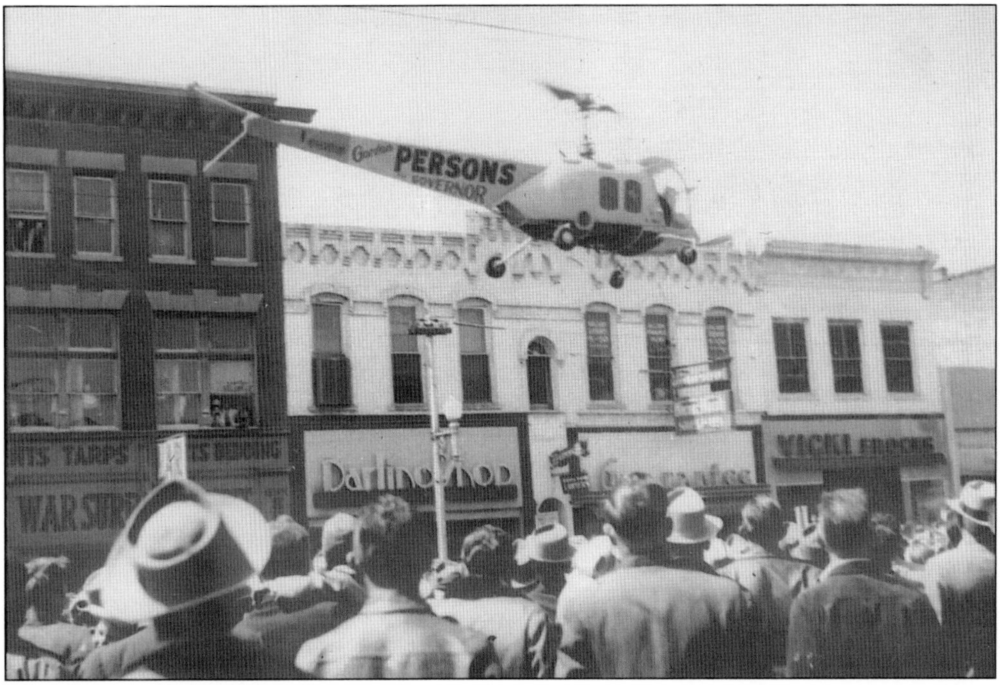

Campaigning for governor of Alabama, Gordon Person made a grand entrance into Gadsden as he landed on Broad Street. All of the stores in this picture have since closed. The War Surplus Store today houses Downtown Gadsden, Incorporated. (Courtesy of Hugh Hall.)

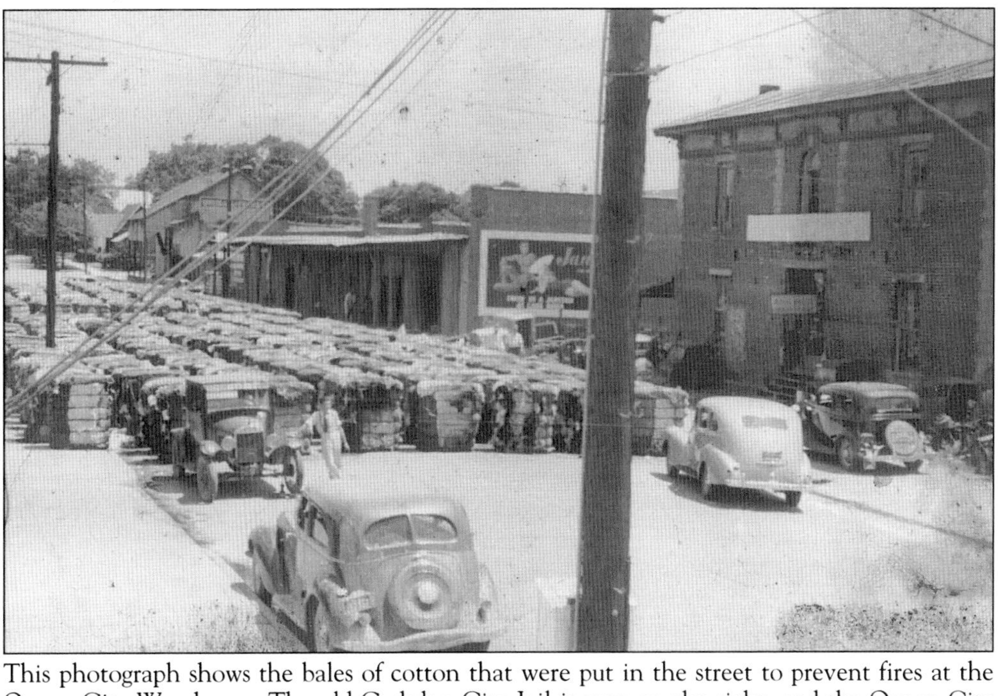

This photograph shows the bales of cotton that were put in the street to prevent fires at the Queen City Warehouse. The old Gadsden City Jail is seen on the right, and the Queen City Gin is located in the background. This image was shot on Chestnut Street between Second and Third Streets.

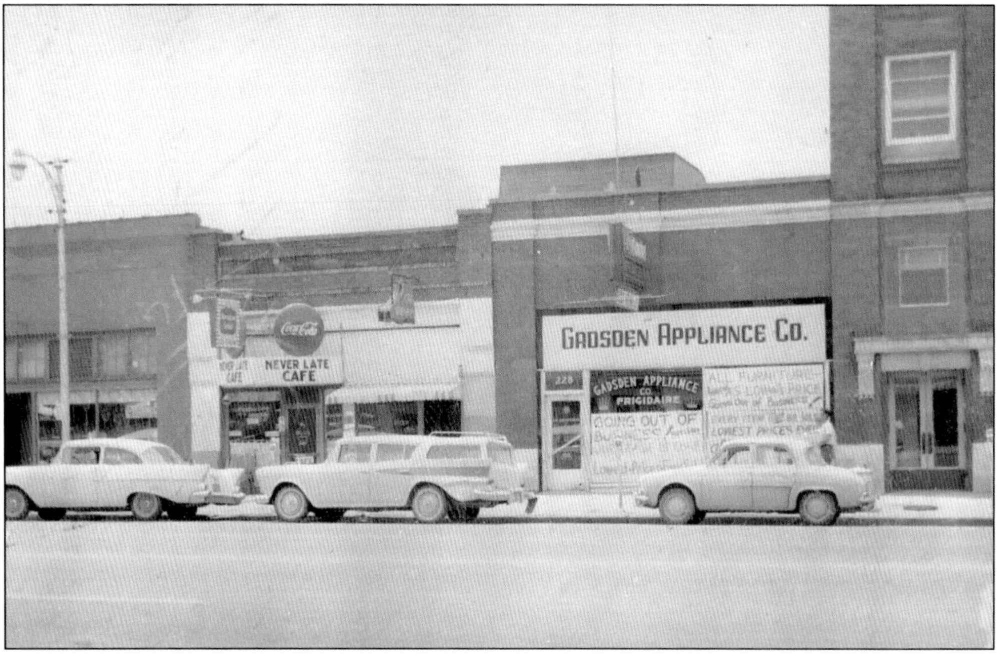

The 200 block of Broad Street included Southern Hardware, the Never Late Cafe, Gadsden Appliance, and the American National Bank when this image was taken in the late 1950s. These buildings have all been torn down and replaced with a new AmSouth Bank and Merrill Lynch office.

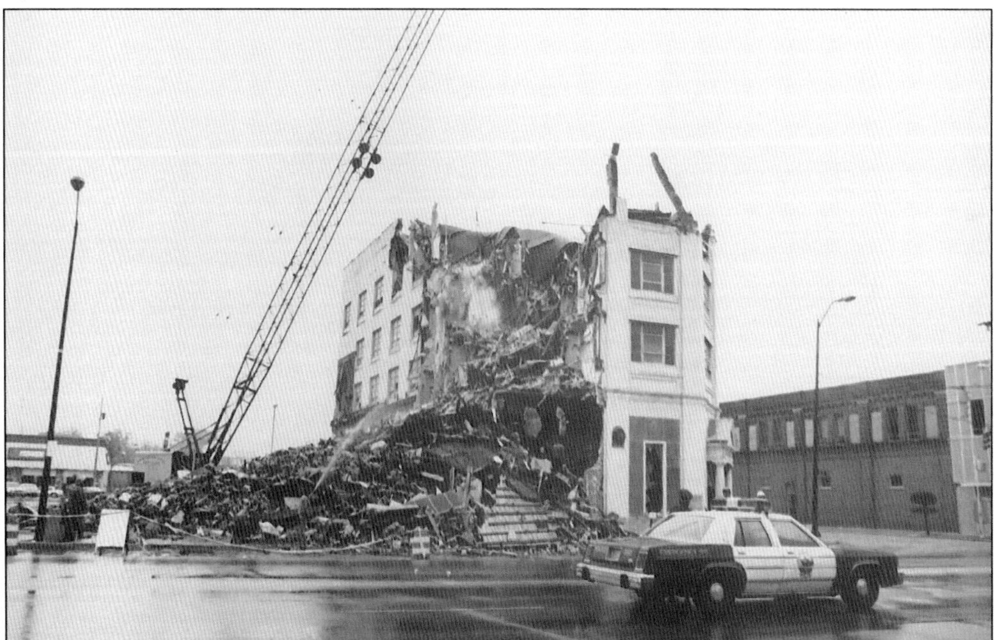

The final walls of Gadsden's American National Bank are seen here being taken down by a wrecking ball. Originally the Etowah Trust and Savings Bank, it once boasted the largest rotating sign in the southeast, which displayed the time and temperature. The bank was torn down to make way for the AmSouth Bank and Merrill Lynch office.

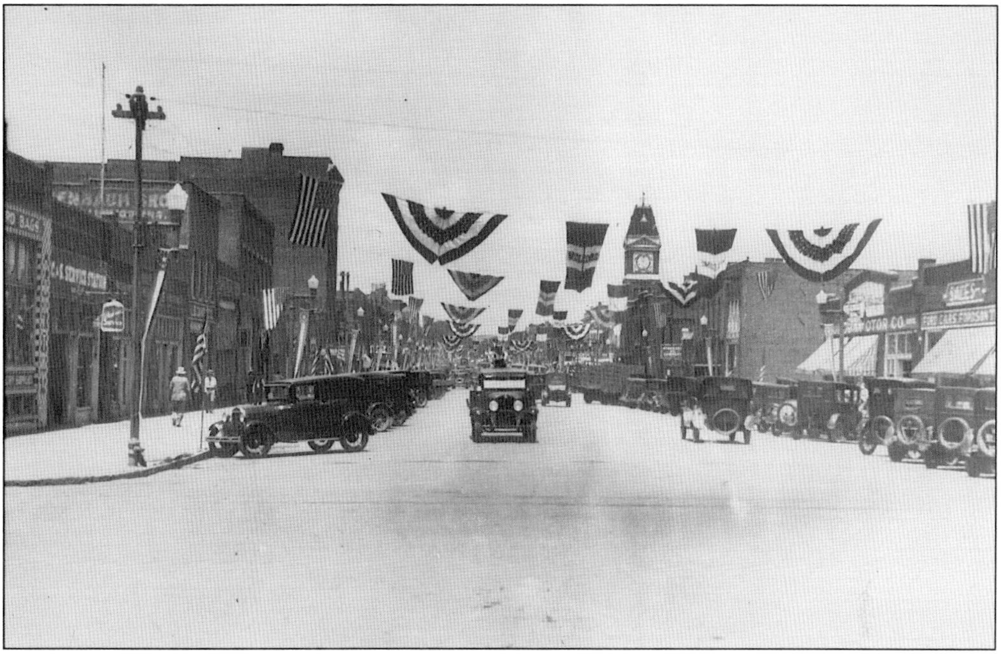

Downtown Gadsden is pictured here on July 11, 1929, the day that Gadsden's Goodyear Tire and Rubber Company plant was dedicated. The entire county celebrated the opening of this plant, which was to become one of the area's largest employers for 70 years. Recent cut-backs at the plant have caused many people to transfer to other plants throughout the southeast.

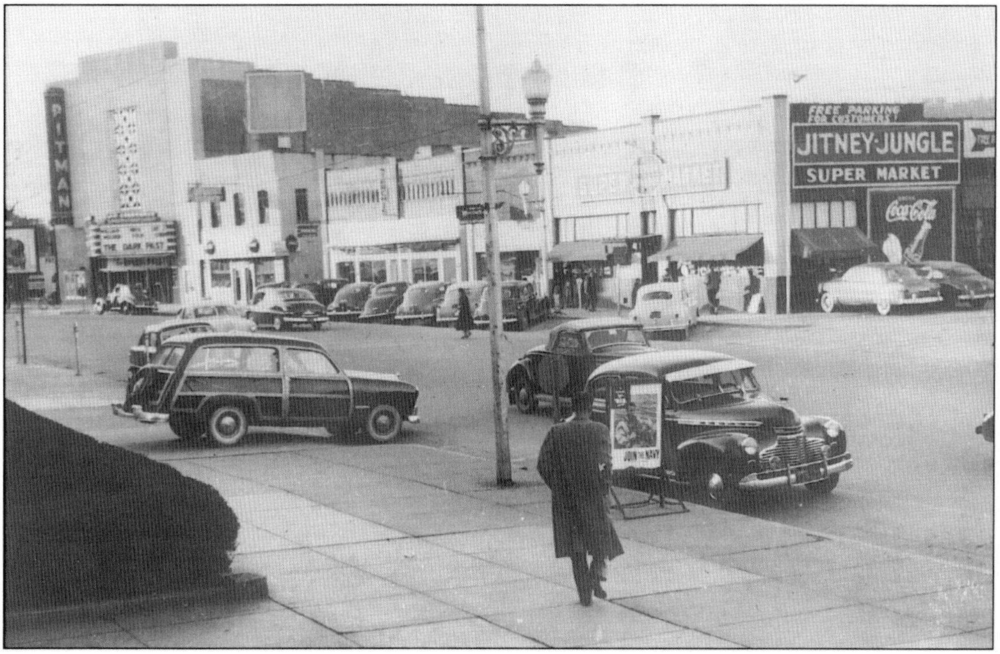

Taken from the steps of Gadsden's Federal Building, this photograph from 1950 shows the north side of the 600 block of Broad Street. The Pitman Theatre, which opened in 1947, is pictured in the upper left-hand corner. It is currently undergoing a total restoration, but all of the other buildings pictured have since been torn down and replaced. (Courtesy of Hugh Hall.)

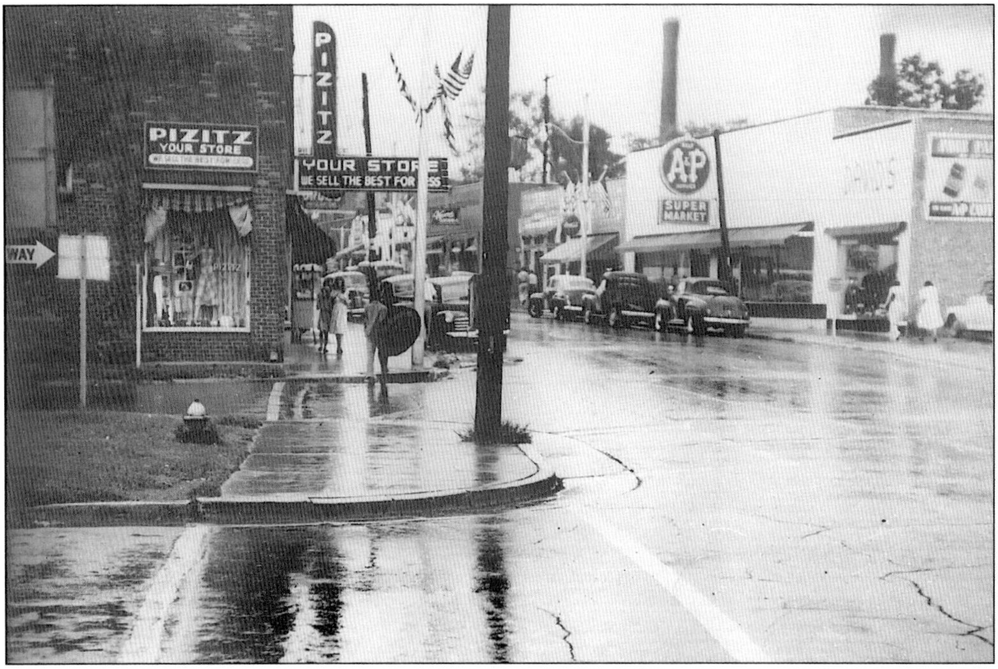

Wall Street, the main business district in Alabama City, is shown here in a photo from 1950. The large smokestacks from the Dwight Cotton Mill can be seen in the background. Alabama City was also the home of a small Pizitz Store. (Courtesy of Hugh Hall.)

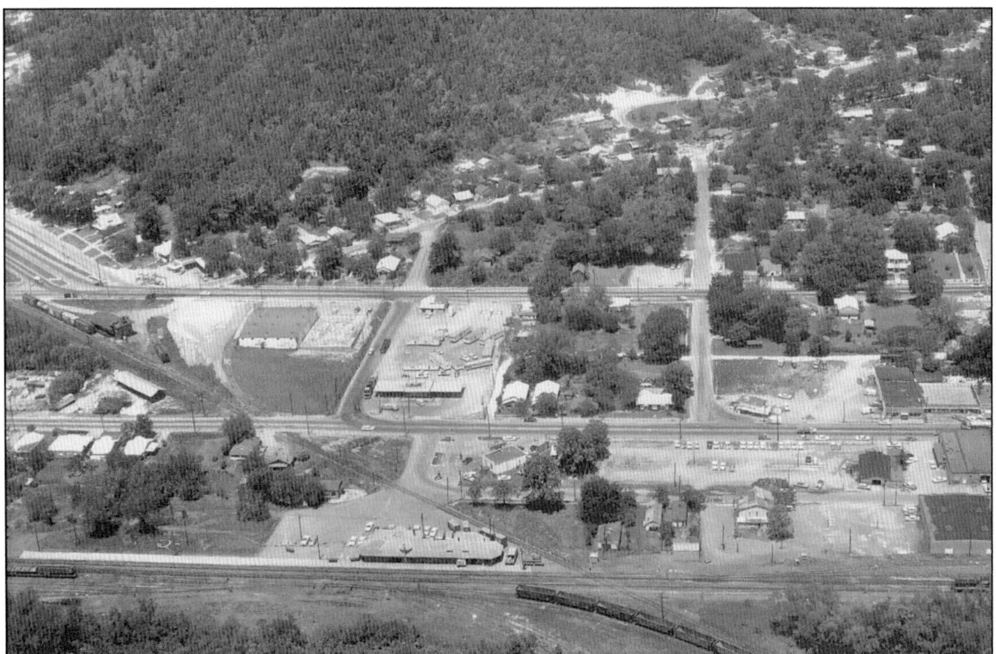

This aerial view shows the railroad center in Attalla, also known as the "Junction" because of the different railroads that came together here. The building at the lower center is the Southern Passenger Depot, and the one in the upper left is the L&N Station. This photograph was taken in early 1960.

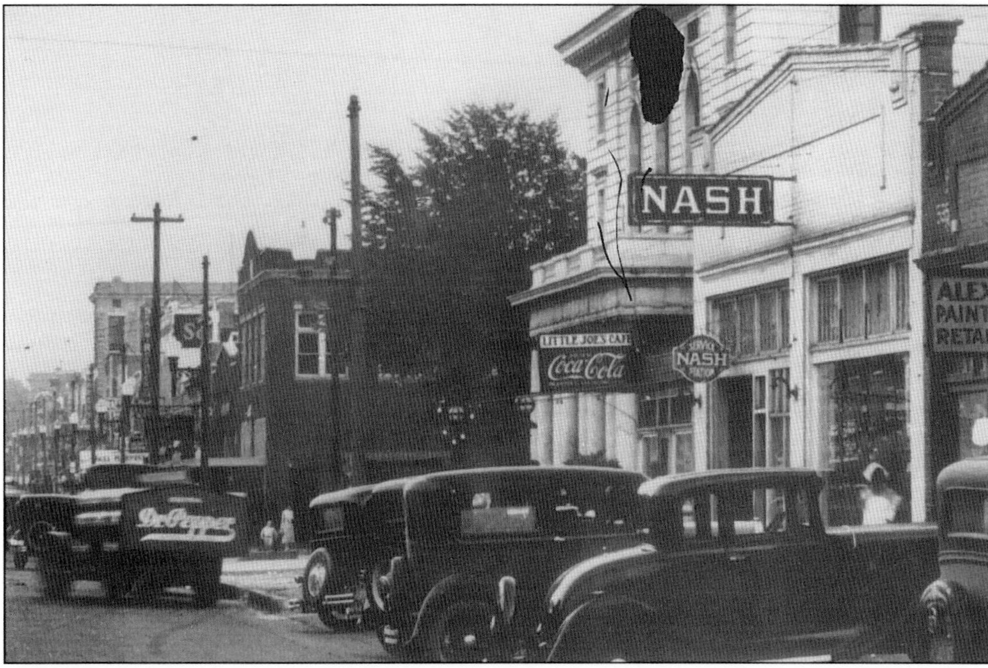

The United States Post Office is shown here in an early 1940 photograph. It sustained moderate damage in a fire in 1958, and a new post office was constructed in 1960. This beautiful Federal Building now houses several government agencies. Also shown in this picture are Little Joe's Café and a Nash automobile dealership.

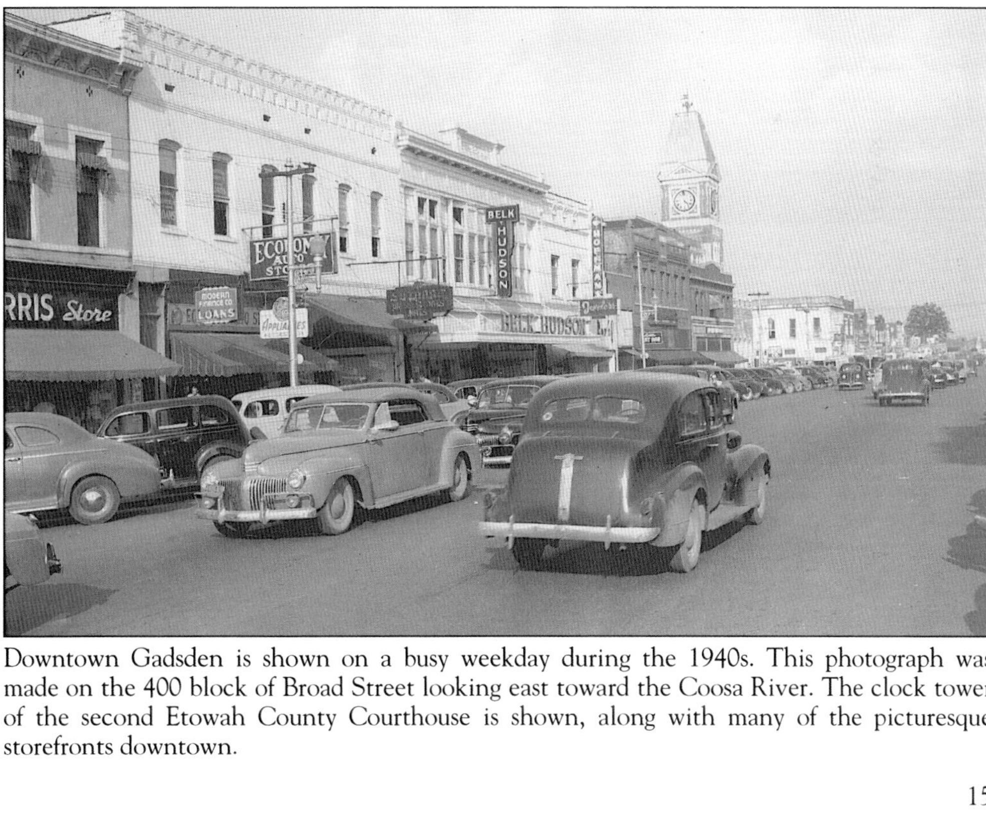

Downtown Gadsden is shown on a busy weekday during the 1940s. This photograph was made on the 400 block of Broad Street looking east toward the Coosa River. The clock tower of the second Etowah County Courthouse is shown, along with many of the picturesque storefronts downtown.

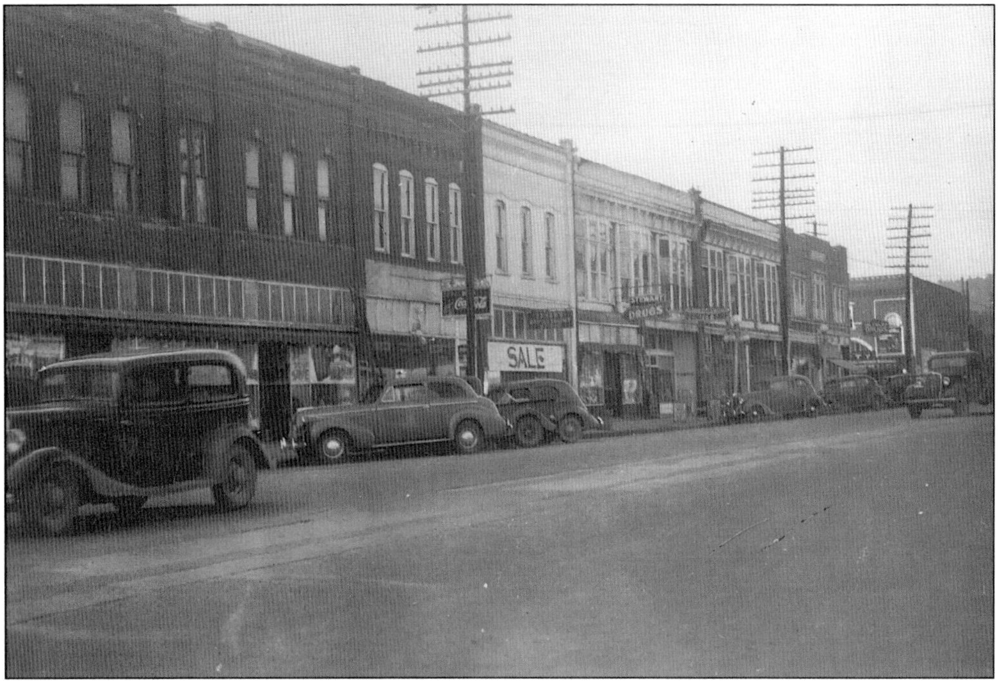

Downtown Attalla is pictured here in a photograph from 1938. Attalla is Etowah County's second largest city. Before it was known as Attalla, this city was also called Newton and the "Junction," because it was a very busy junction of the railroads of Etowah County. Among the buildings pictured here are Stewart Drugs, Walker Drugs, and the Liberty Theatre at the far right.

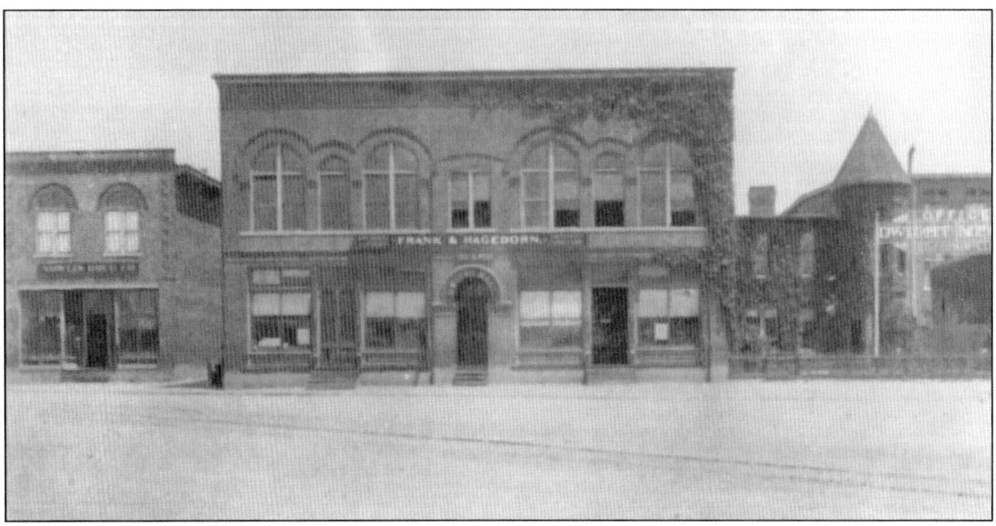

A large industrial center in Etowah County, Alabama City was home to Dwight Manufacturing Company. This photograph depicts Dwight Square at the main entrance to the company, the Nowlin Drug Company, and Frank and Hagedorn, which was the company general store and the mill office. Dwight Hall, the company union hall, was located upstairs.

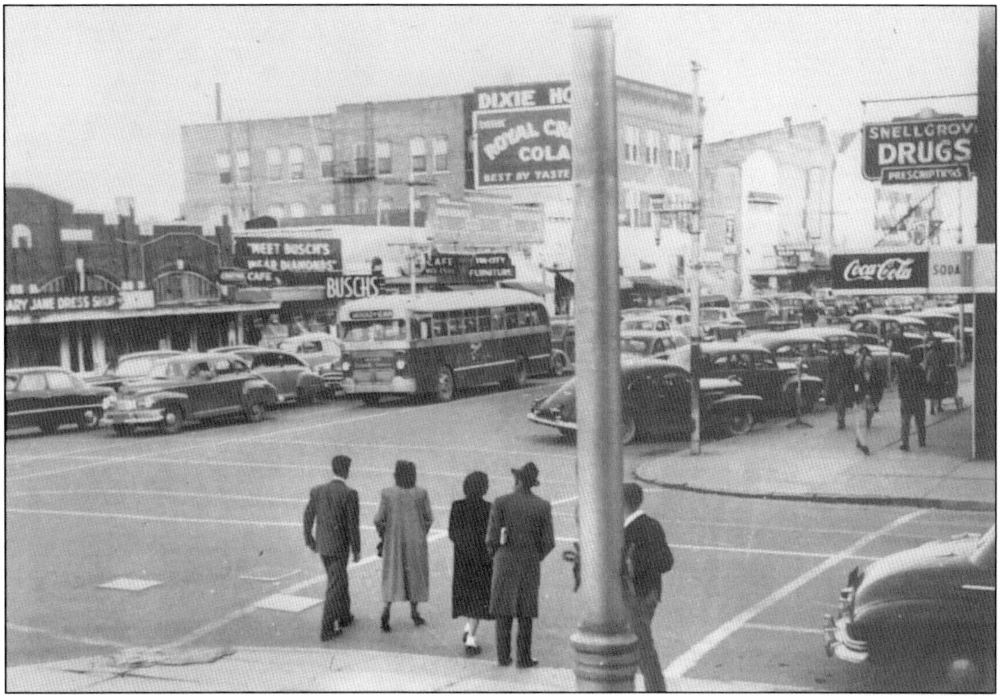

Pictured here is the corner of Sixth and Broad Streets, where Snellgrove Drugs was in operation until 1993. The Dixie Hotel is also shown in this photograph, as well as one of the hourly buses that ran in the Gadsden and Attalla areas. The buses replaced streetcar travel until this mode of transportation became unprofitable. (Courtesy of Hugh Hall.)

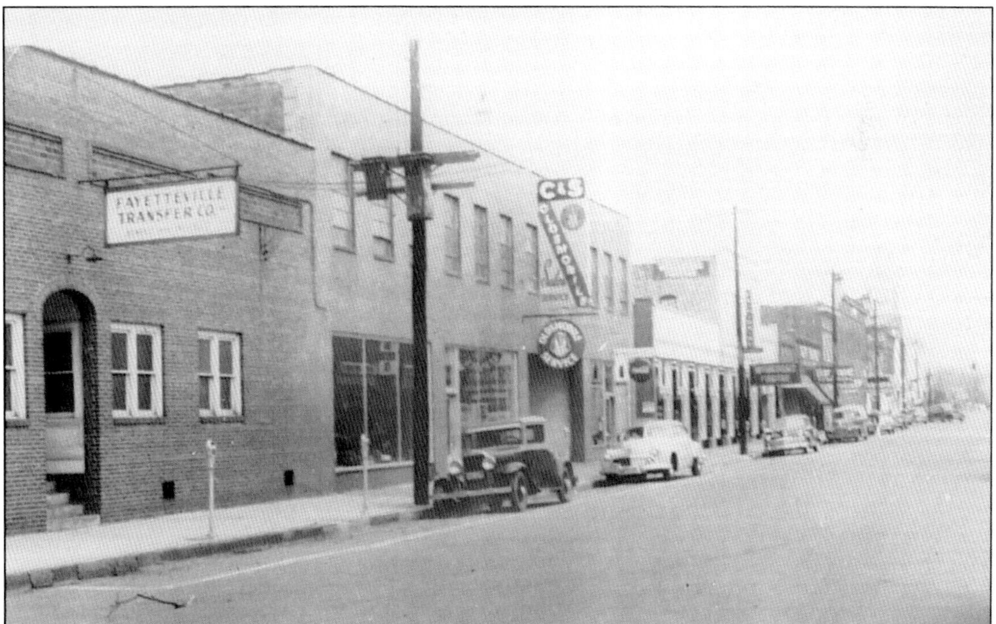

This photograph from 1950 shows C&S Oldsmobile and the Fayetteville Transfer Company. C&S Oldsmobile was a Gadsden car dealership for many years, and was located on the southwest side of Fourth Street. (Courtesy of Hugh Hall.)

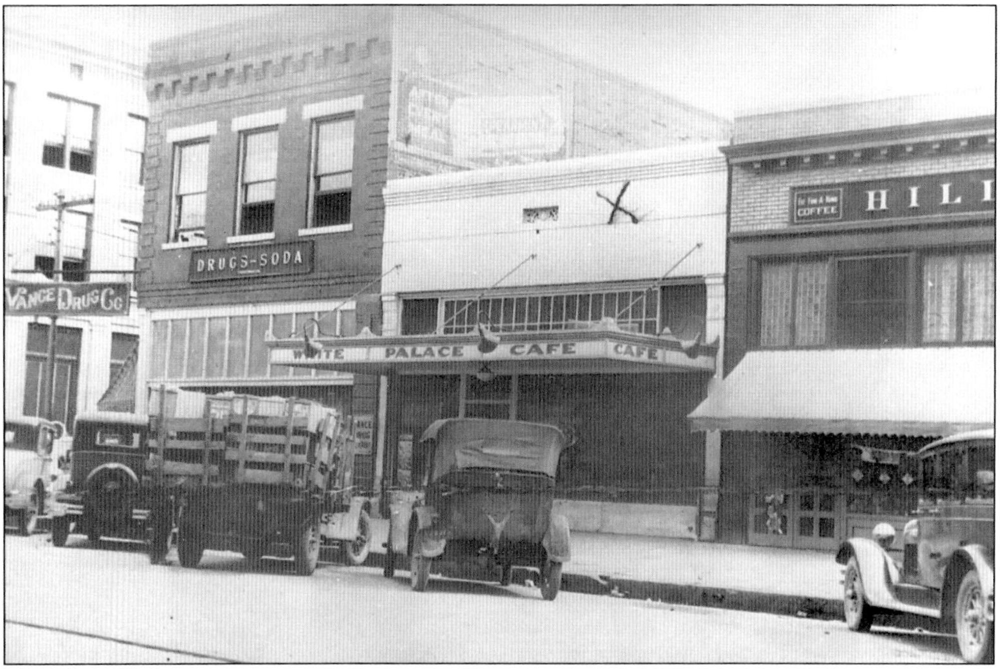

Downtown Gadsden was a busy place during the mid-1920s. The corner of Broad and Fifth Streets was a very popular area with Vance Drug Store and the White Palace Cafe. Hill's Grocery was located next to the White Palace Cafe in the building that housed the Alamo Theatre and later the Lyric Theatre. The Cafe, complete with its beautiful art-deco entrance, is still located on Broad Street.

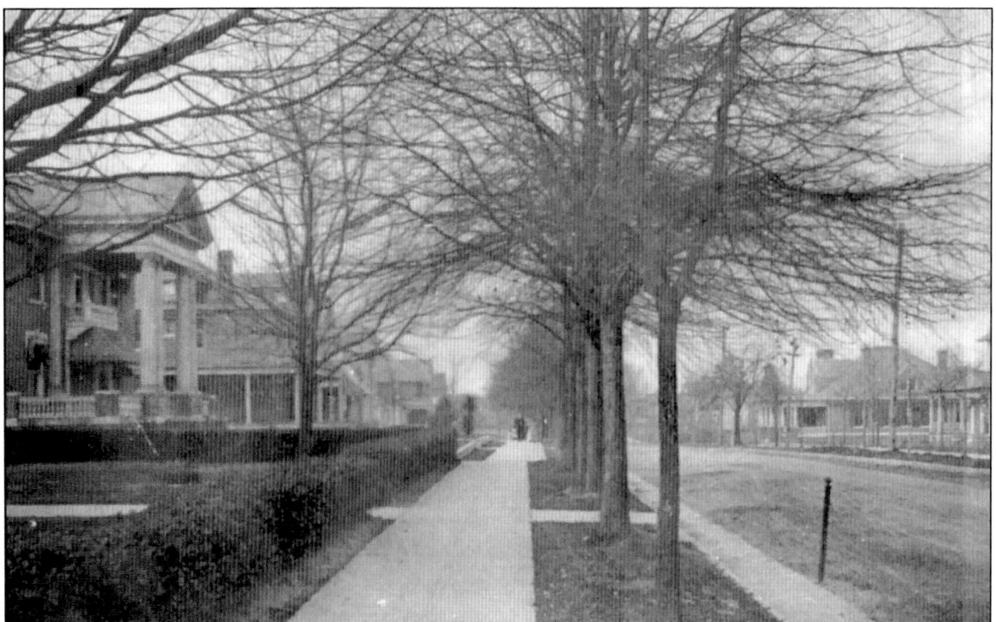
Turrentine Avenue is one of the most beautiful areas in downtown Gadsden. Best known for its elegant mansions and some of the oldest homes in the area, it was originally part of Gen. D.C. Turrentine's farm. General Turrentine was one of the early prominent leaders in Gadsden.

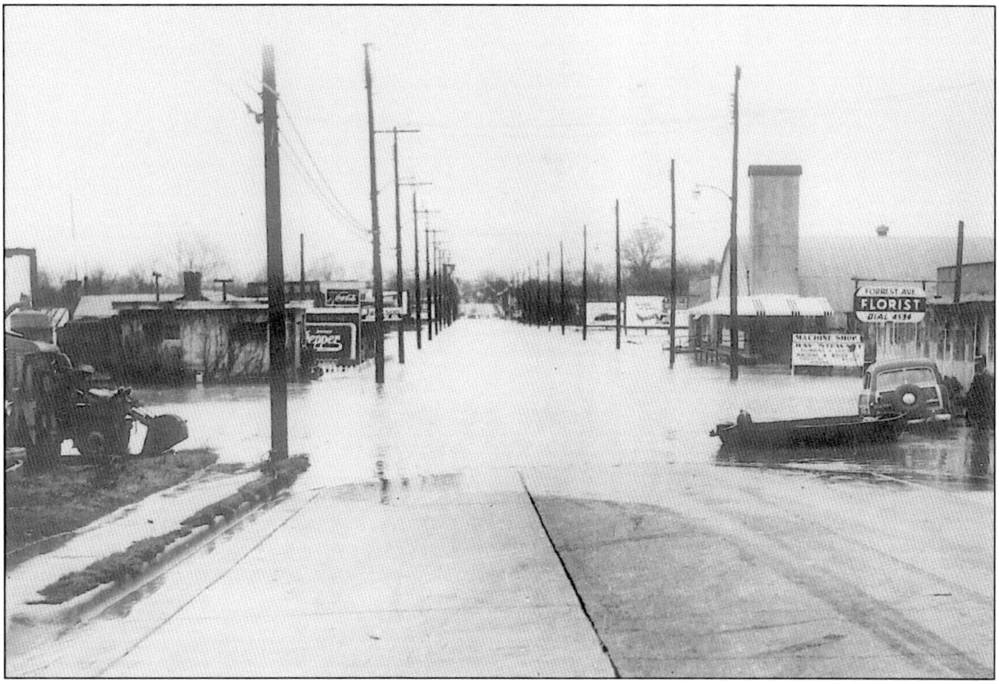

This photograph shows Forrest Avenue at a time when Black Creek was well above its banks. The creek would flood the streets during the spring following heavy rains, and Forrest Avenue, Tuscaloosa Avenue, Chestnut Street, South Eleventh Street, and Rainbow Drive would be closed by several feet of water. During these floods, people would have to go through Attalla and across the mountain to get to town. (Courtesy of Hugh Hall.)

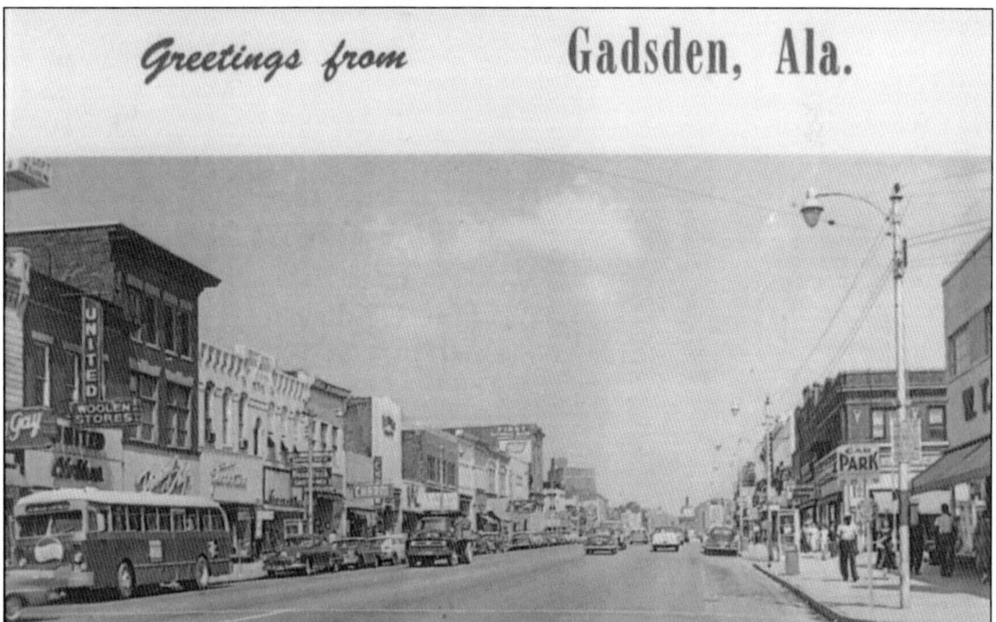

During the 1950s, downtown Gadsden was where Etowah Countians went to shop. Shown in this 1955 photograph are the W.T. Grant store and one of the many buses that ran in the area.

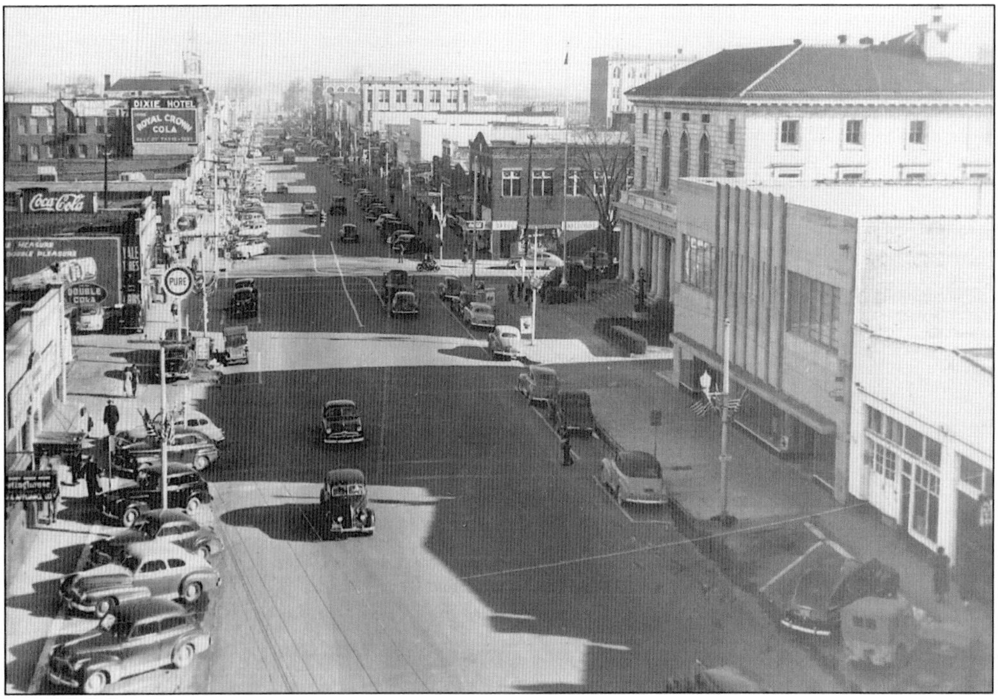

An important area for many people in Etowah County, Gadsden's business district is pictured in this 1949 view of Broad Street. The Federal Building is the large three-story building on the right, with Snellgrove Drug Store located across Sixth Street. A trip to "town" on Saturday was always a big event for people growing up in Gadsden.

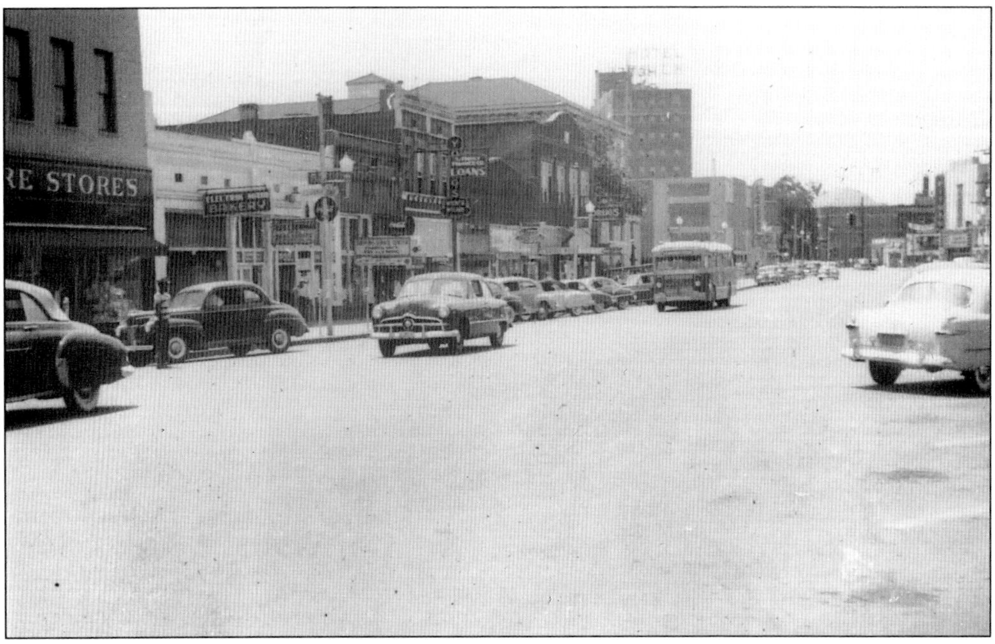

The south side of the 500 block of Broad Street is shown here with views of the V.J. Elmore Store and Snellgrove's Drugstore. Also shown is one of the buses operated by Crescent Motor Lines, and the Reich Hotel, which can be seen in the background.

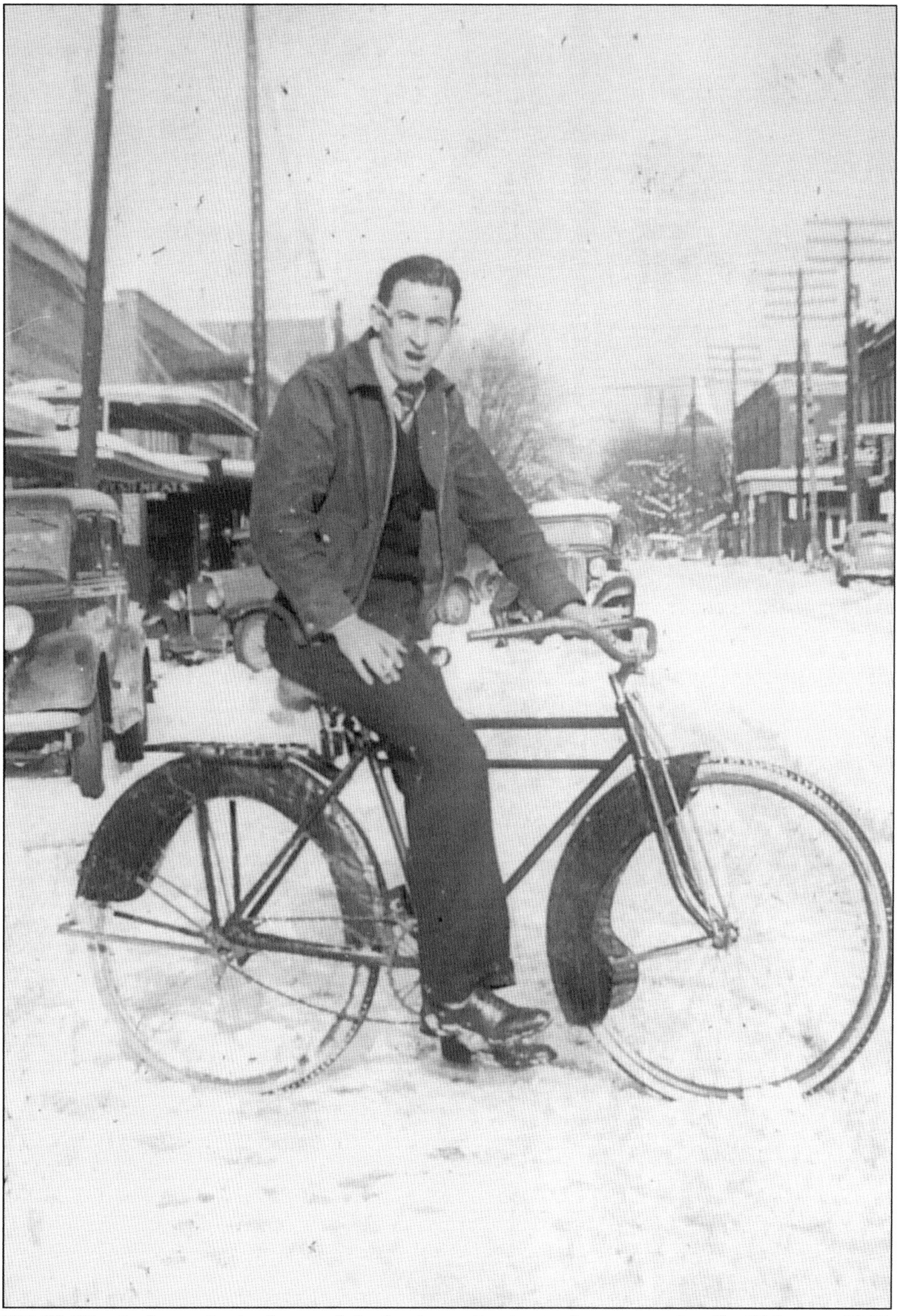

J.T. Phillips is shown in the heart of the business district in downtown Attalla. Taken in 1940, this photograph depicts an unusually heavy snowfall for Etowah County. A total of 12 inches of snow crippled the entire county for a week.

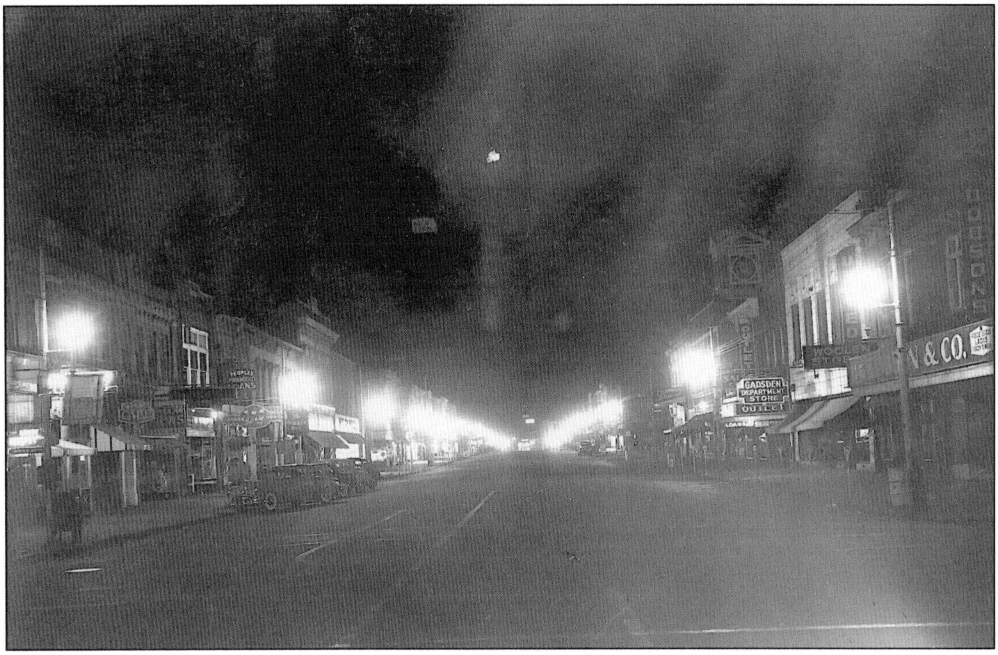

The late 1940s and early 1950s saw a great business district grow in the downtown area of Gadsden. Many stores, restaurants, and theatres were located on or near Broad Street. Although many of the businesses diminished during the 1970s, the 1990s have brought a great turnaround for this district.

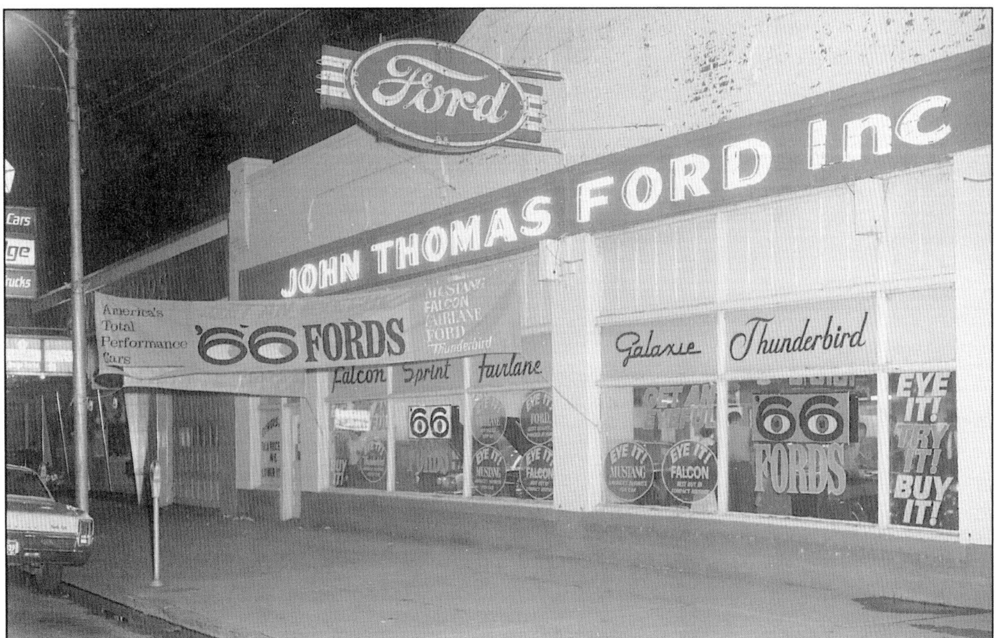

A family-owned business, John Thomas Ford was located on Broad Street for many years. John N. Thomas was the owner, with John D. Thomas as president, Mercer Thomas as vice president and treasurer, and Henry Ella Barrow as secretary. The family later retired and closed this business in 1983.

Two

SCHOOLS AND CHURCHES

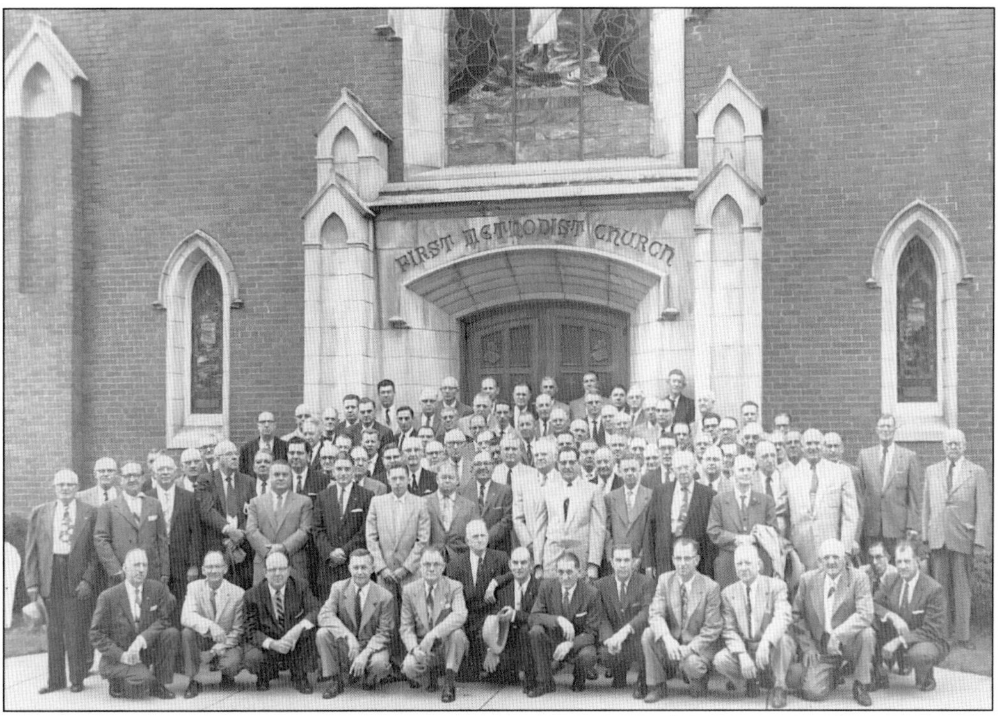

This 1950 photograph shows a men's Sunday school class at Gadsden's First Methodist Church, the city's oldest church, located at the corner of Fifth and Chestnut Streets. The church has recently undergone a major expansion with a huge addition being built.

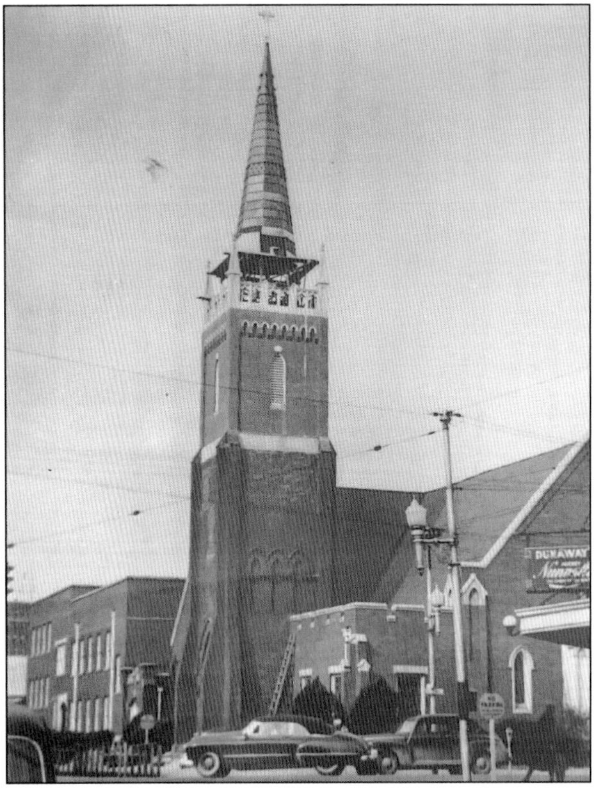

Another view of First Methodist Church from 1948 shows the church following some renovations. Still active in the community after over a hundred years, the First Methodist Church congregation is one of Gadsden's strongest.

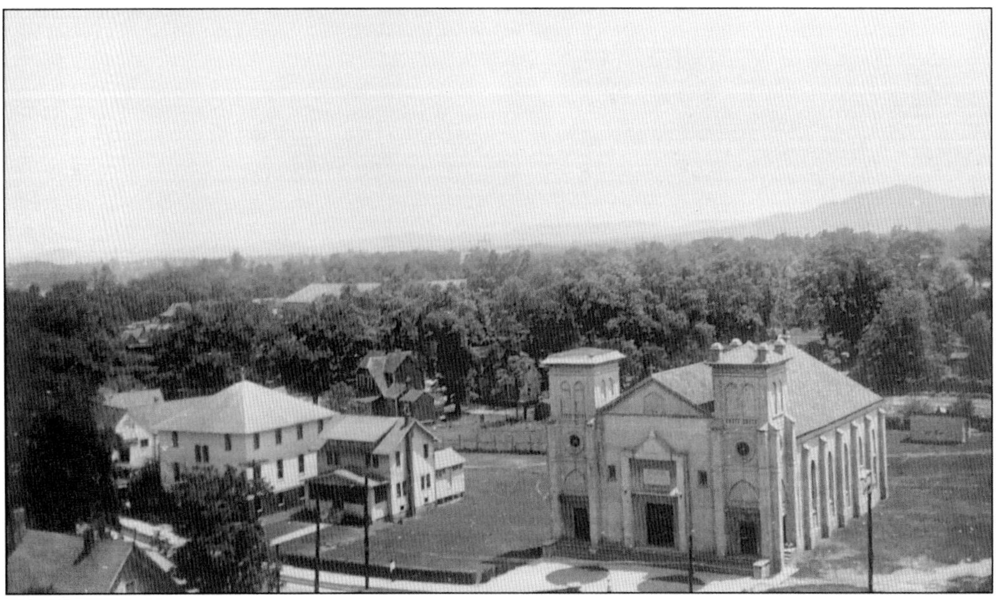

The Saint James Catholic Church is shown here with the rectory located next door. On the left is the Saint James Catholic School. The rectory was a mail-order home that could be ordered from the Sears and Roebuck catalog. The church moved into this new building, located at the corner of Seventh and Chestnut Streets, in 1927.

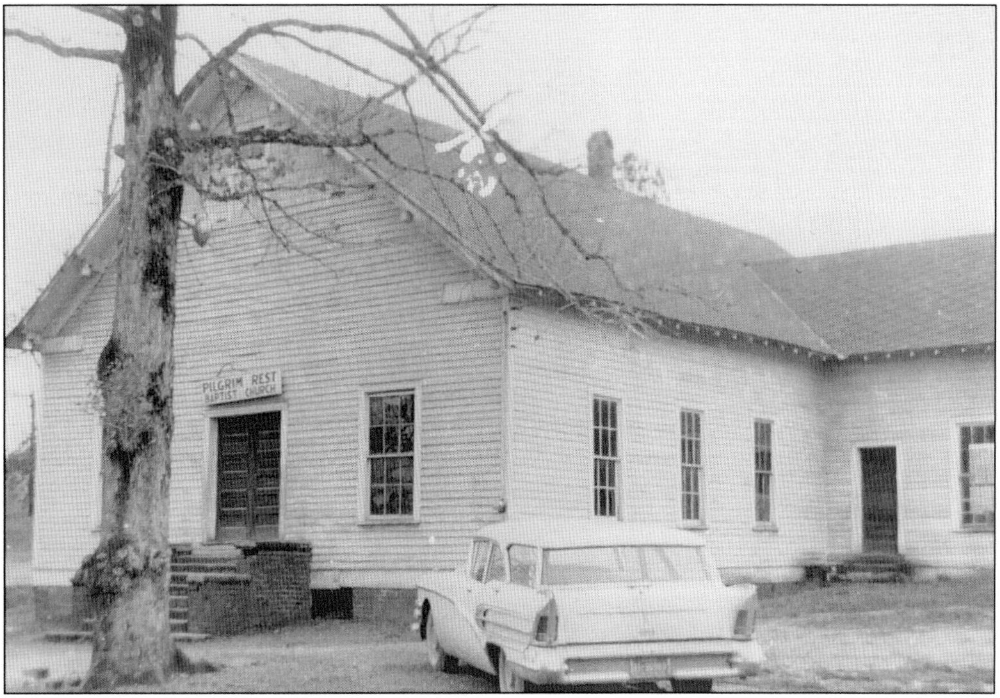

Etowah County boasts many fine churches of all denominations and sizes. This photograph from the late 1950s shows the Pilgrims Rest Baptist Church, located in the Southside Area. From its beginnings, Etowah County has founded many churches.

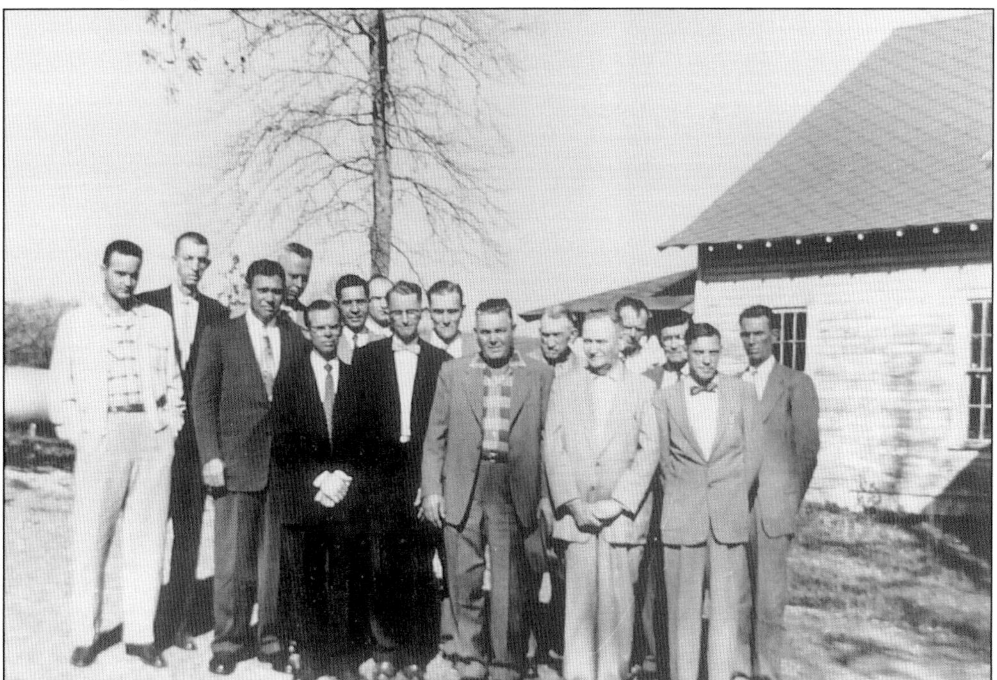

Another view of the Pilgrims Rest Baptist Church depicts a men's Sunday school class. Strong Sunday school programs are indicative of the many churches found throughout the county.

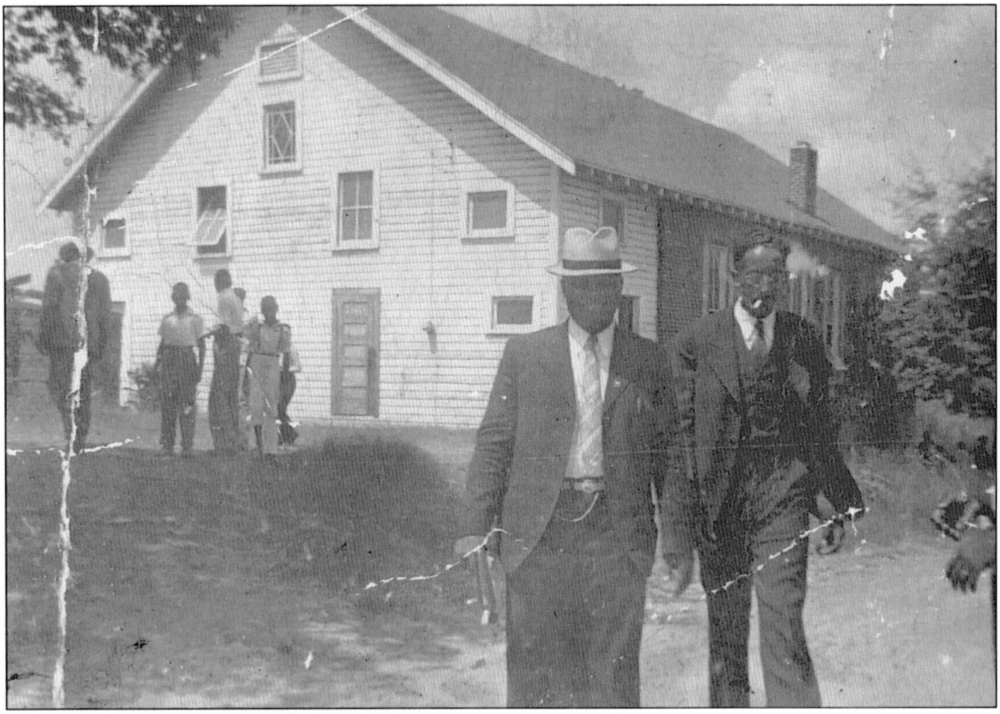

Several members of the congregation of the Galilee Baptist Church are shown here after a service in the summer of 1916. Located on the corner of Sixteenth and Peachtree Streets in West Gadsden, the Galilee Baptist Church was one of the many strong black churches in the area.

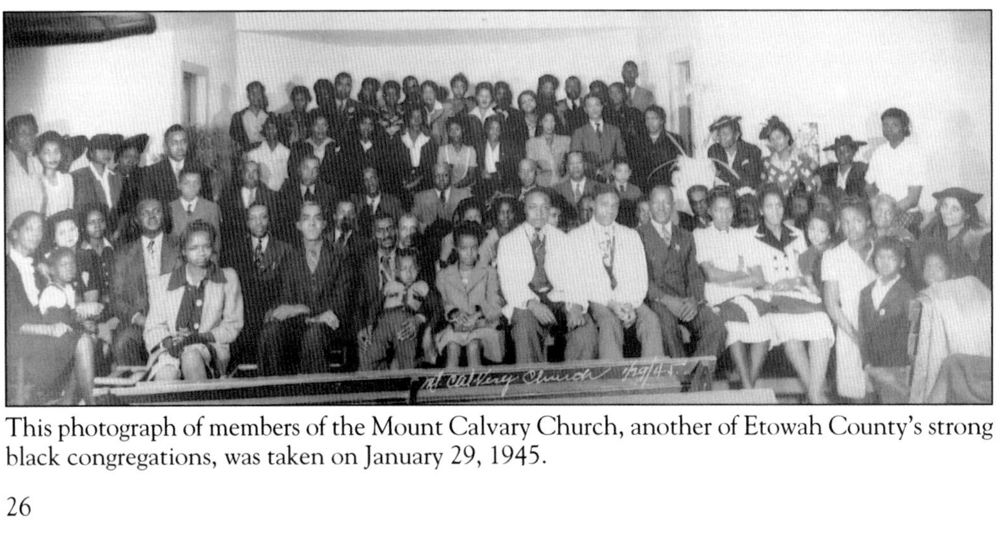

This photograph of members of the Mount Calvary Church, another of Etowah County's strong black congregations, was taken on January 29, 1945.

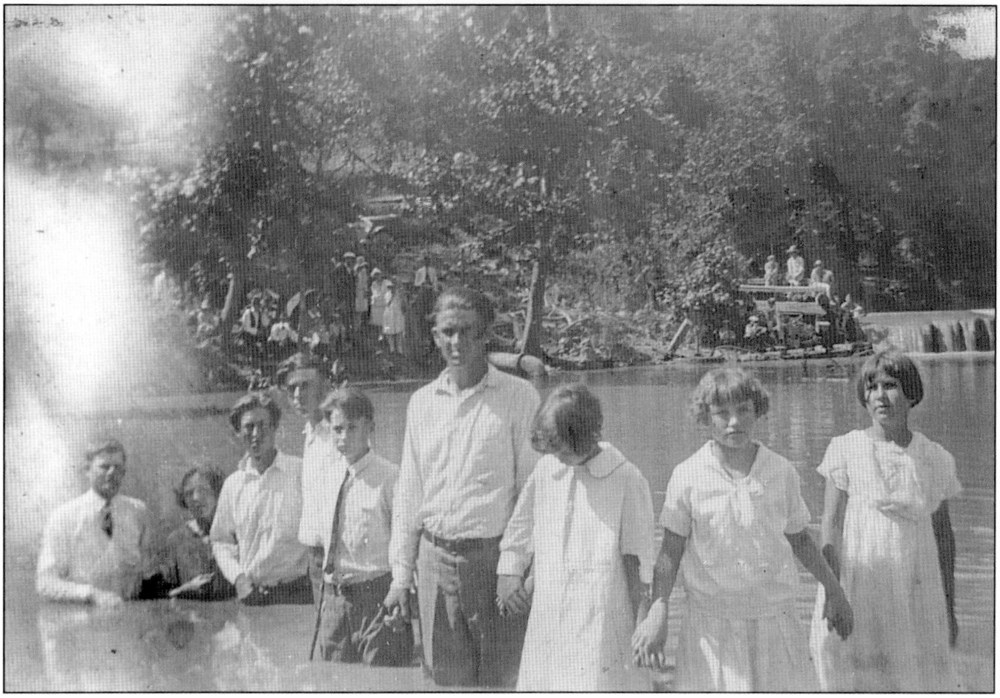

Clayton's Mill Pond, located on Black Creek in Alabama City, was a popular place for local churches to hold baptisms. Shown here are members of the Forrest Avenue Cumberland Presbyterian Church baptizing new members in 1925. Baptisms were often held in creeks and lakes in the days before churches had indoor baptisteries.

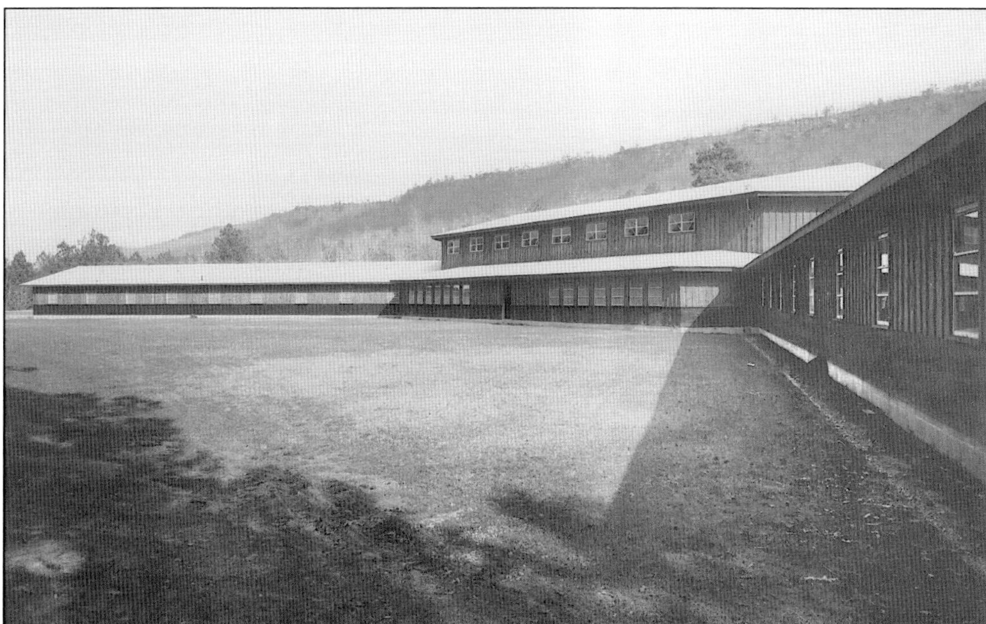

The Lodge Building at Camp Sumatanga is shown in this photograph from early 1960. Operated by the Methodist Church and a popular place in the Etowah County area, the building burned during the early 1960s.

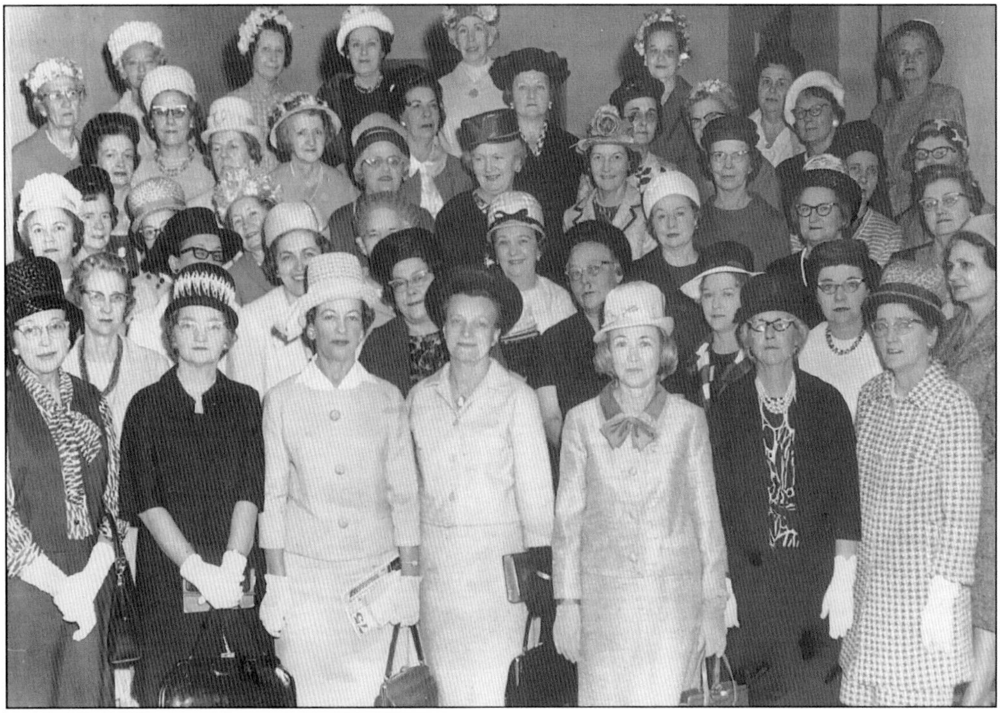

"True, Trusted, and Tried" is the motto of the Tri-T Sunday School Class at the First Baptist Church of Gadsden. This is one of the many adult classes, photographed here in 1966, at the downtown church. Note that many of the ladies are wearing hats and gloves.

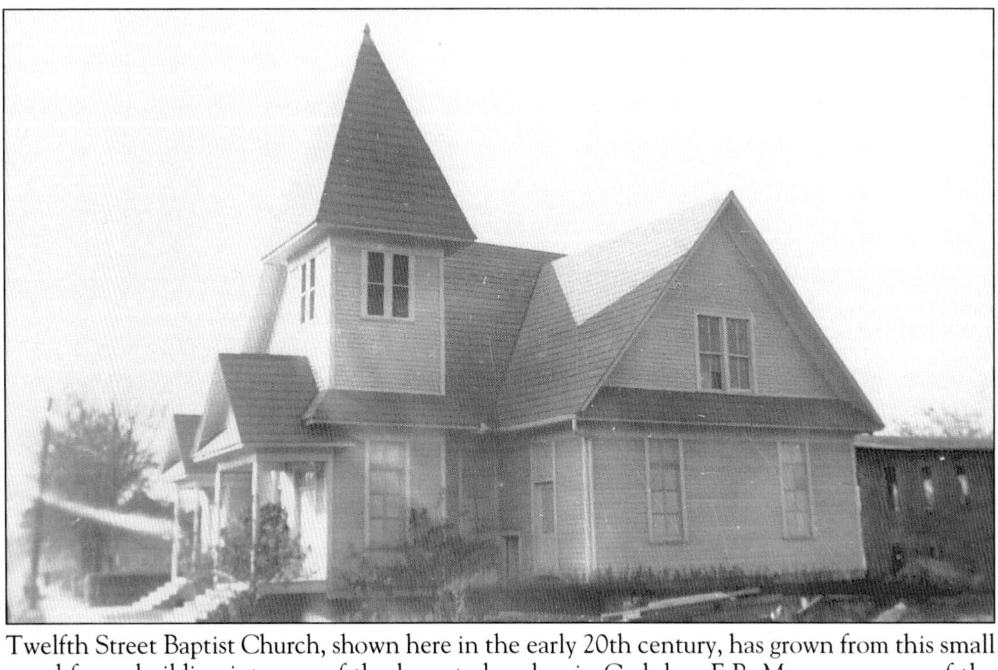

Twelfth Street Baptist Church, shown here in the early 20th century, has grown from this small wood frame building into one of the largest churches in Gadsden. E.B. Moore was one of the church's early pastors. Moore later served several other churches in Etowah County, and was also elected circuit clerk.

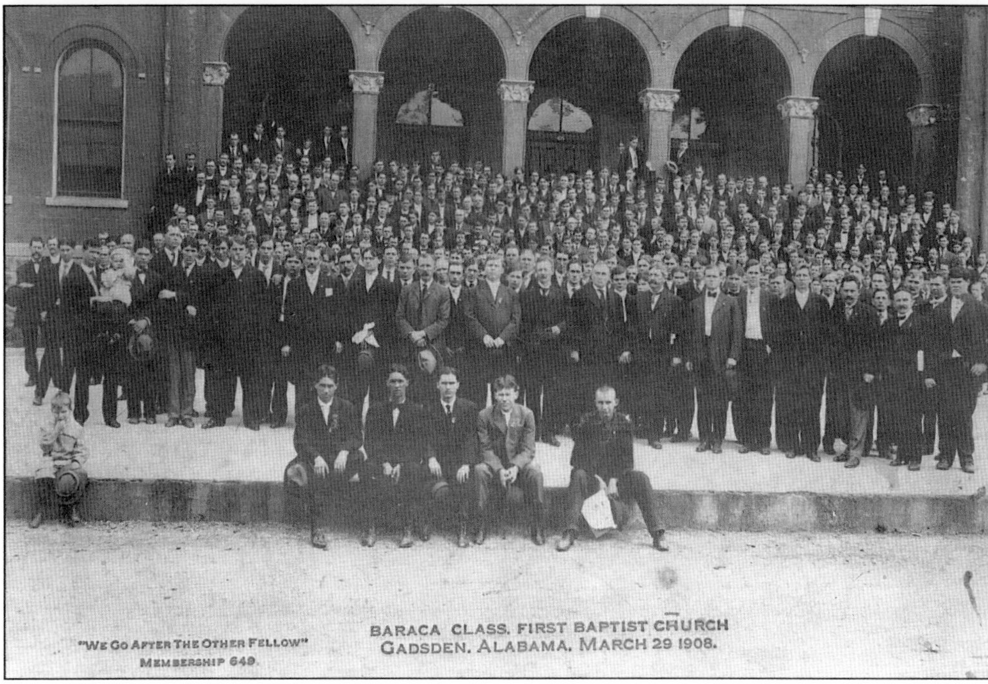

Over 640 members of the Baraca Sunday School Class are shown on the steps of the early Etowah County Courthouse in March of 1908. First Baptist Church was located a few blocks away in a beautiful structure on the corner of Seventh and Broad Streets.

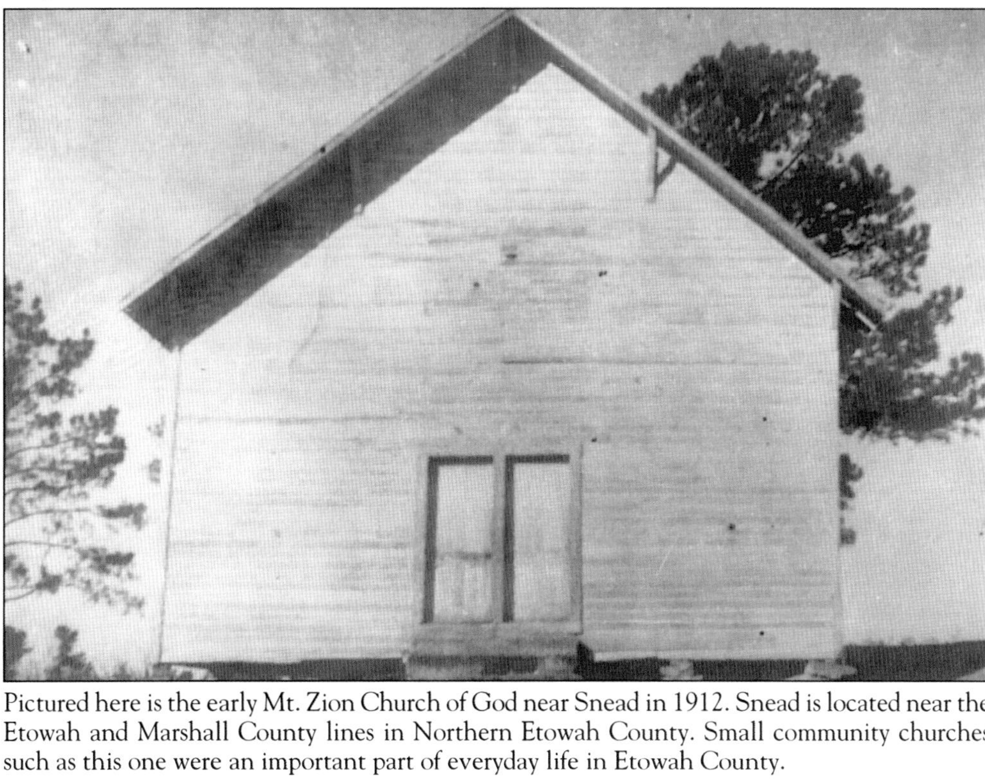

Pictured here is the early Mt. Zion Church of God near Snead in 1912. Snead is located near the Etowah and Marshall County lines in Northern Etowah County. Small community churches such as this one were an important part of everyday life in Etowah County.

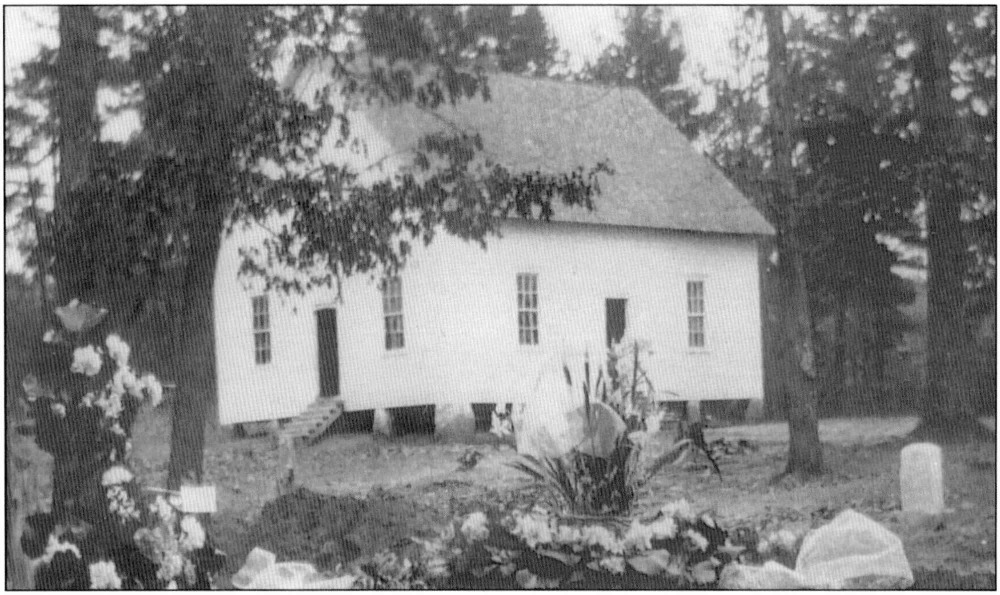

This is the early home of Fairview Baptist Church on Lookout Mountain. Built in 1854 on Fairview Road near Noccalula Falls, this small wood frame building has long since been replaced by a more modern structure. The Fairview Baptist Church congregation is still meeting and worshipping on Lookout Mountain.

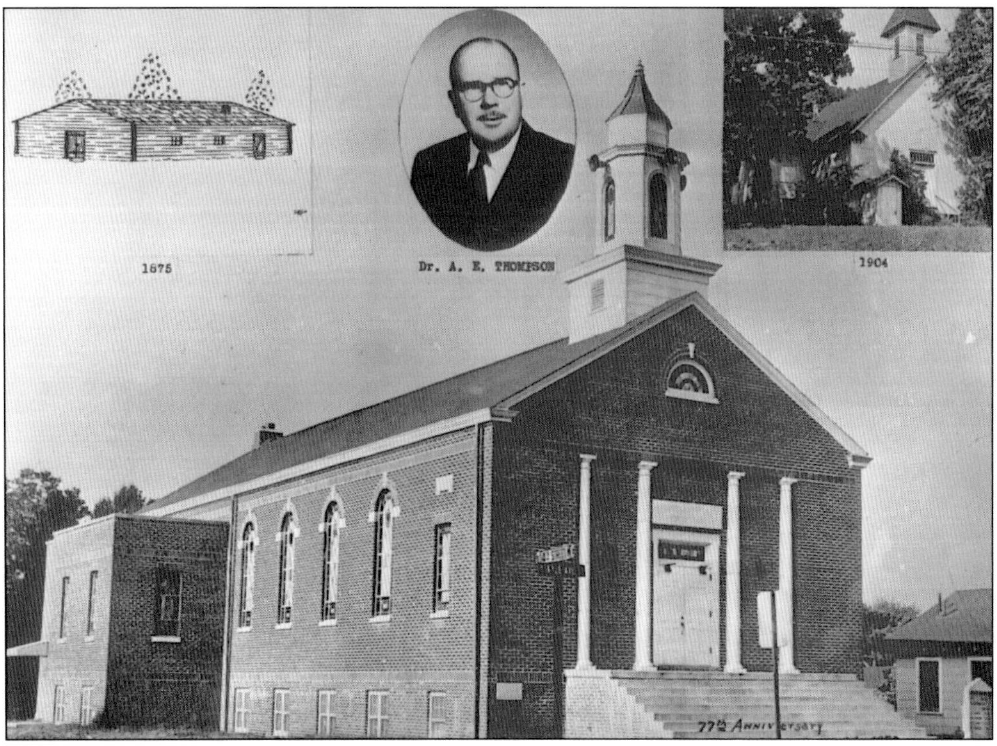

Gadsden's Mt. Carmel Baptist Church is shown here on its 77th anniversary in 1942. The church was founded in a small building in 1875, and is nearing its 125th anniversary in the year 2000. It is located on the corner of Kyle Avenue and Fourteenth Street.

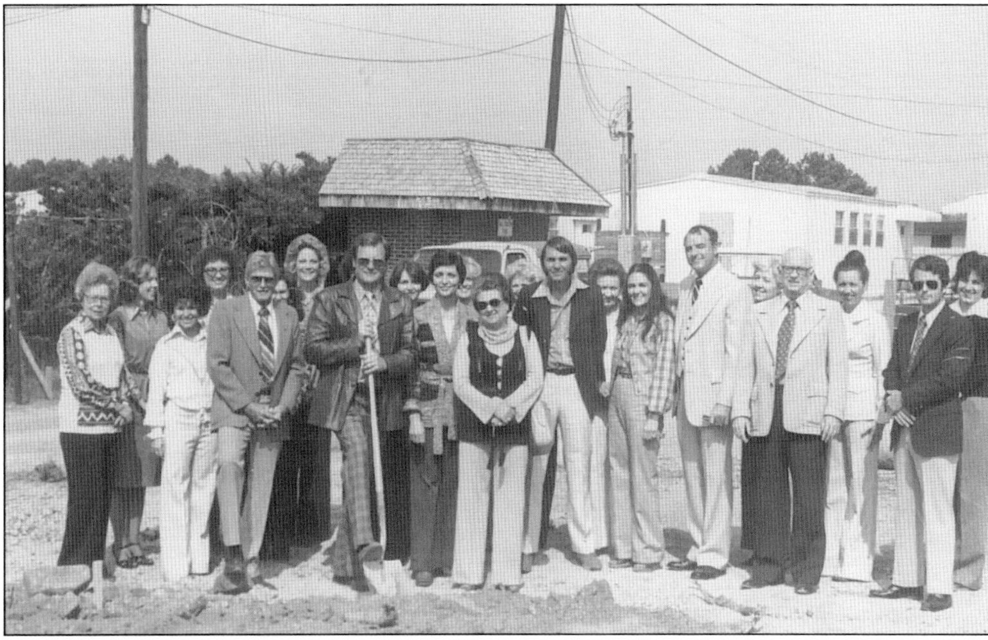

A large group gathers for the groundbreaking of the new Southside School. One of the fastest growing areas in Etowah County, Southside boasts some of the finest schools in the area. Among the people pictured here is E.C. "Baldy" Wilson, superintendent of Etowah County Schools.

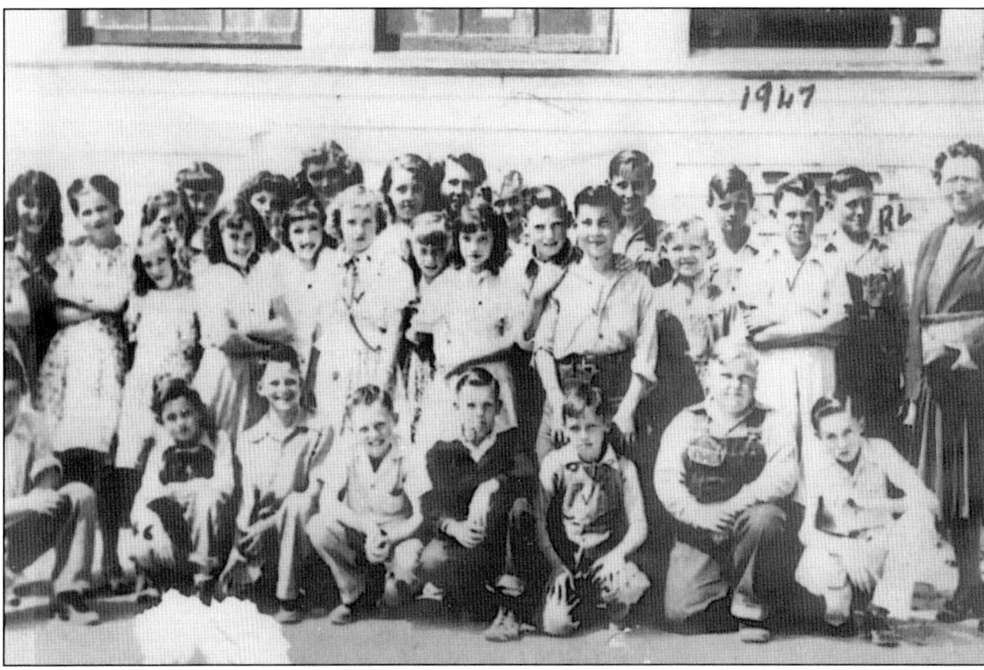

Students from the fifth and sixth grade classes of the Black Creek Grammar School are pictured in this photograph from the 1947-1948 school year. Their teacher, Mrs. Mae Raley, is pictured at the far right. The Black Creek Grammar School was located in rural Etowah County just above Noccalula Falls on Lookout Mountain.

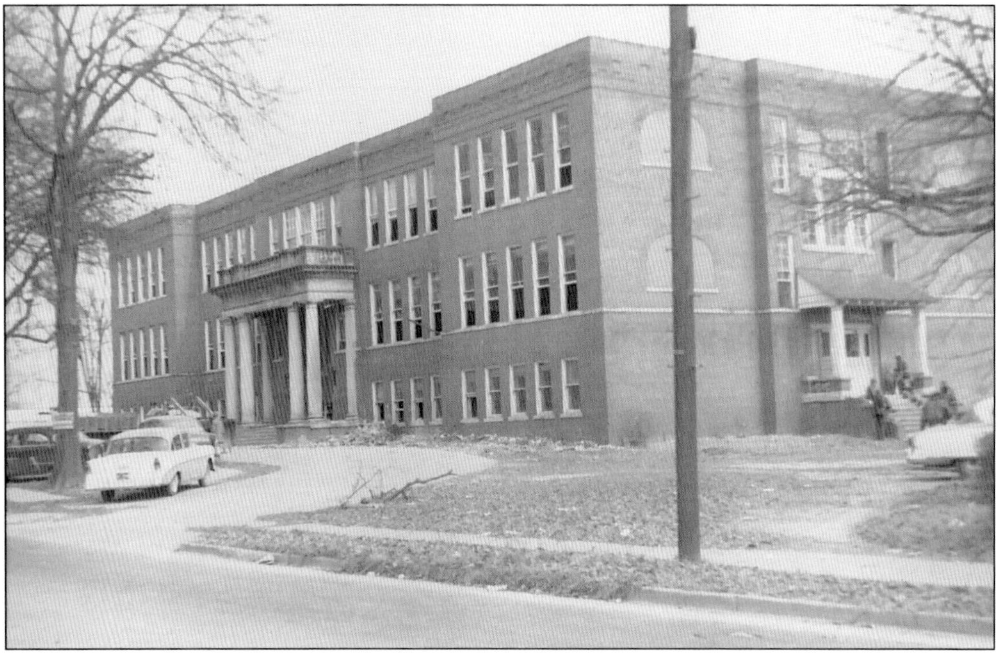

Gadsden's Striplin Elementary School, a beautiful brick structure built in 1910, contained 16 classrooms and had a capacity of 640 students. Located behind Disque High School near the present site of Gadsden's Public Library, the school was later torn down after a newer and more modern structure was built. It was originally known as the College Street School until the name was changed in 1912 in honor of Walter E. Striplin, who had done so much for public education in Gadsden.

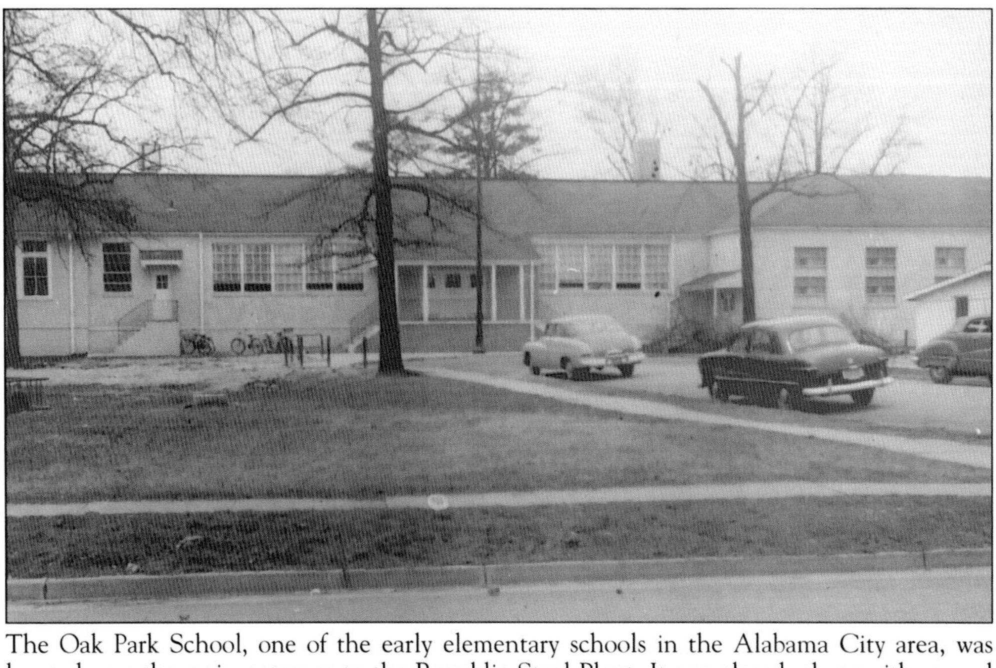

The Oak Park School, one of the early elementary schools in the Alabama City area, was located near the main entrance to the Republic Steel Plant. It was closed, along with several other small schools, when the G.W. Floyd Elementary School was built on Black Creek.

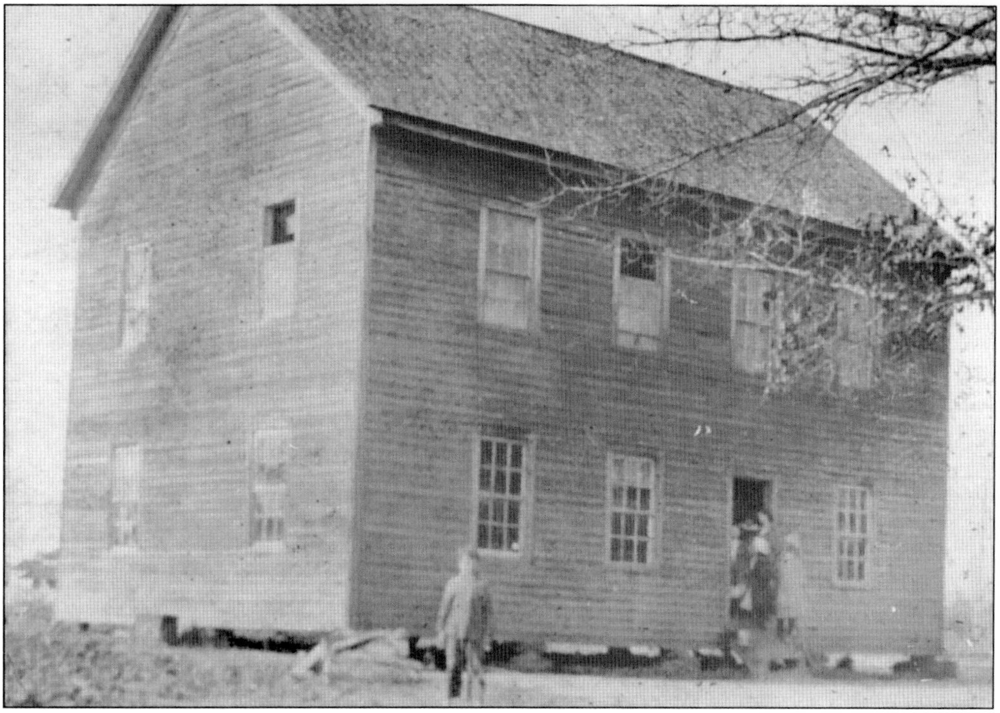

Pictured here is the Whorten Bend School, located in the bend of the Coosa River near Southside, Alabama. Small wooden schoolhouses such as this one were common in Etowah County in the early part of the 20th century; however, the advent of the county school system and the buses it provided caused such schools to slowly fade into the history of the county.

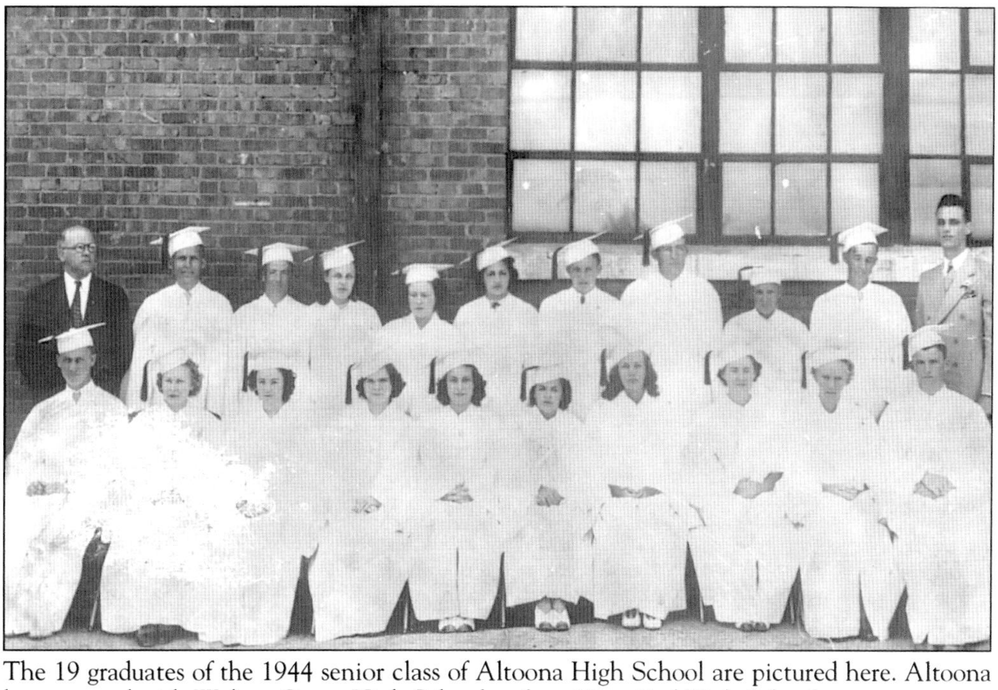

The 19 graduates of the 1944 senior class of Altoona High School are pictured here. Altoona later merged with Walnut Grove High School to form West End High School.

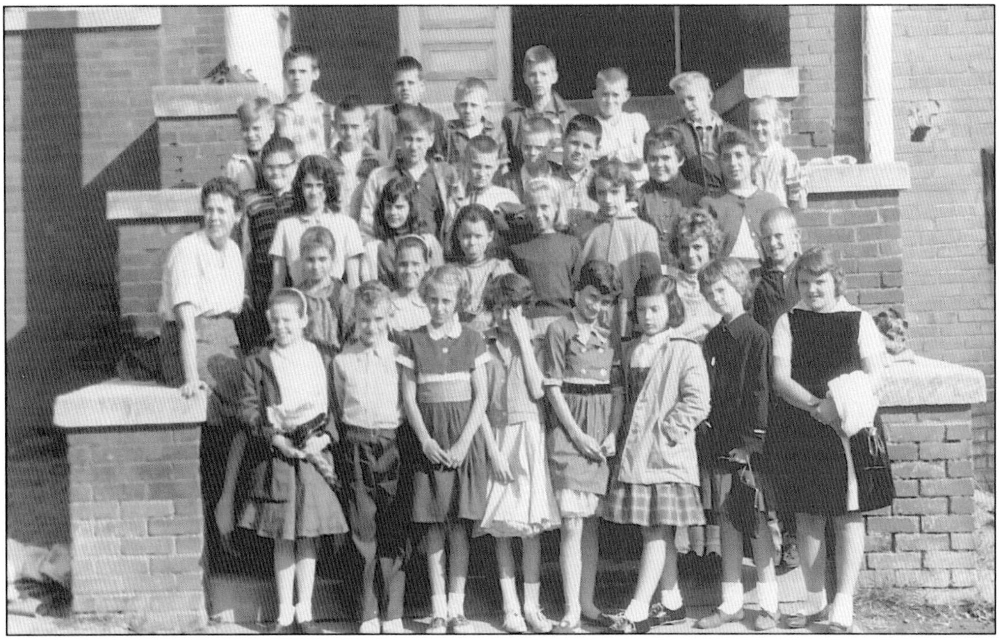

Pictured above are the members of Mrs. John K. Weaver's fifth grade class at the Eleventh Street School. The entire class attended school for one month without an absentee in October 1960, which was the first time such a record had been set, according to Mrs. Elizabeth Shores, the principal.

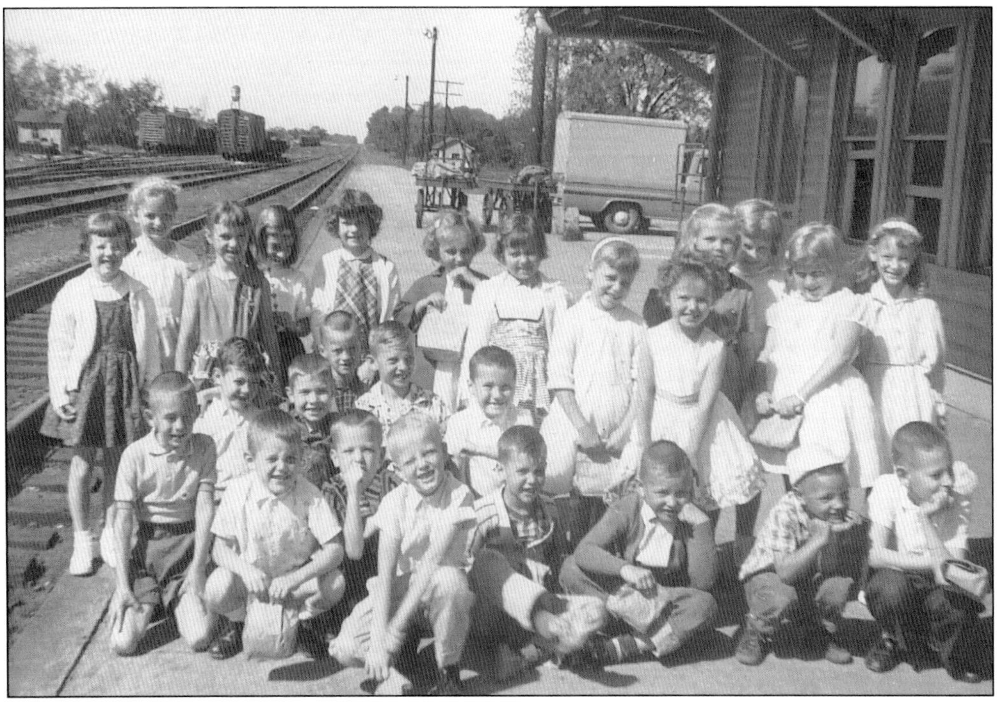

This photo, taken at the train station in Fort Payne during the early 1960s, shows a group from Mitchell Elementary School taking a trip to Fort Payne. Mitchell Elementary is located on Lookout Mountain in Gadsden across from Noccalula Falls.

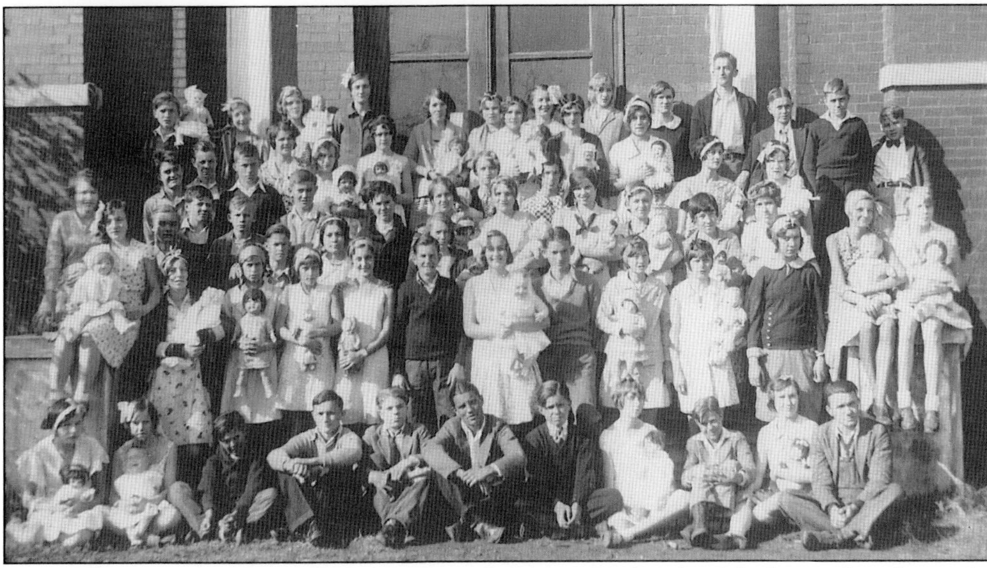

Pictured here are the 65 students of the Etowah County High School freshman class during the 1930-1931 school year. Located in Attalla, Etowah County High School is one of the larger high schools in the area and is known for its excellent curriculum and sports program.

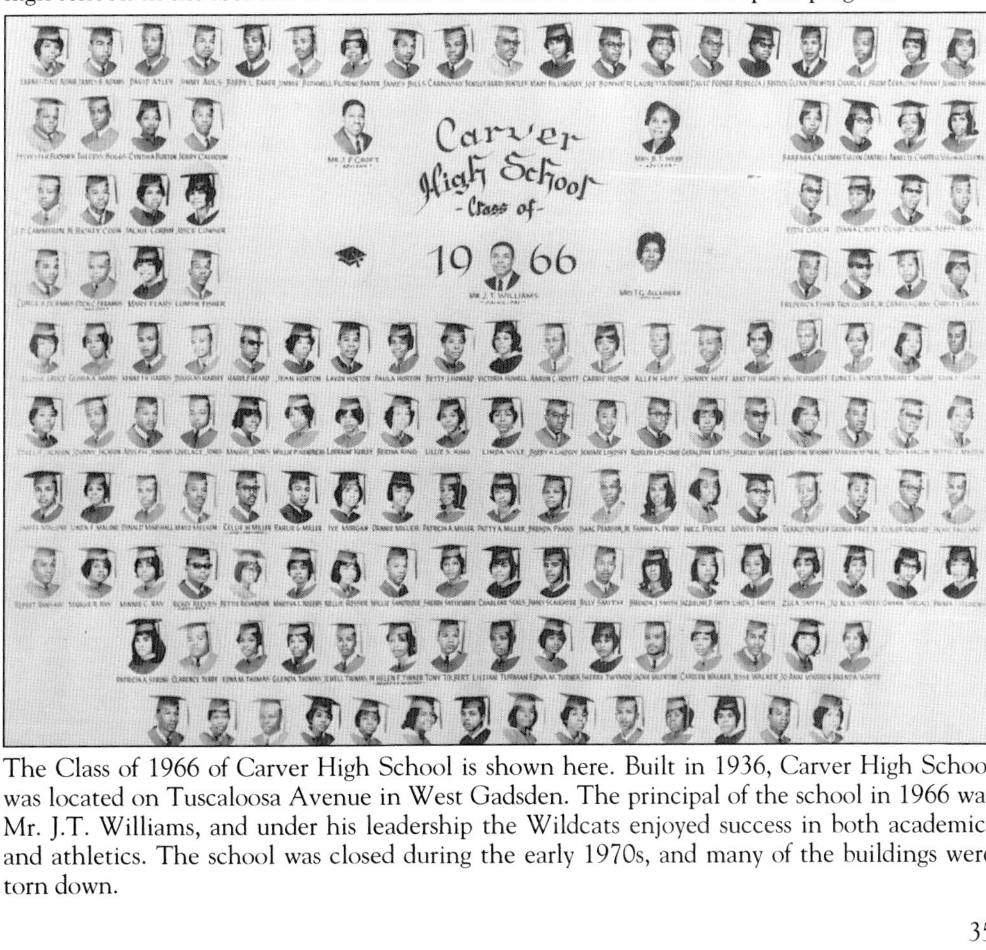

The Class of 1966 of Carver High School is shown here. Built in 1936, Carver High School was located on Tuscaloosa Avenue in West Gadsden. The principal of the school in 1966 was Mr. J.T. Williams, and under his leadership the Wildcats enjoyed success in both academics and athletics. The school was closed during the early 1970s, and many of the buildings were torn down.

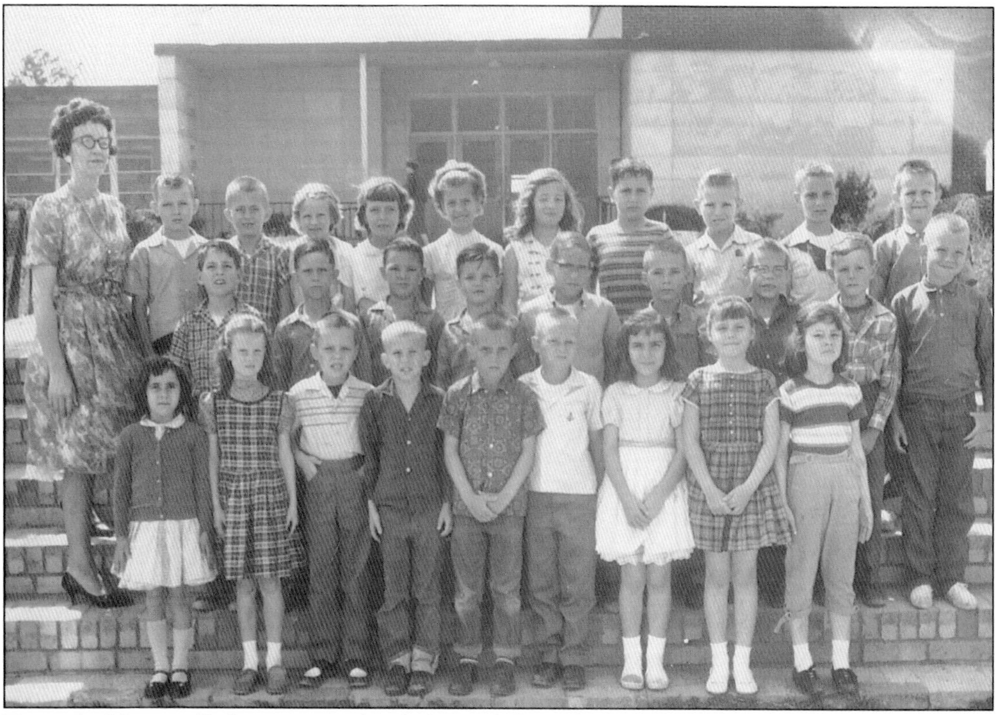

Typical of the small elementary schools located throughout Etowah County was the Curtiston School. This photograph of Curtiston students was taken in 1961. Curtiston is located in the Attalla area between Attalla and Steele.

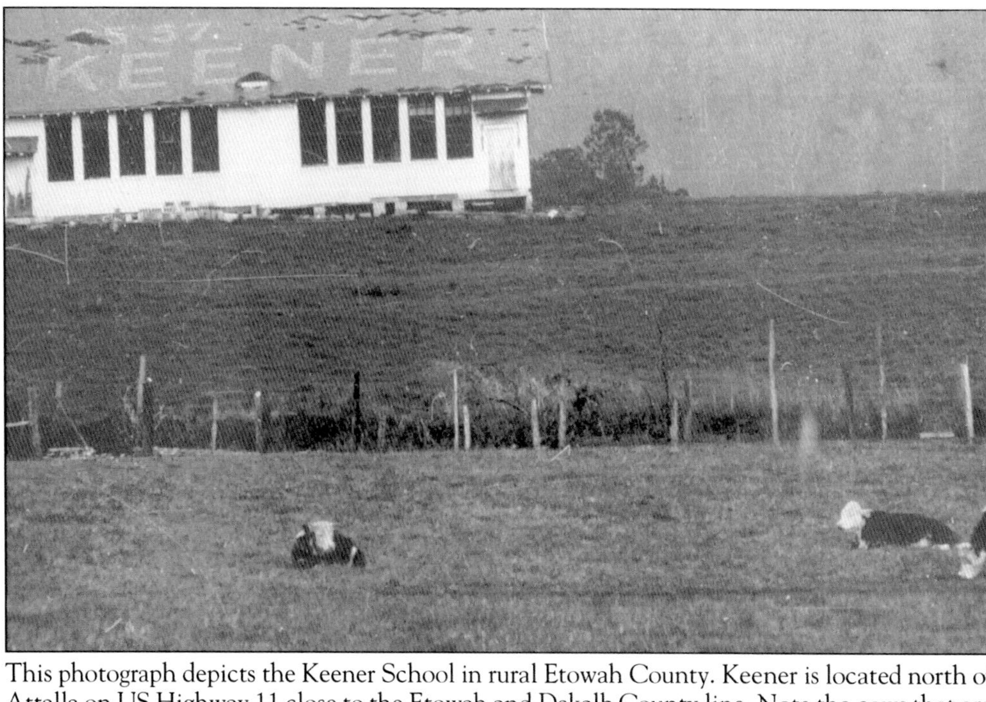

This photograph depicts the Keener School in rural Etowah County. Keener is located north of Attalla on US Highway 11 close to the Etowah and Dekalb County line. Note the cows that are also pictured in the pasture near the school. This photo was taken in 1959.

Three

Retail Merchants

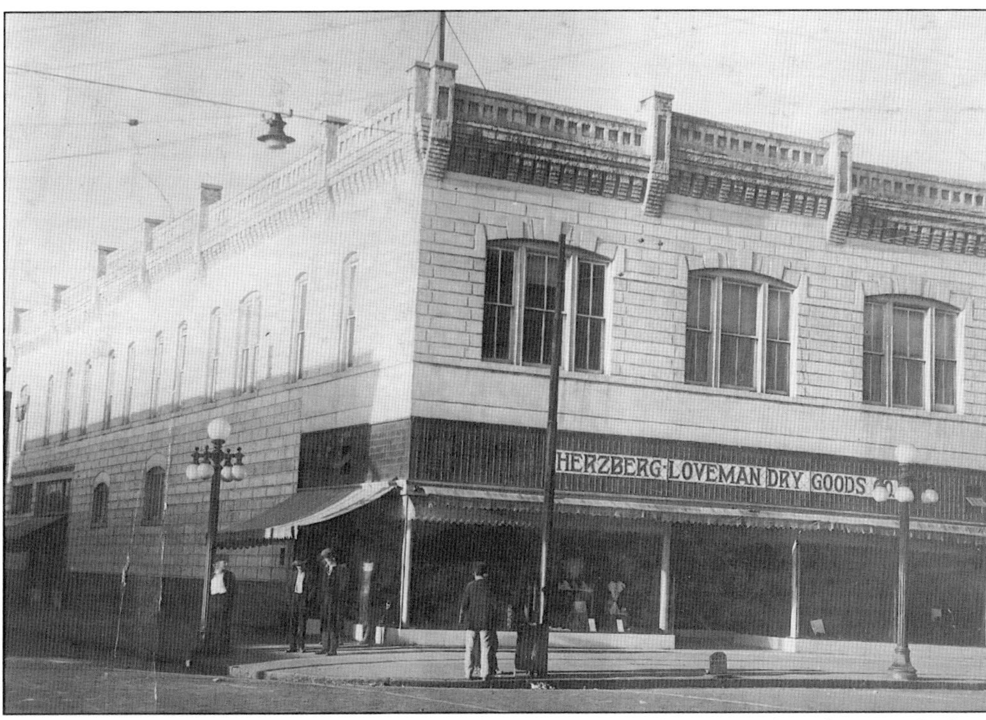

The beautiful Herzberg-Loveman Dry Goods Company is shown in this photograph from the late 1930s. This popular store was located on the southwest corner of Broad and Fourth Streets—the present location of the Gadsden Jewelry and Loan Company.

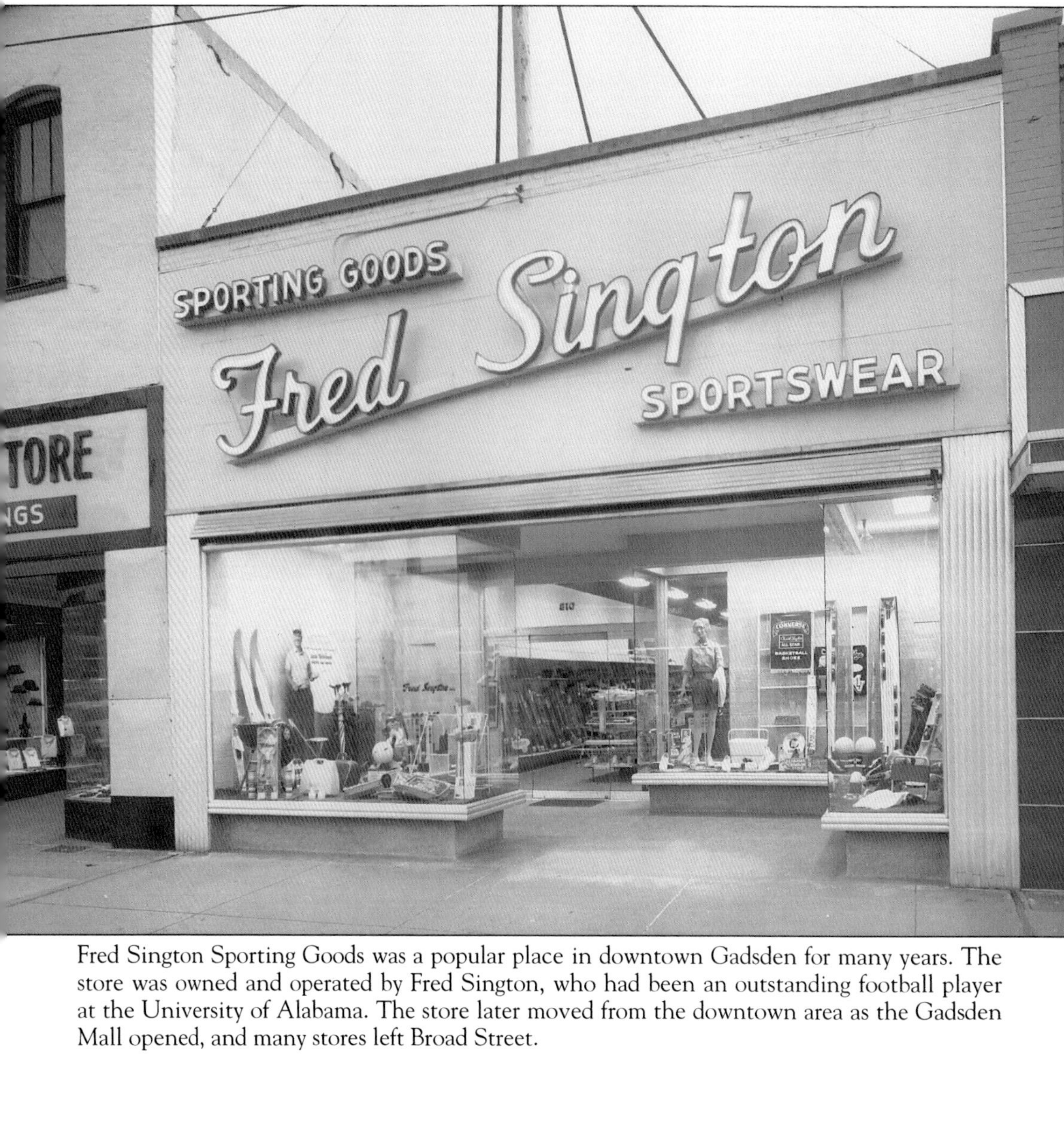

Fred Sington Sporting Goods was a popular place in downtown Gadsden for many years. The store was owned and operated by Fred Sington, who had been an outstanding football player at the University of Alabama. The store later moved from the downtown area as the Gadsden Mall opened, and many stores left Broad Street.

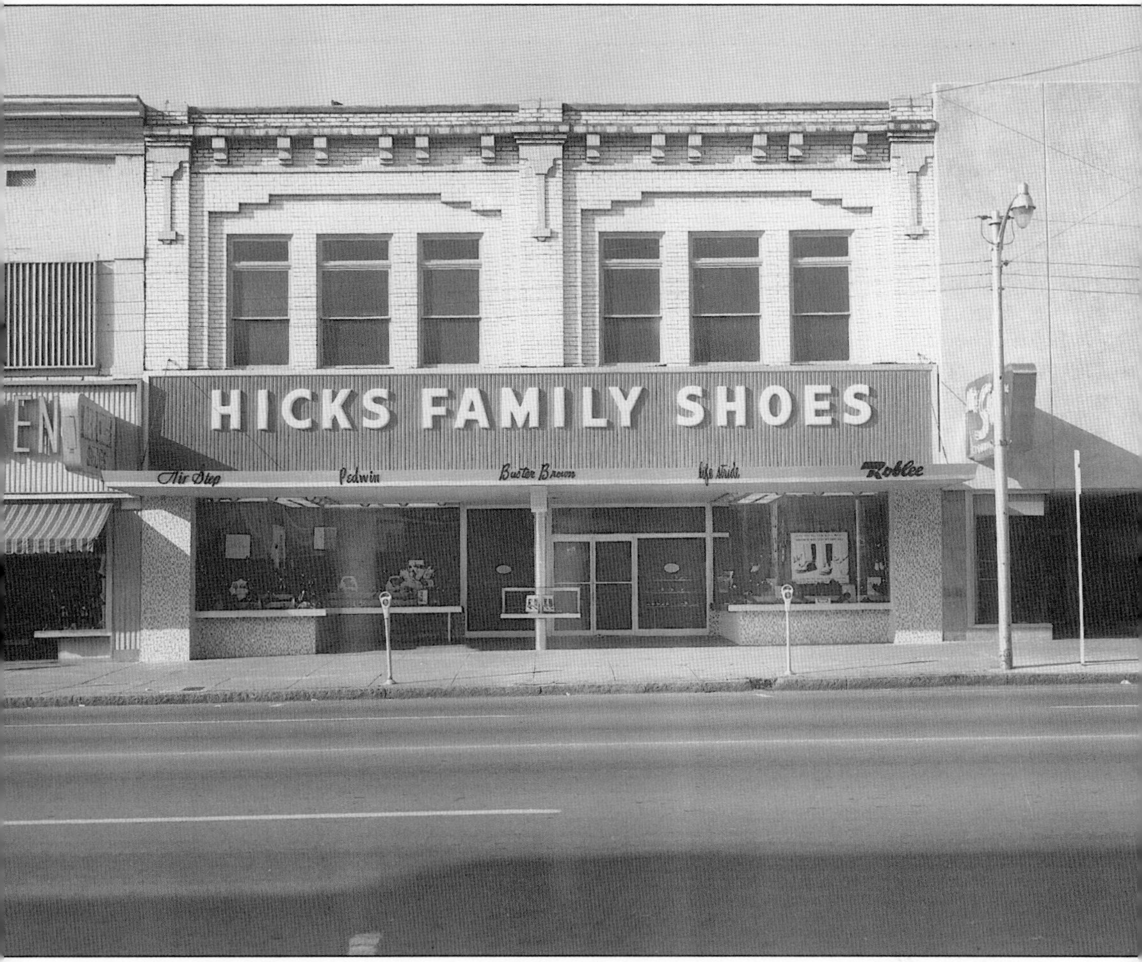

Located on Broad Street in downtown Gadsden, the Hicks Shoe Store is shown at the former site of the F.W. Woolworth Store in this photo from 1961. This beautiful building was originally the site of the Kyle Opera House, which burned, and the third floor was removed during renovation.

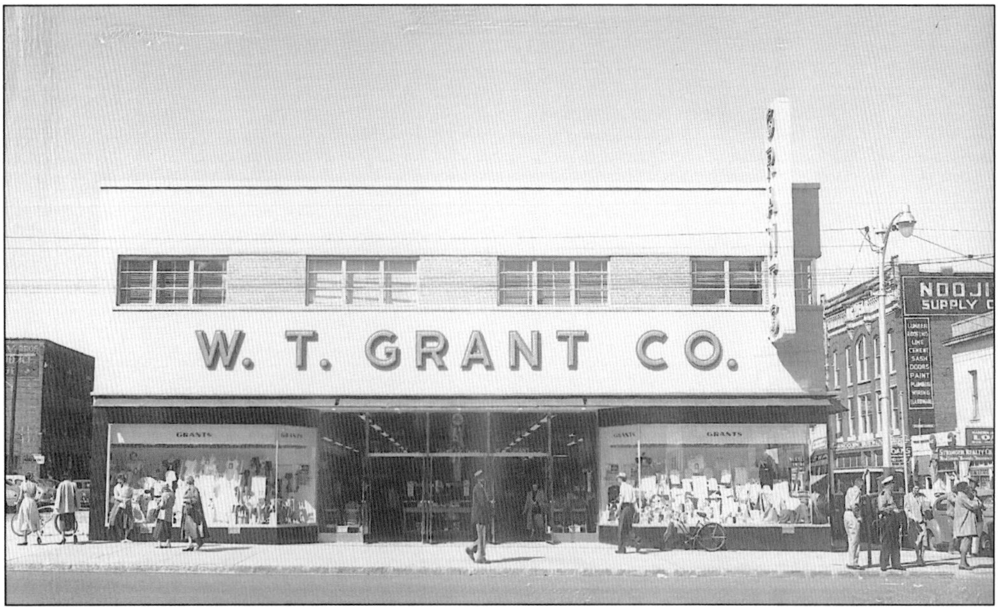

A popular department store in downtown Gadsden for many years, the W.T. Grant Company was built on the corner of Broad and Fourth Streets on the site of Etowah County's early courthouse. The courthouse was moved in the 1940s, and the old building was demolished. This building is presently the site of Railroad Furniture.

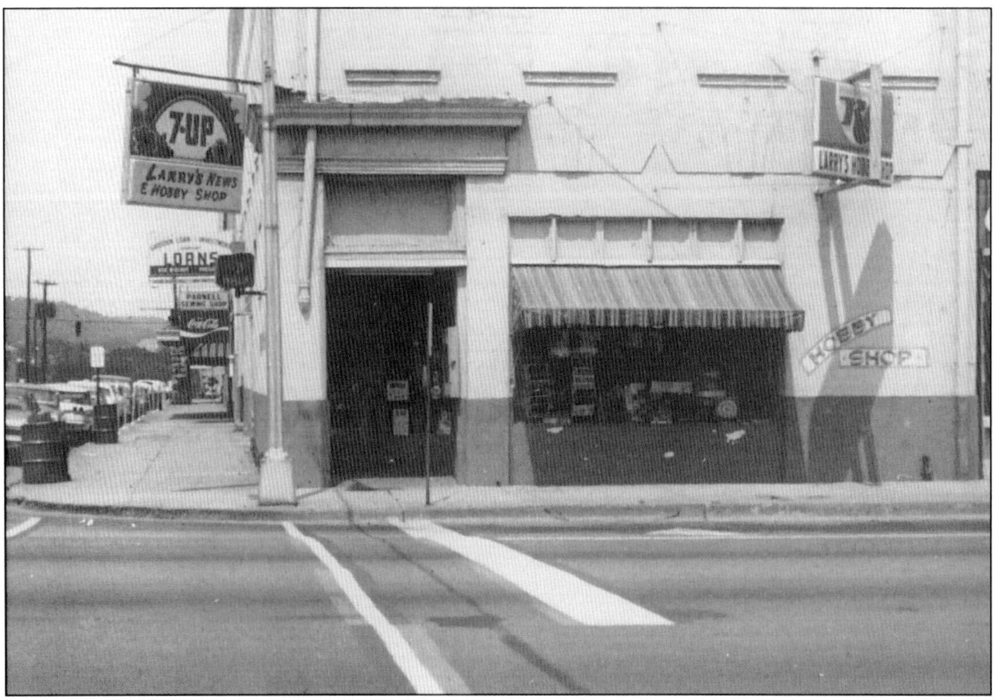

Larry's News and Hobby Shop was located on the northeast corner of Broad and Fourth Streets during the early 1970s. This newsstand carried the latest in magazines, newspapers, and a complete line of hobby supplies. Typical of the popular newsstands of the 1950s and 1960s, this business closed in the mid-1970s and the building was torn down.

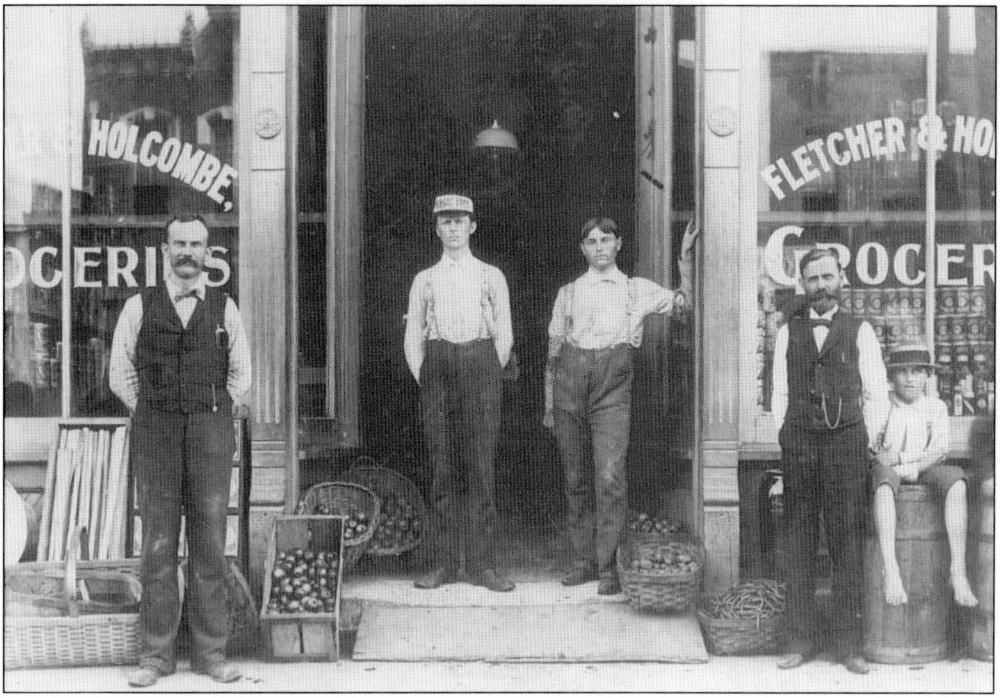

Fletcher and Holcombe Grocery was located on the 300 block of Broad Street in the early 1900s. Among those pictured in this photo include Claude Small at left and Cliff Little at right standing in the doorway.

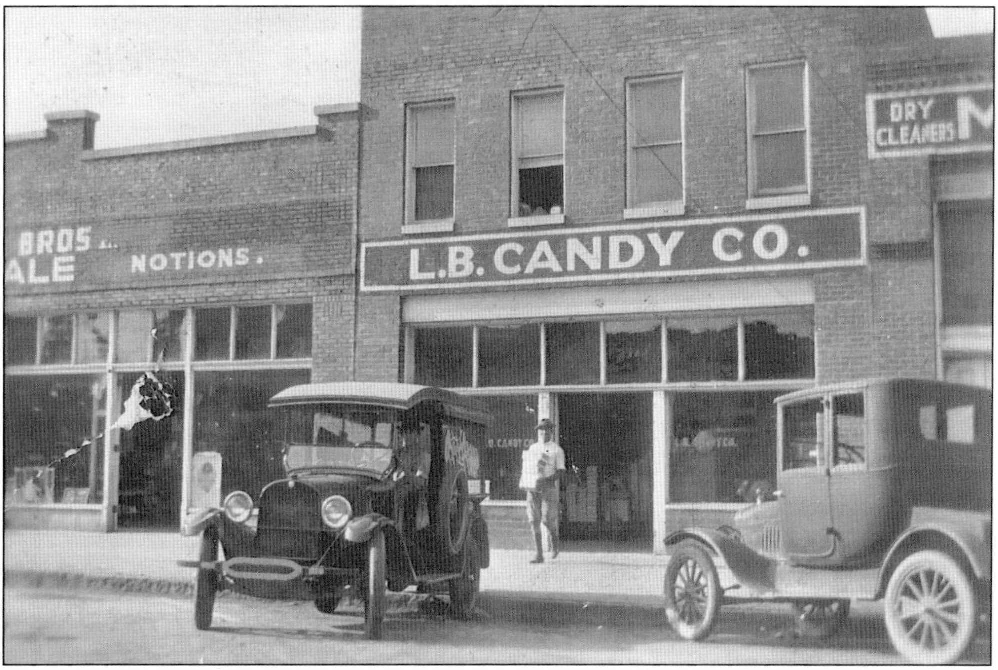

Shown in an early 1930s photograph is the L&B Candy Company, a favorite candy wholesaler in the Gadsden area. It was located on the south side of Broad Street between Second and Third Streets.

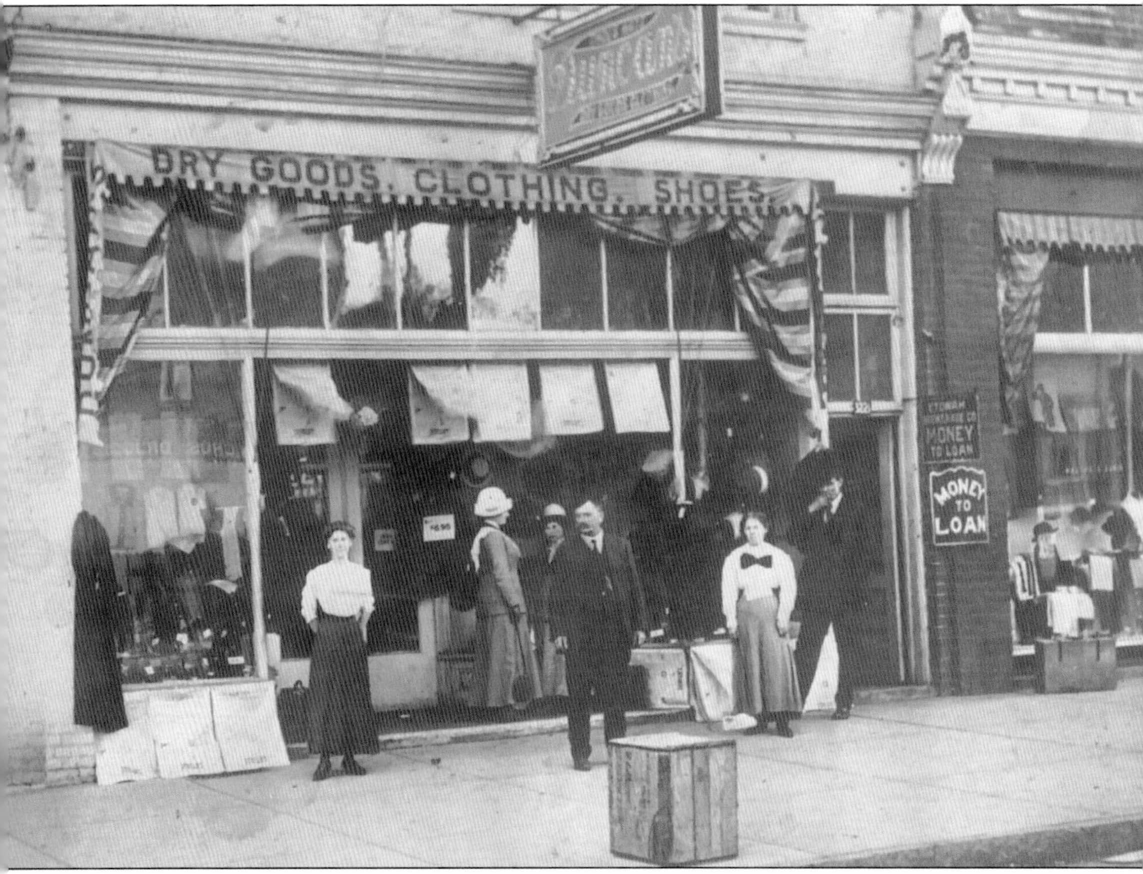

Duncan's Dry Goods is shown in this photograph from the early 1900s. Duncan's was a very popular clothing store in the downtown Gadsden area. Next door, the Etowah Brokerage Company advertises "money to loan." These businesses were located across the street from Cross Drug Company during the early part of the 20th century.

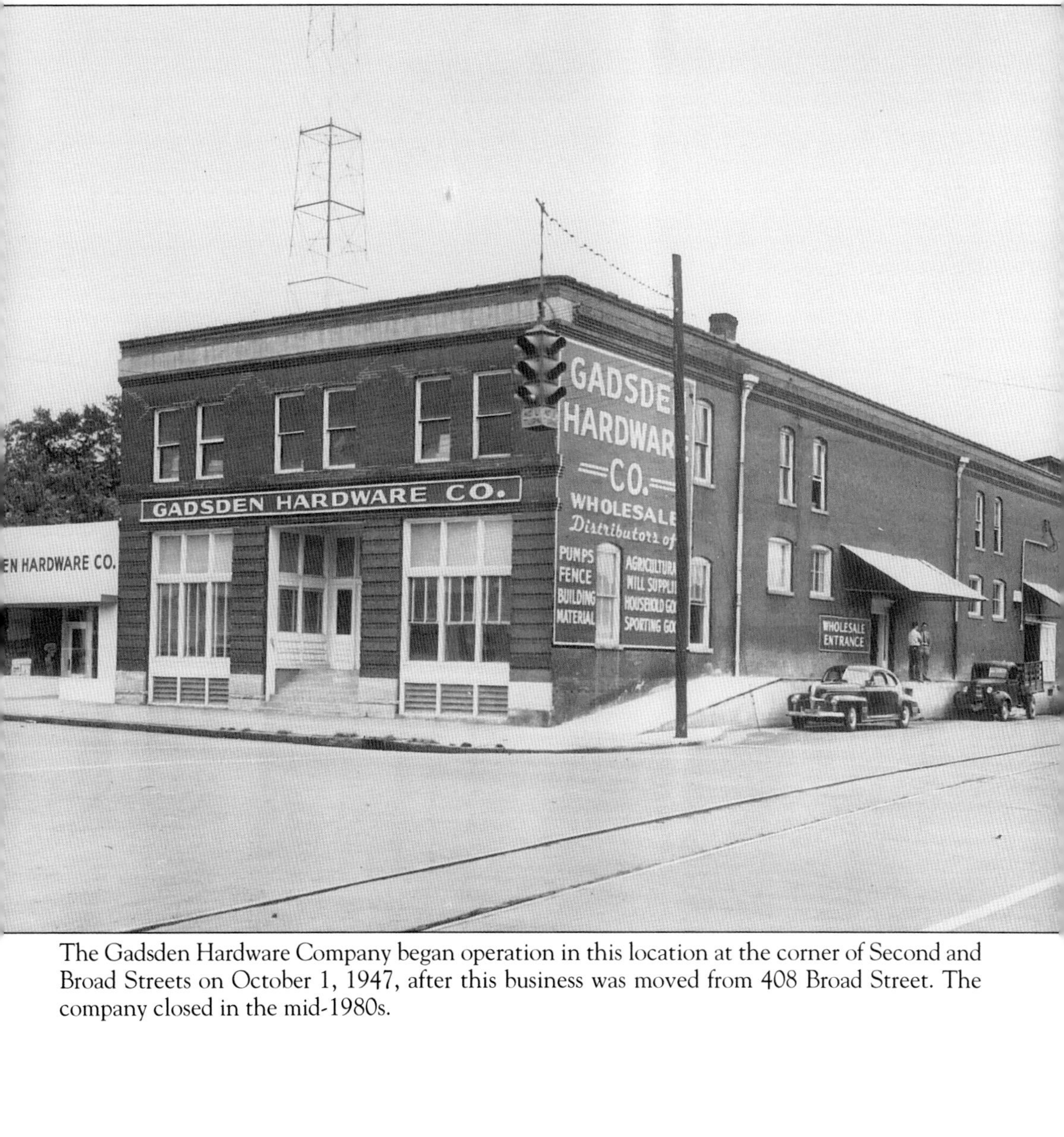

The Gadsden Hardware Company began operation in this location at the corner of Second and Broad Streets on October 1, 1947, after this business was moved from 408 Broad Street. The company closed in the mid-1980s.

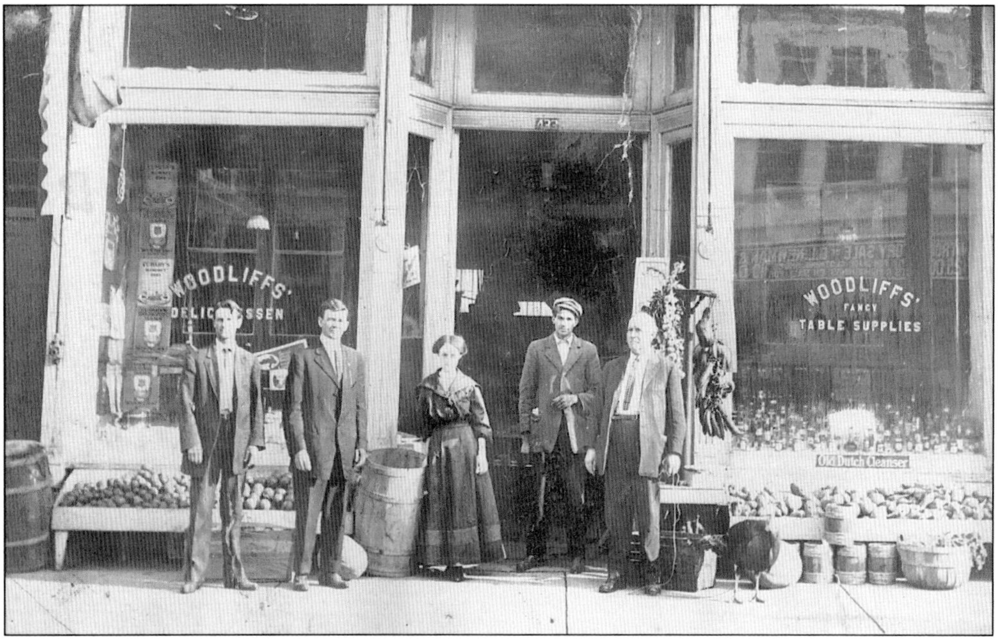

The Woodliffs, a prominent family in Gadsden, owned this delicatessen along with several other businesses. Shown in this early 1900 photograph, Woodliffs' Delicatessen also offered "fancy table supplies." It was located on Broad Street between Fourth and Fifth Streets.

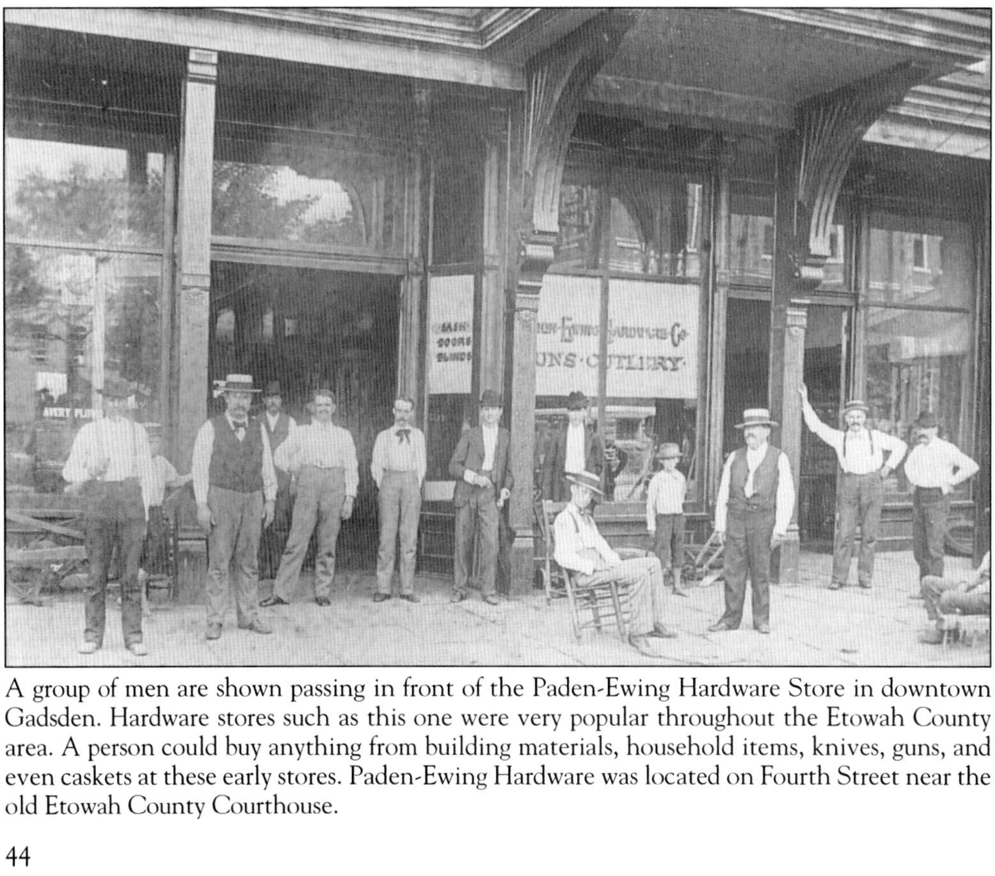

A group of men are shown passing in front of the Paden-Ewing Hardware Store in downtown Gadsden. Hardware stores such as this one were very popular throughout the Etowah County area. A person could buy anything from building materials, household items, knives, guns, and even caskets at these early stores. Paden-Ewing Hardware was located on Fourth Street near the old Etowah County Courthouse.

Michael's Jewelers was a locally owned and operated credit jewelry store. Ruby Kay Pevsner opened her first store on Broad Street in 1953, and went on to open several other stores through the years. Many Gadsden residents had charge accounts at these stores, which closed in 1999 following the death of Ms. Pevsner.

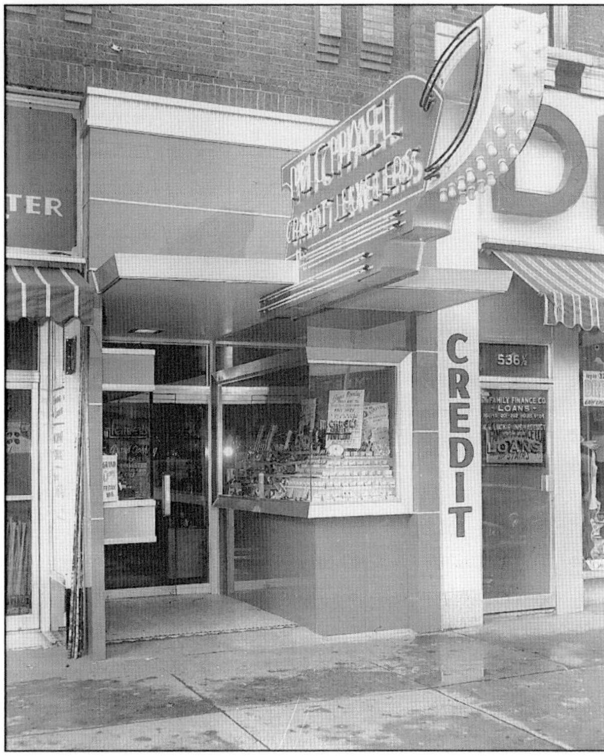

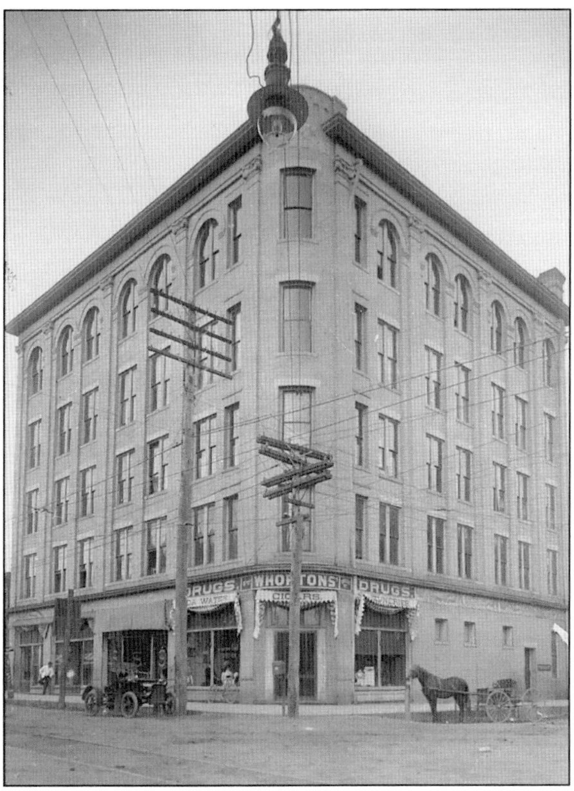

One of Gadsden's first skyscrapers, the Stock's Building was located on the corner of Fifth and Chestnut Streets. This five-story building housed several medical offices and Whorton's Drug Store, which lead people to call it the "medical building." Note the early automobile and the horse and buggy parked outside.

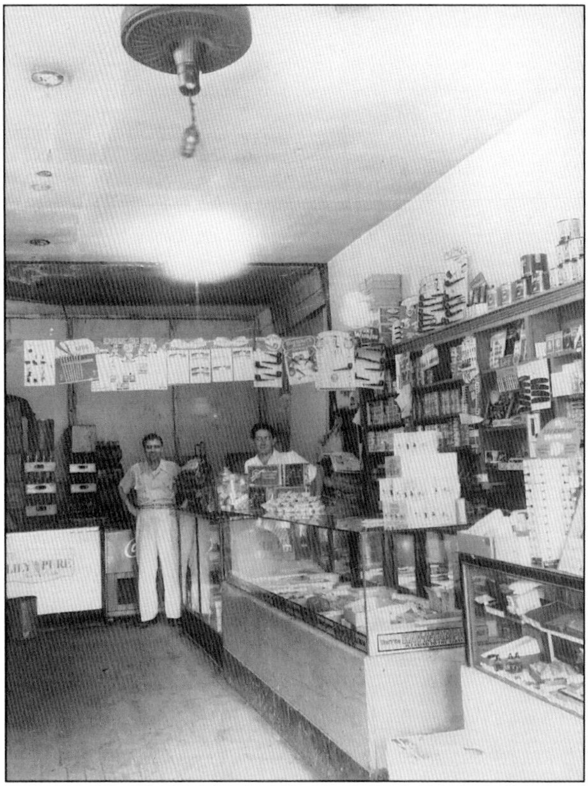

Pictured here is the original location of Baker's Sundries on the corner of Sixth and Broad Streets. Wallace Baker, the gentleman on the left, opened this business in 1946 and has operated it for over 50 years, longer than any other business on Broad Street.

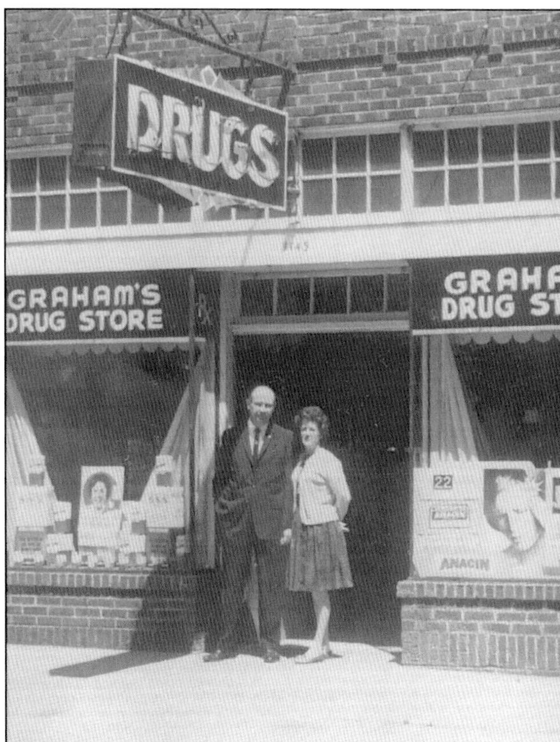

Typical of the neighborhood drugstores throughout Etowah County was Graham's Drugs on Walnut Street. Doc Graham is shown here in the doorway of his store, a popular retreat for Gadsden High School students at lunchtime or while skipping classes.

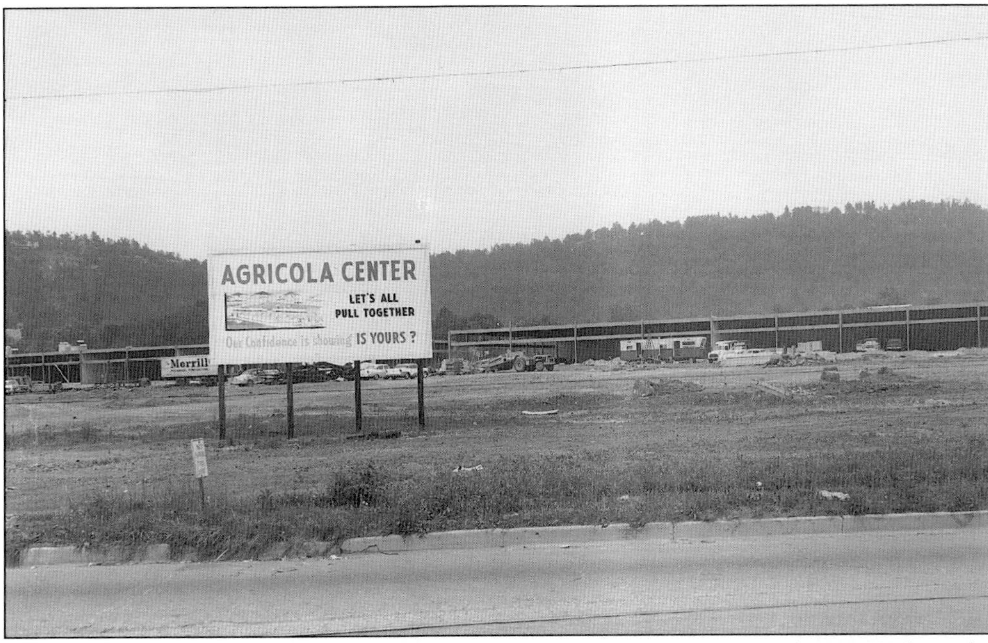

The Agricola Shopping Center is shown here under construction in May of 1962. Built on the former site of the Agricola Furnace Works, the center contained two groceries, a W.T. Grant's store, a G.C. Murphy's store, and several smaller stores. Located on North Twelfth Street, it is now known as the Old America Center.

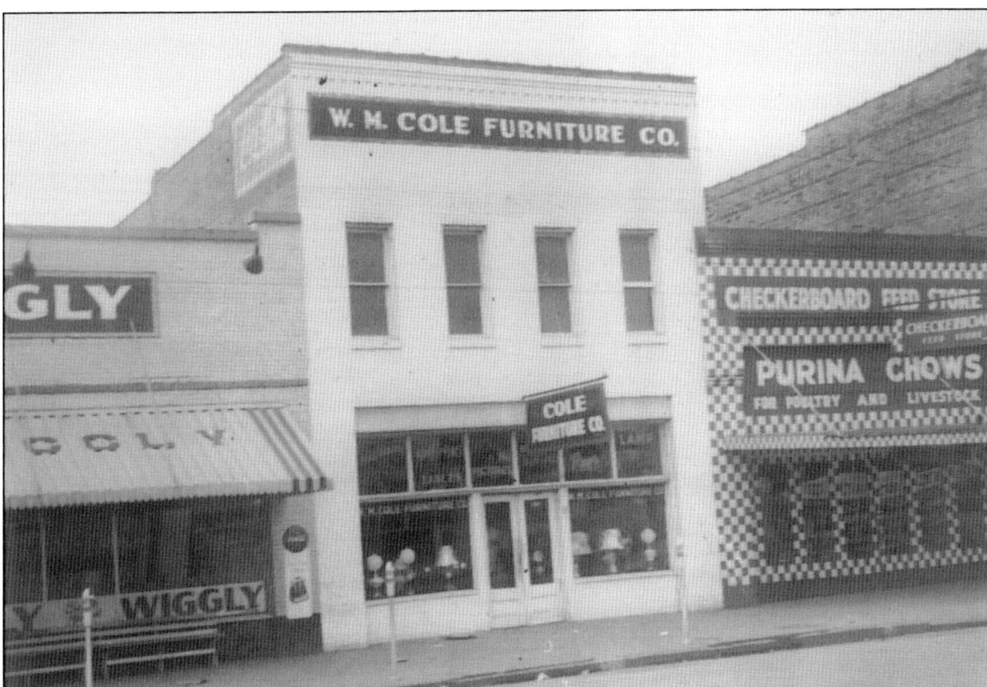

Pictured in a 1950 photograph is the W.M. Cole Furniture Company. Piggly Wiggly is located on the left and the Checkerboard Feed Store is on the right. These stores were located on Broad Street between Second and Third Streets on the south side. (Courtesy of Hugh Hall.)

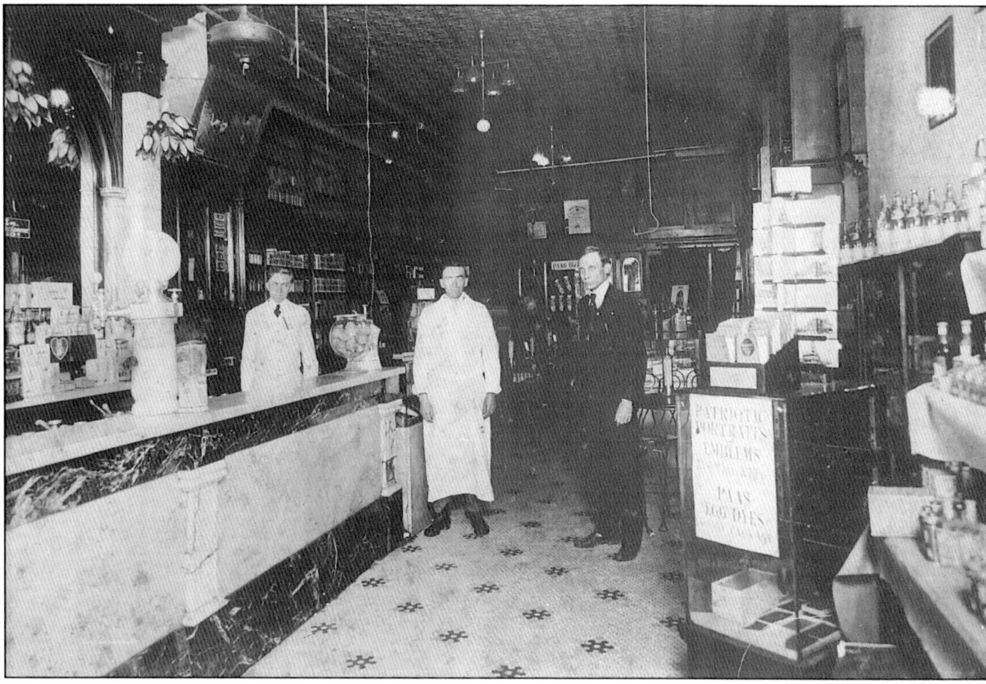

Located on the corner of Fifth and Chestnut Streets, Whorton's Drug Store opened for business in Gadsden in 1904.

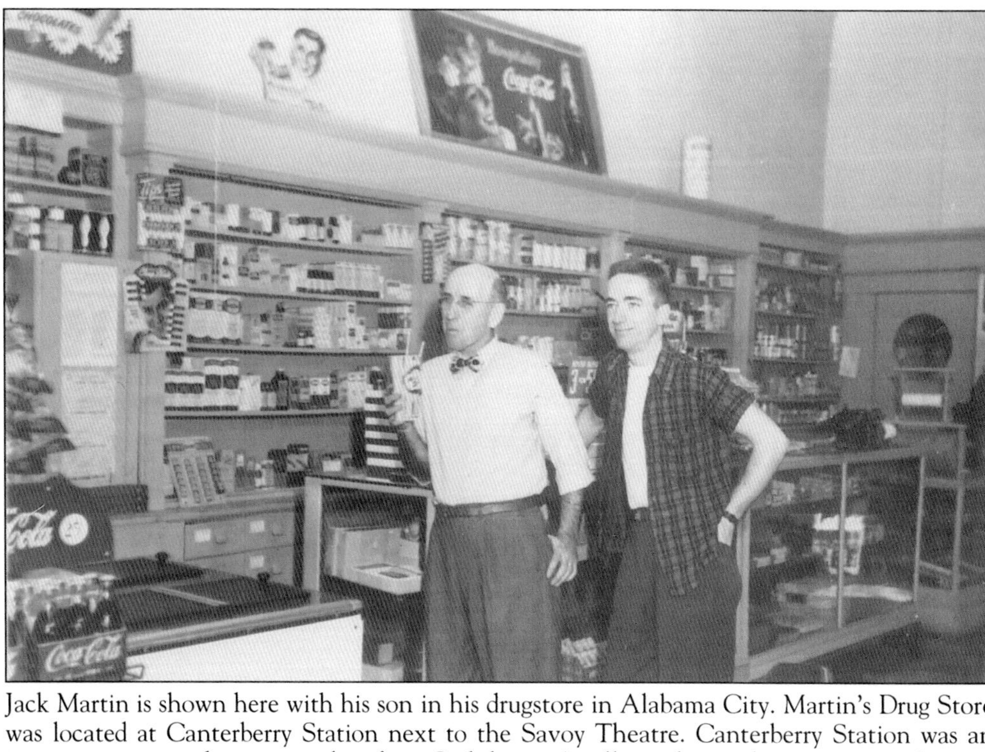

Jack Martin is shown here with his son in his drugstore in Alabama City. Martin's Drug Store was located at Canterberry Station next to the Savoy Theatre. Canterberry Station was an important stop on the streetcar line from Gadsden to Attalla, and many businesses were located here in the early 20th century.

Four

Businesses

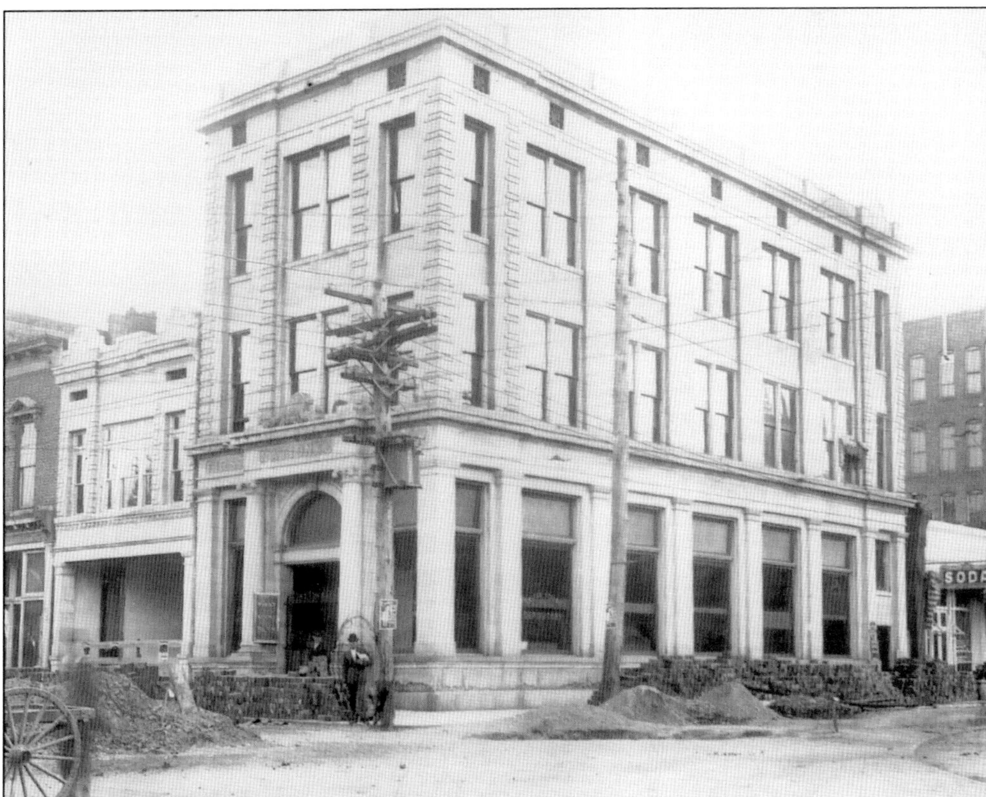

The beautiful First National Bank is shown in this photograph from early 1910. Bricks that were used to pave Broad Street are shown stacked on the sidewalk in front of the bank. These bricks were large and extremely heavy, each weighing 10 pounds. The bank was located at the corner of Fifth and Broad Streets.

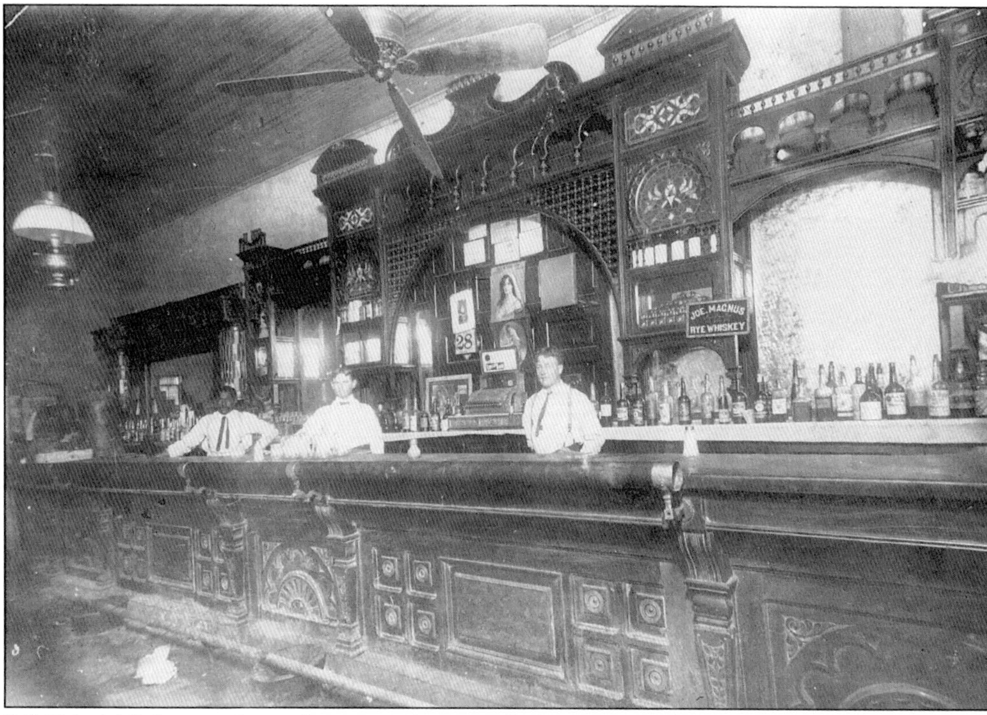

Bill Echols' Saloon is shown here in a photograph from 1907. Saloons such as these were found throughout downtown Gadsden on Broad Street and Chestnut Street. Echols' Saloon and Motlow's Saloon were two of the most popular, located in the 400 block of Broad Street. The saloons closed when the residents of Gadsden voted the city "dry."

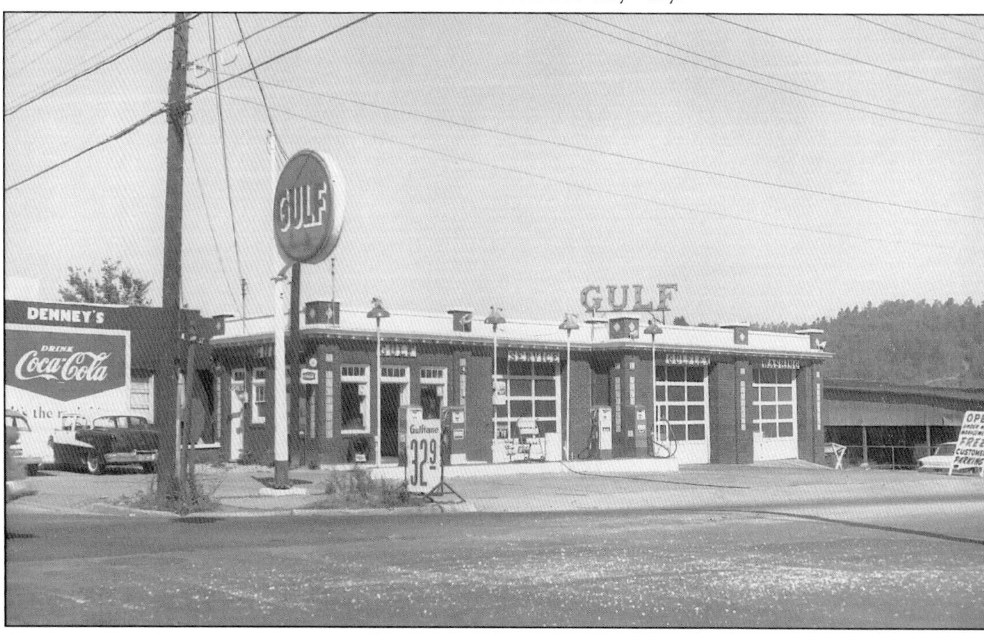

Gulftane Gasoline was 32.9¢ per gallon in October of 1963. This popular station was located on the corner of Third and Locust Streets in downtown Gadsden at the present site of Byrd Lock and Key.

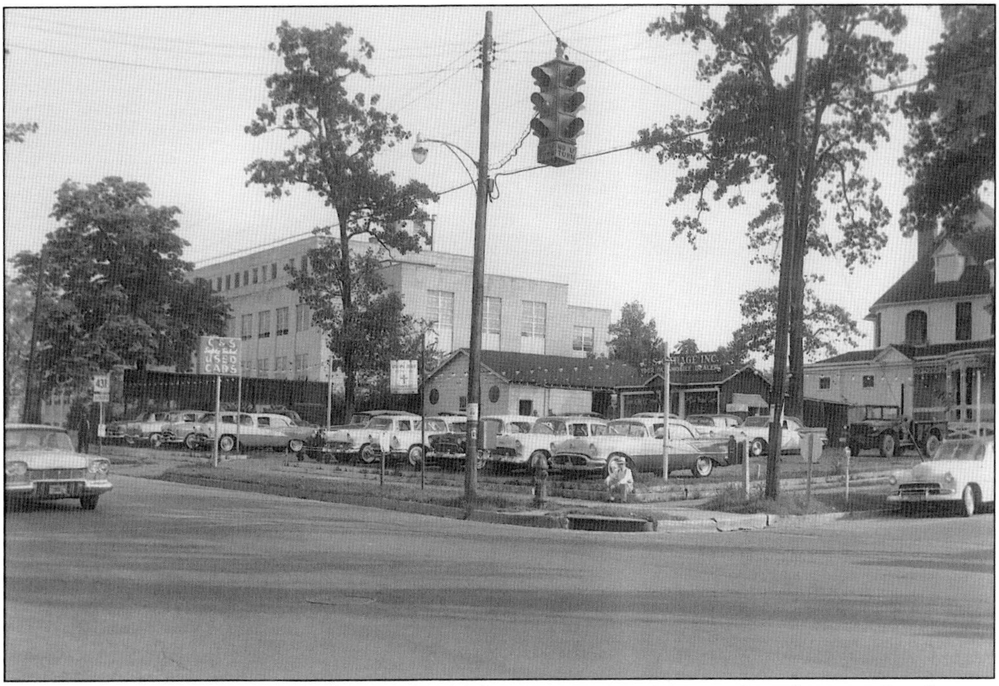

Gadsden's accelerated growth during the 20th century is evident in this photograph taken at the intersection of Ninth Street and Forrest Avenue. The new Etowah County Courthouse is seen in the background, and the Kyle home is also located in the rear of a used car lot.

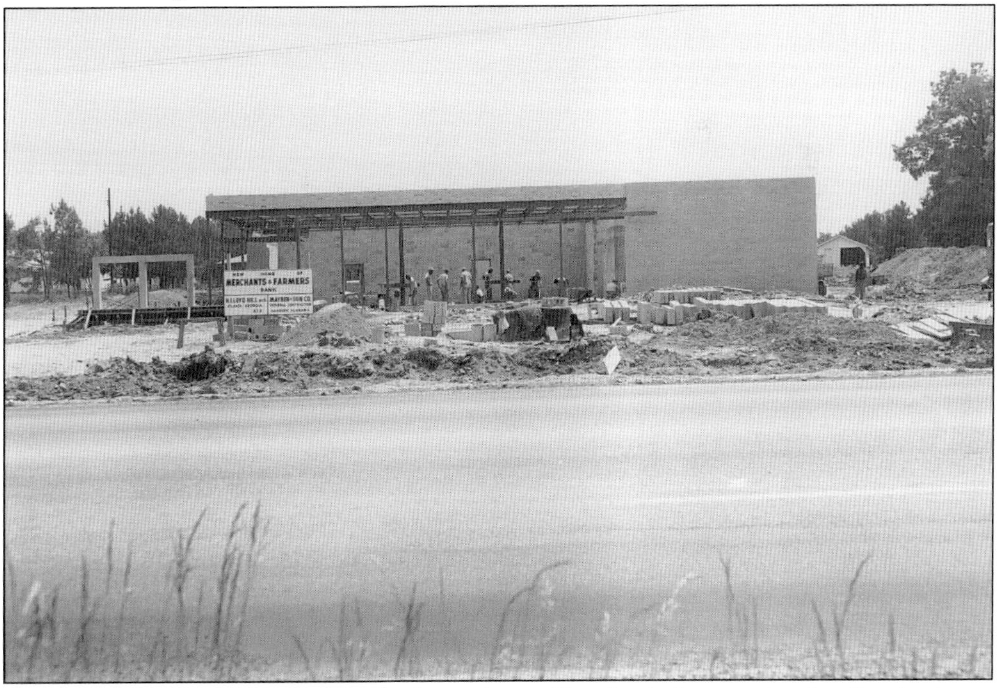

The Merchants and Farmers Bank, located on Cleveland Avenue in Attalla, is shown here under construction. Built in May of 1962, it is currently the home of the Exchange Bank of Attalla.

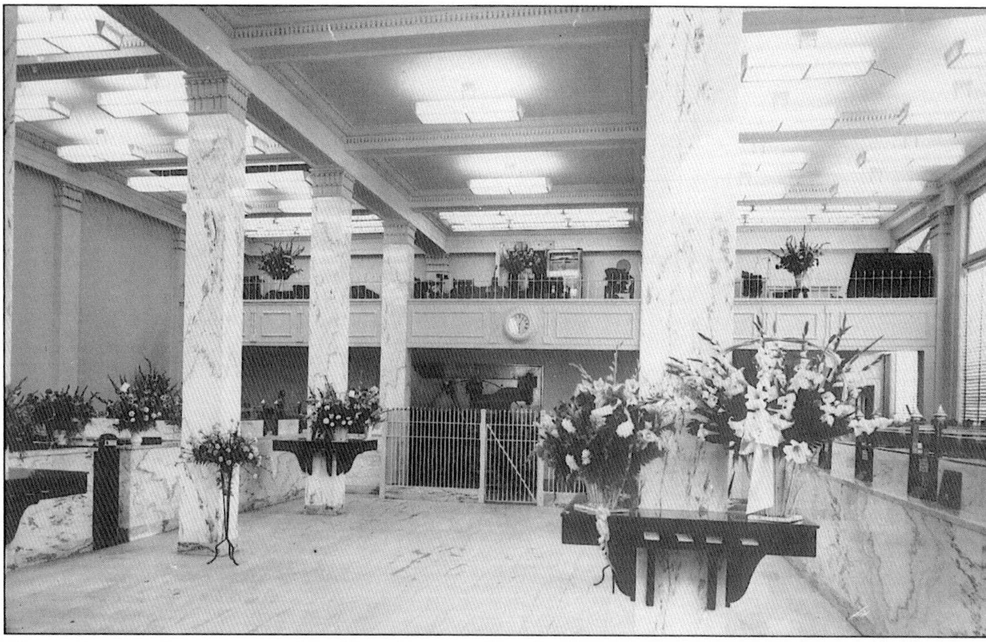

Shown here is the interior of the First National Bank of Gadsden, located on the corner of Fifth and Broad Streets. This bank was the scene of "Silver Dollar Day" when the local steel plant, Republic Steel, paid each of their employees in silver dollars. This building was later the home of Ike Saks, and now houses the Gadsden Christian Book Store.

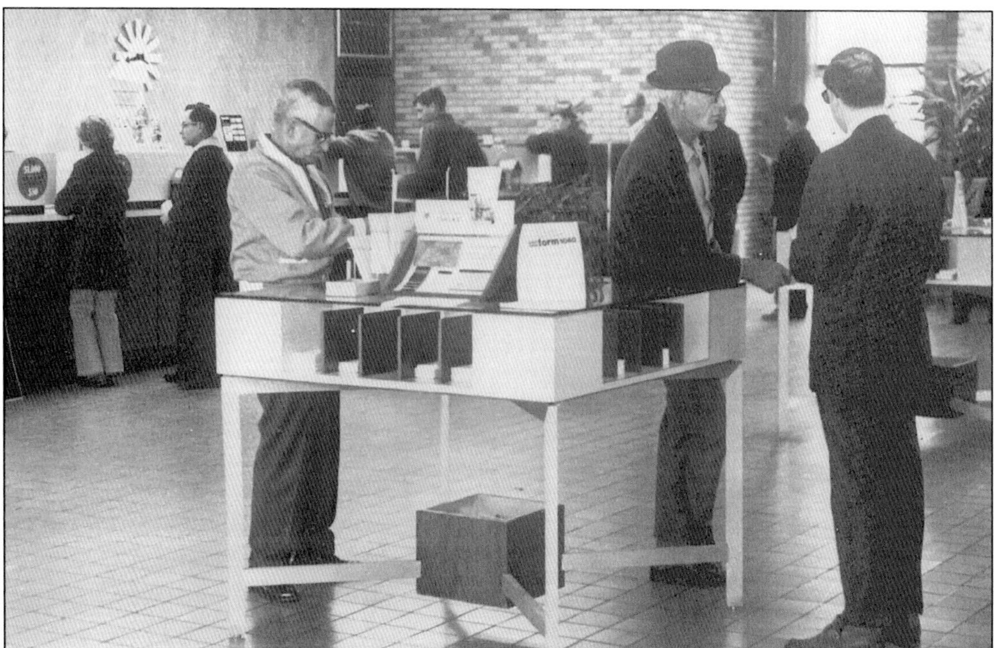

A group of customers are pictured in the Alabama City Bank. For many years this bank was located on Twenty-Seventh Street or "Wall Street." A new modern structure was built near the original bank during the mid-1960s, and this interior is pictured above. Once a locally owned bank, it is now owned by SouthTrust Bank.

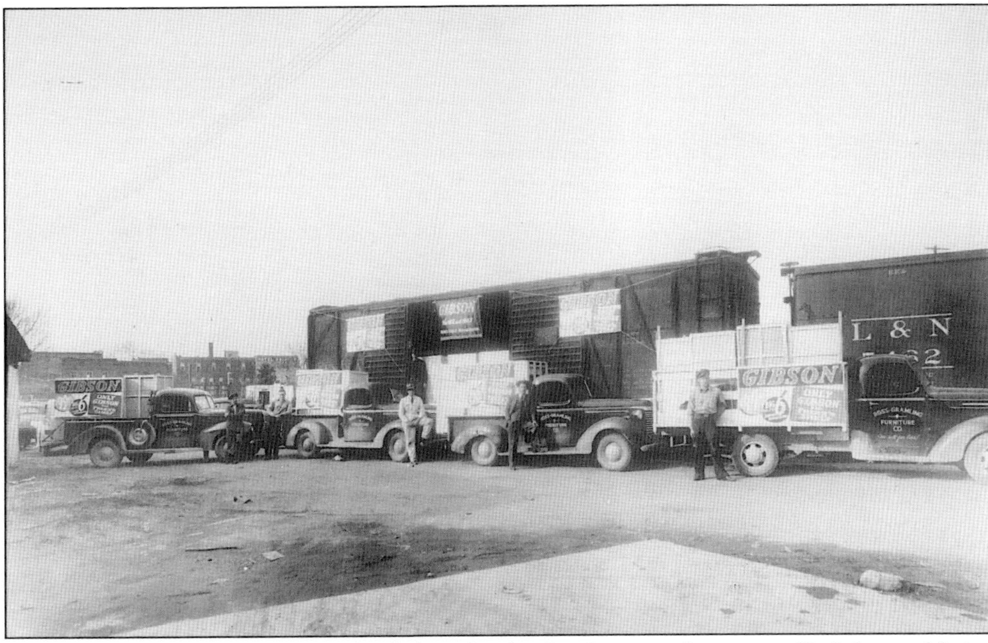

A large load of refrigerators is unloaded at the freight depot in downtown Gadsden and being transported to the Ross Gramling Furniture Company, a popular downtown store for many years. During the 1940s and 1950s, many people depended on large items being shipped by rail.

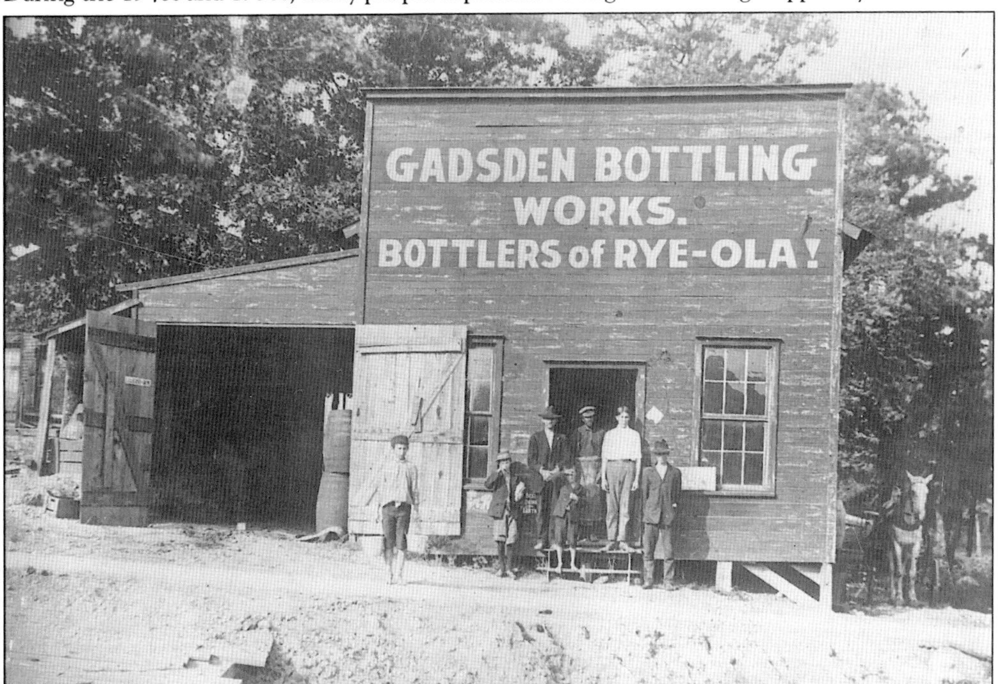

Located on North Twelfth Street near the present site of Meighan Boulevard, the Gadsden Bottling Works was a locally owned soft drink bottling company that bottled a cola known as Rye-Ola. During the early 1900s, there were several small bottling works in the Etowah County area.

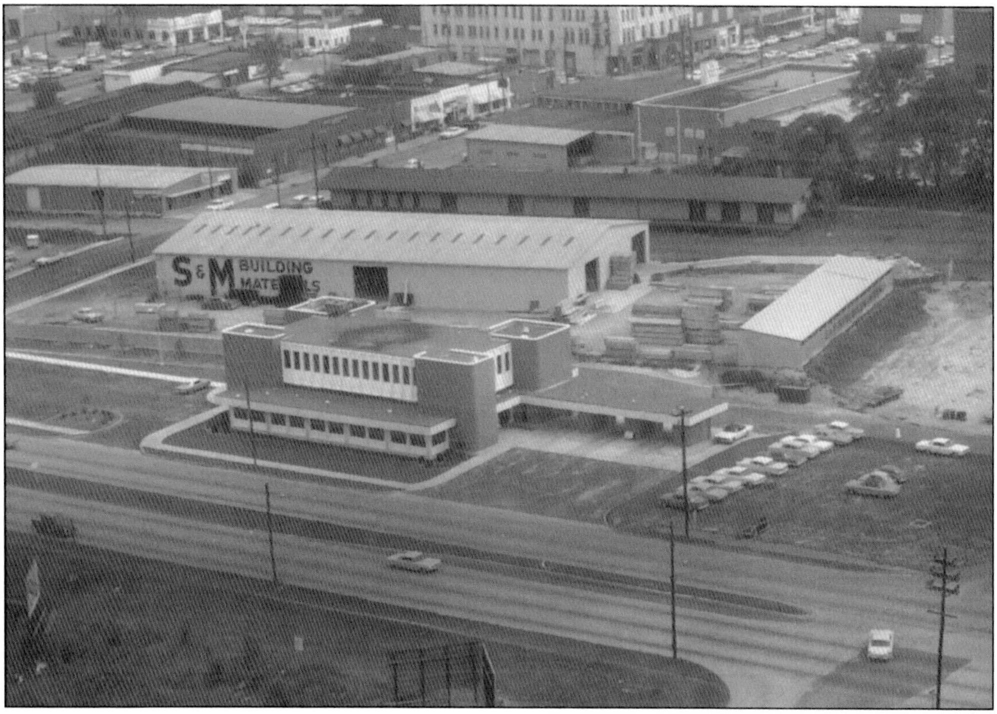

The newly constructed First City National Bank, known today as Regions Bank, is shown here located on Meighan Boulevard in downtown Gadsden. Located directly behind the bank is the S&M Building Supply and the old freight depot, which runs parallel to S&M. Gadsden's Printup Hotel is located in the upper center of the photograph.

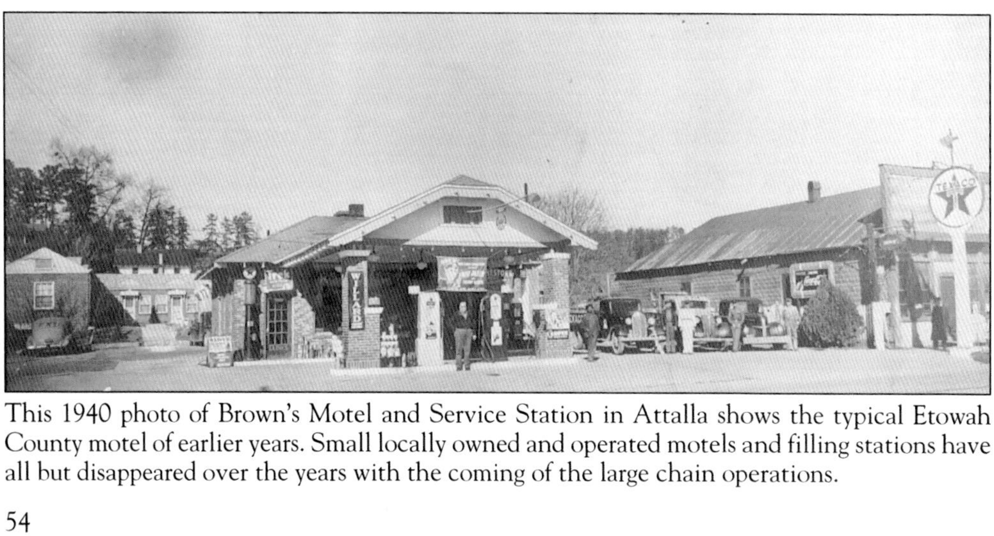

This 1940 photo of Brown's Motel and Service Station in Attalla shows the typical Etowah County motel of earlier years. Small locally owned and operated motels and filling stations have all but disappeared over the years with the coming of the large chain operations.

The Philipson Building is shown here under construction. This seven-story office building was later known as the Noojin Building and is located on Chestnut Street. The original building, located between Fifth and Sixth Streets, was built in front of the old Gadsden General Hospital. First Presbyterian Church of Gadsden is located next to the Philipson Building.

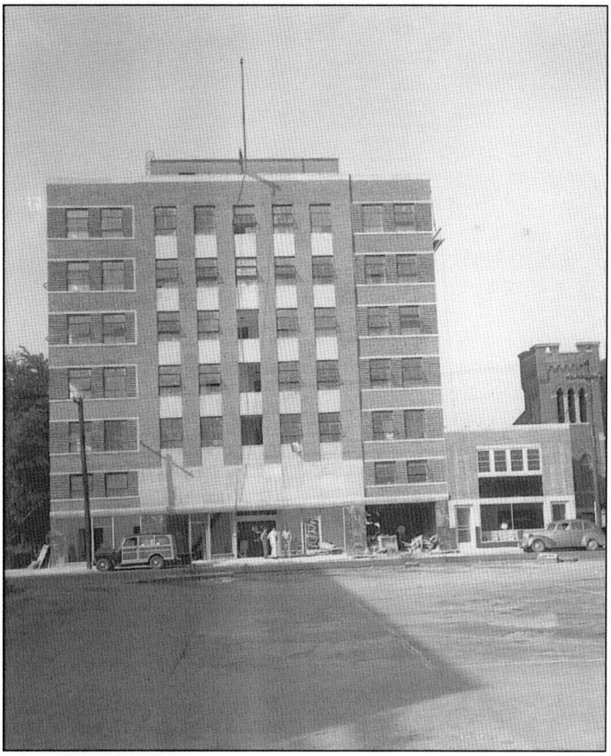

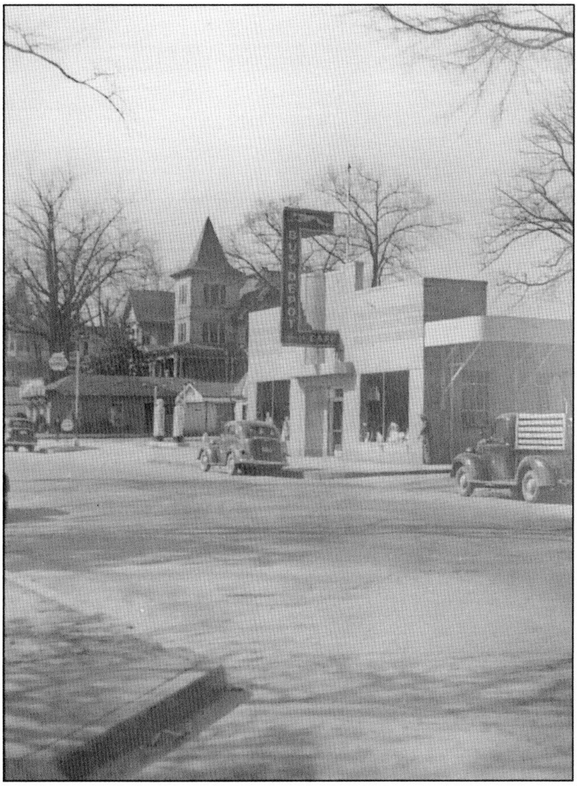

The Greyhound Bus Depot is shown here in a photo from the late 1940s. It was located on Forrest Avenue in downtown Gadsden for many years. Also shown are two old homes on Forrest Avenue that were eventually torn down, along with the bus station.

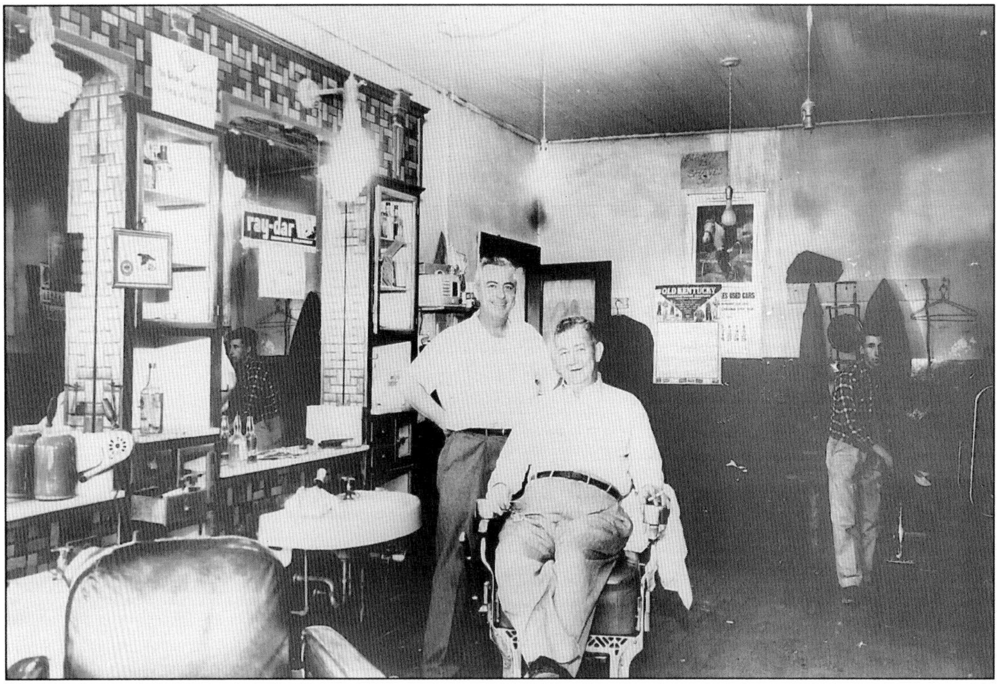

This is an interior scene of one of the many barber shops located throughout the Etowah County area. Paul Barnes' Barber Shop was located on Sansom Avenue in Alabama City. Located at the rear of the shop was a shoe shine stand, a typical feature in barber shops throughout the area. Paul Barnes worked as a barber in the Alabama City area for many years.

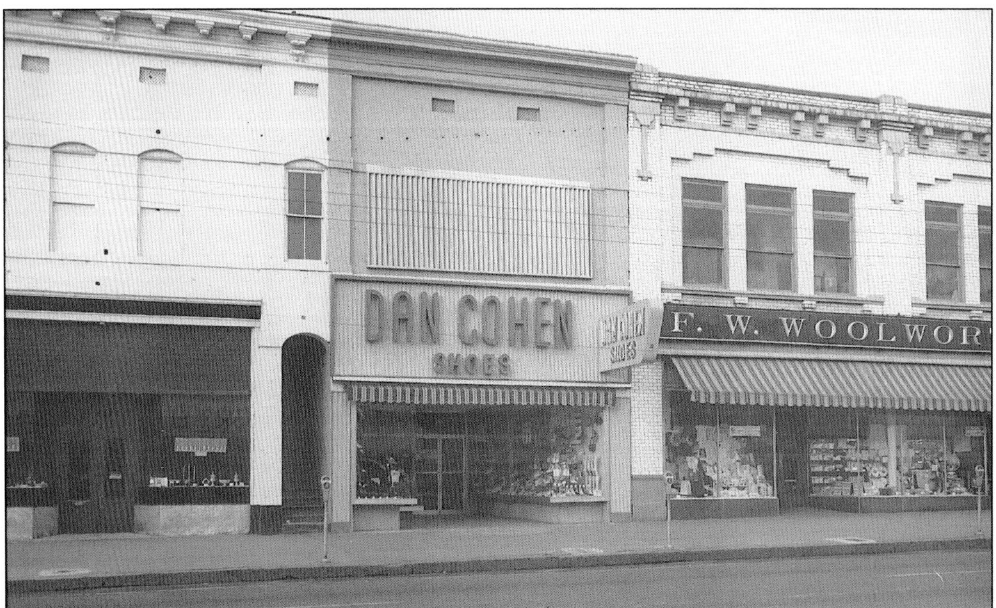

Downtown Gadsden is pictured in May of 1956. The Dan Cohen Shoe Store and the F.W. Woolworth Store were located on the south side of Broad Street in the 400 block. Cross Jewelers is also located next to the Dan Cohen Shoe Store. These stores have long since faded into the history of downtown Gadsden.

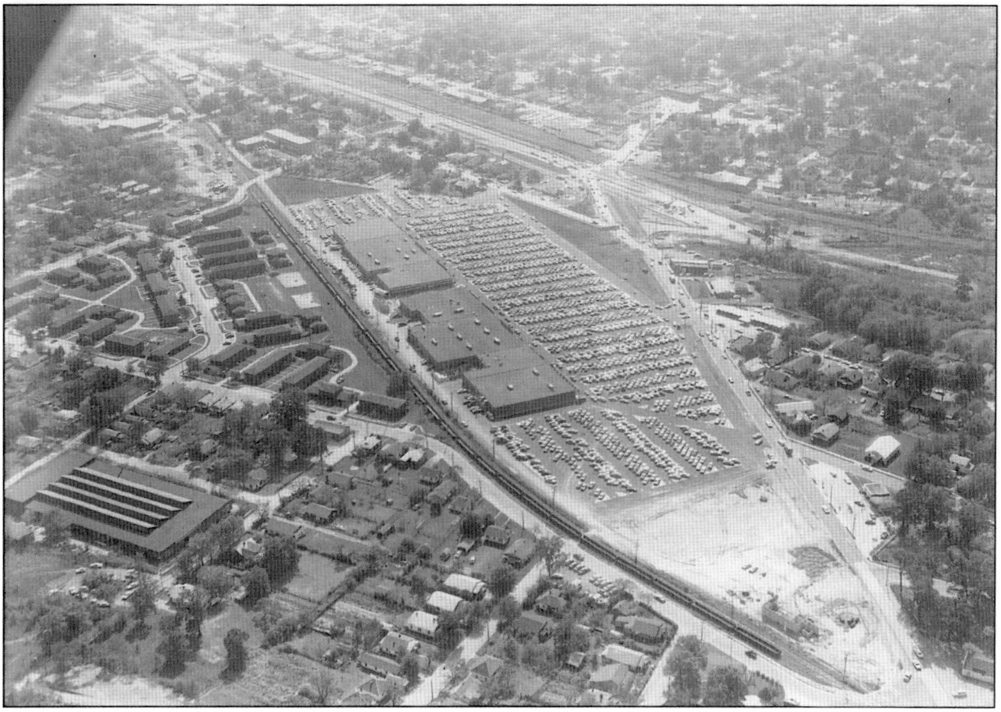

This aerial view of Gadsden shows the Agricola Shopping Center on opening day in December of 1964. One of the first of such shopping centers to open in Etowah County, it was built on property owned by the Agricola family and was once the home of the Elliott Car Works and the Agricola Furnace Works. This shopping center is still in operation 35 years later.

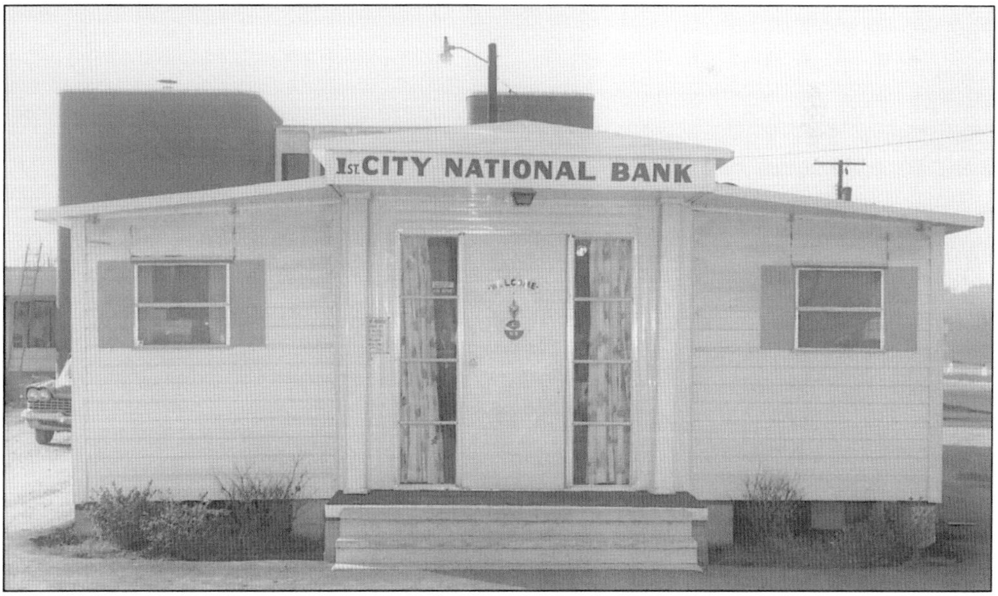

This small mobile home served as the first building of the First City National Bank. Built on Meighan Boulevard during the early 1960s, this popular financial institution is currently part of the Regions Financial Network. The bank is located in downtown Gadsden on Meighan Boulevard between Fourth and Fifth Streets.

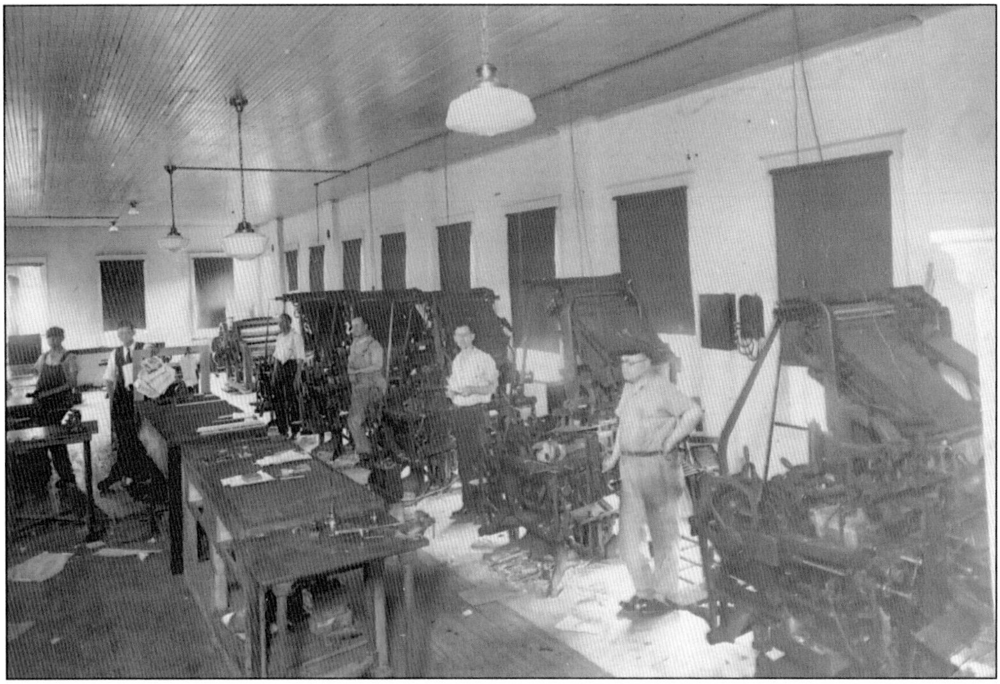

Shown here is the interior of the composing room at the *Gadsden Times*. Several of the *Times* employees are pictured in this 1947 photo. Etowah County's oldest employer, the *Gadsden Times* dates back to 1867. It is presently located on Locust Street in downtown Gadsden.

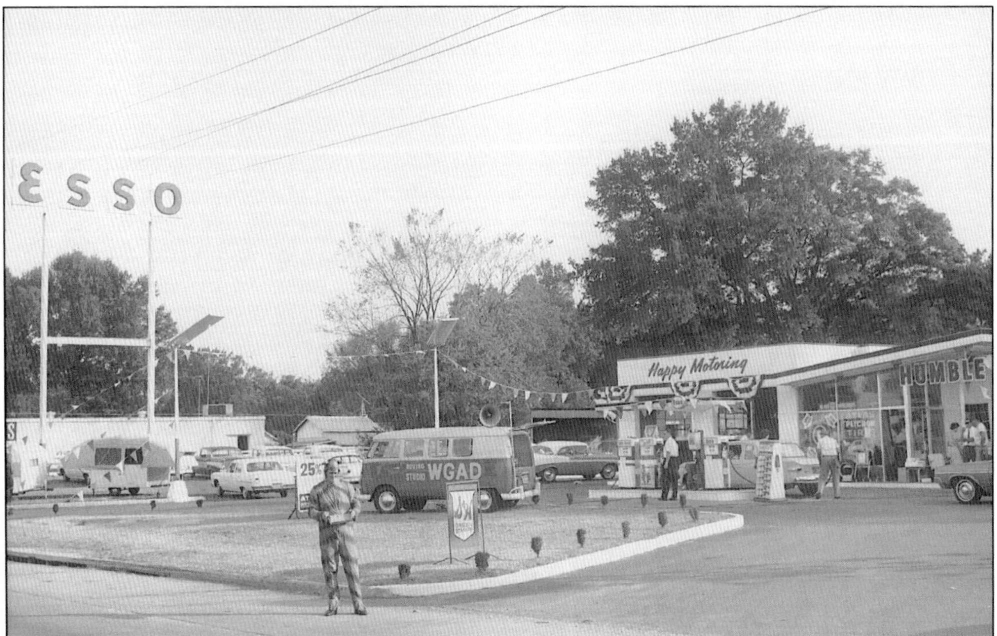

The ESSO Station is shown here on the corner of Hood Avenue and East Meighan Boulevard. Service stations such as this Humble Oil Station offered many promotional items to entice motorists to purchase gasoline at their stations. The WGAD news van is seen at this live remote broadcast from 1960.

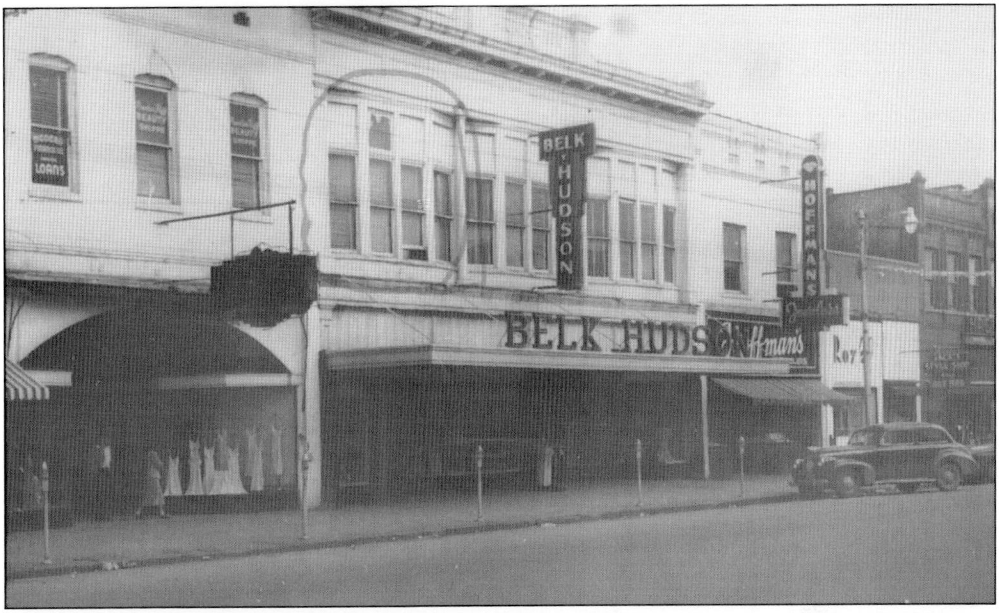

The Belk Hudson Store, located at the time of this photograph in the Hughes Building, is shown in the 400 block of Broad Street. The Hughes Building was built by longtime Gadsden physician M.P. Hughes. Also located on this block were Hoffman's Jewelers and Hagedorns. Jack Saks clothing is located to the left of the Belk Hudson Store.

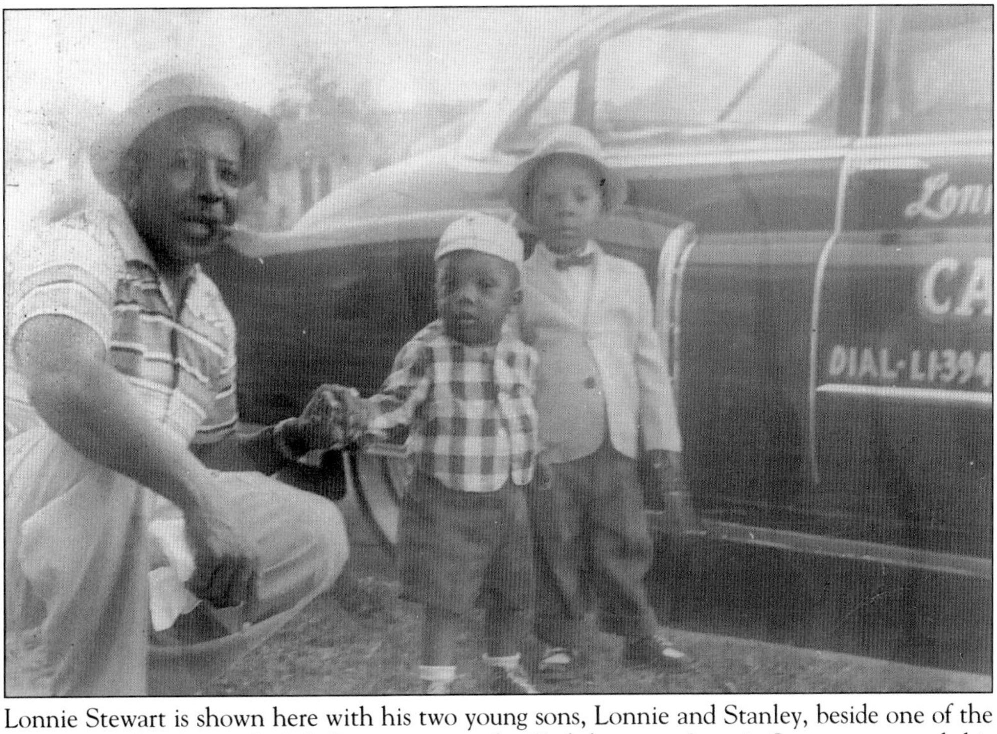

Lonnie Stewart is shown here with his two young sons, Lonnie and Stanley, beside one of the many taxis that Lonnie's Cab Service ran in the Gadsden area. Lonnie Stewart operated this very successful service during the 1950s and 1960s, and it was located on North Sixth Street in downtown Gadsden.

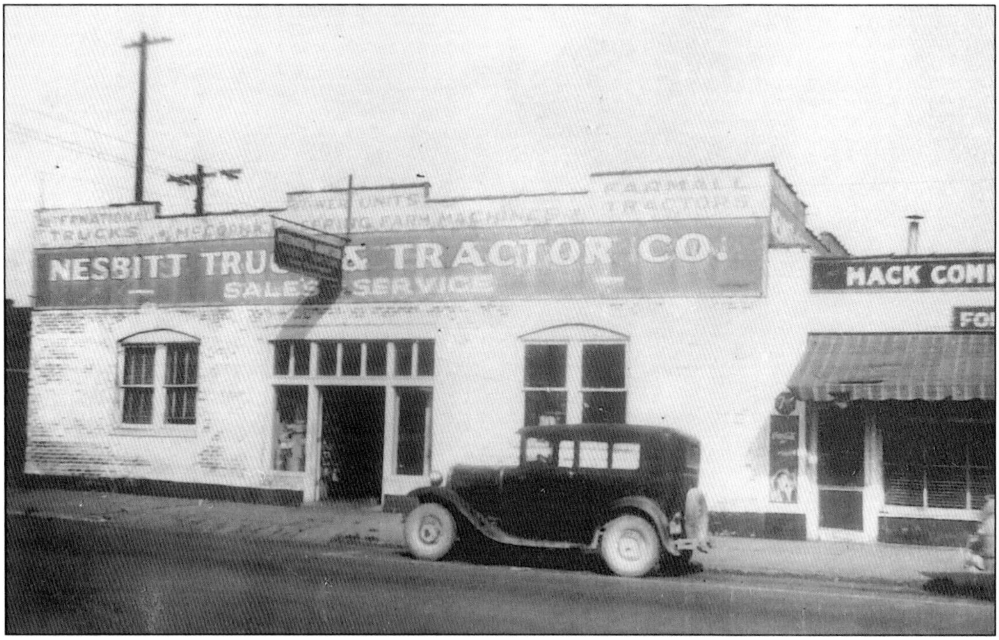

Nesbitt Truck and Tractor Company is shown here in a photo from the 1940s. Located on the southeast corner of Third and Locust Streets, it was a popular place for Etowah Countians to purchase tractors and farm equipment.

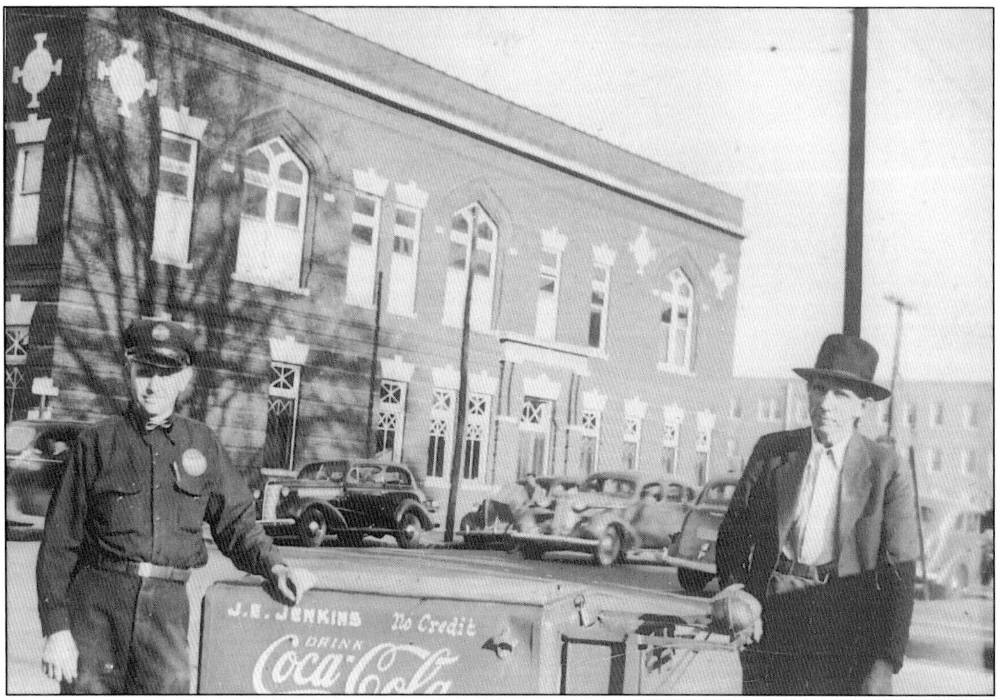

J.E. Jenkins, pictured on the right, is shown with the Coca-Cola cart he pushed around in downtown Gadsden. Downtown workers could purchase soft drinks, candy, potato chips, chewing gum, and fruit from Jenkins. When he came by, everyone knew it was time to take a break from work. This photo was taken on South Sixth Street.

Five

PUBLIC SERVICE

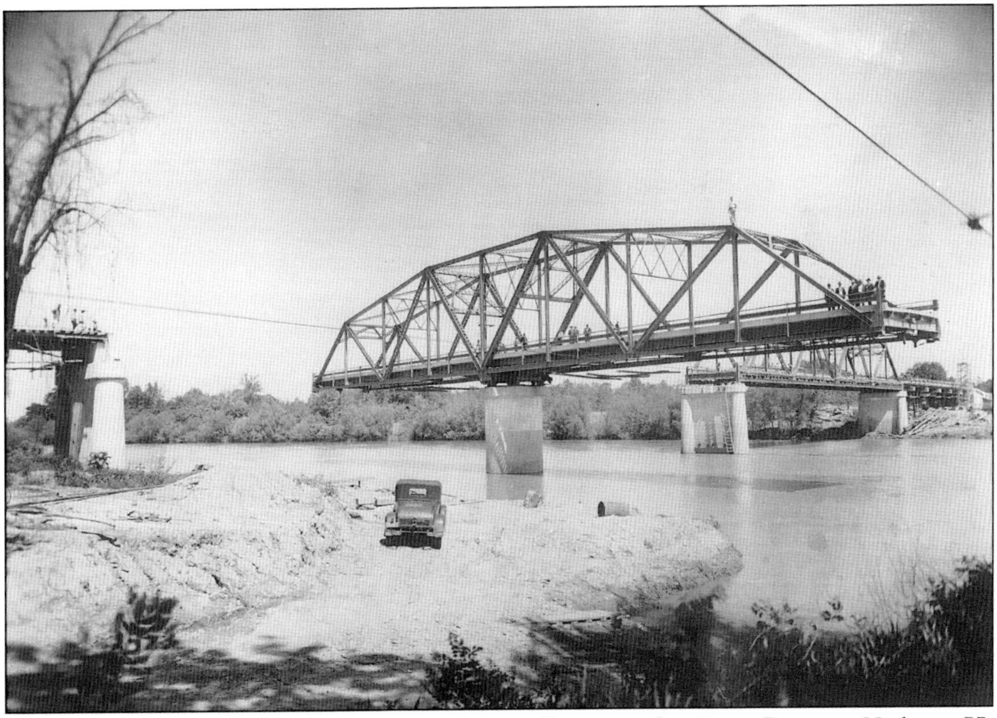

Built to handle the ever-increasing automobile traffic across the Coosa River on Highway 77, the Mark Smith Bridge in Southside is shown here under construction. The bridge featured a turning mechanism to allow riverboats to pass, and replaced the ferry that operated here for many years.

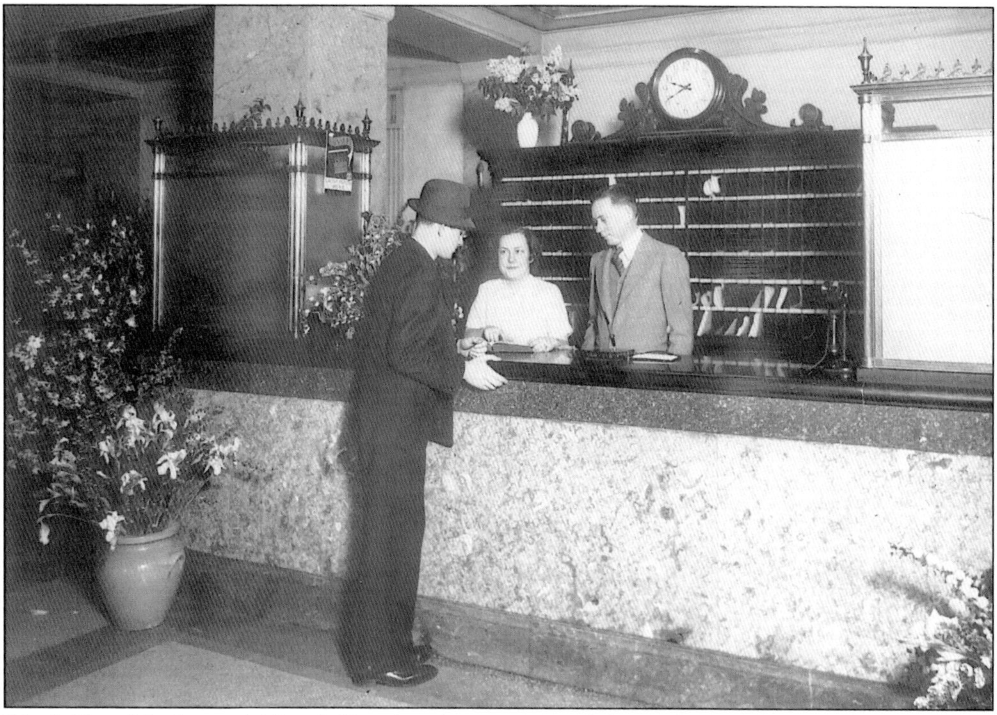

The lobby of the beautiful Reich Hotel in downtown Gadsden is shown in this early photograph. Vera Springfield is registering a guest as Mr. Coates, the hotel manager, looks on. Gadsden's first skyscraper, the hotel was built and operated by Mr. Adolph Reich. Vera Springfield worked at the hotel during its entire 50 years of operation.

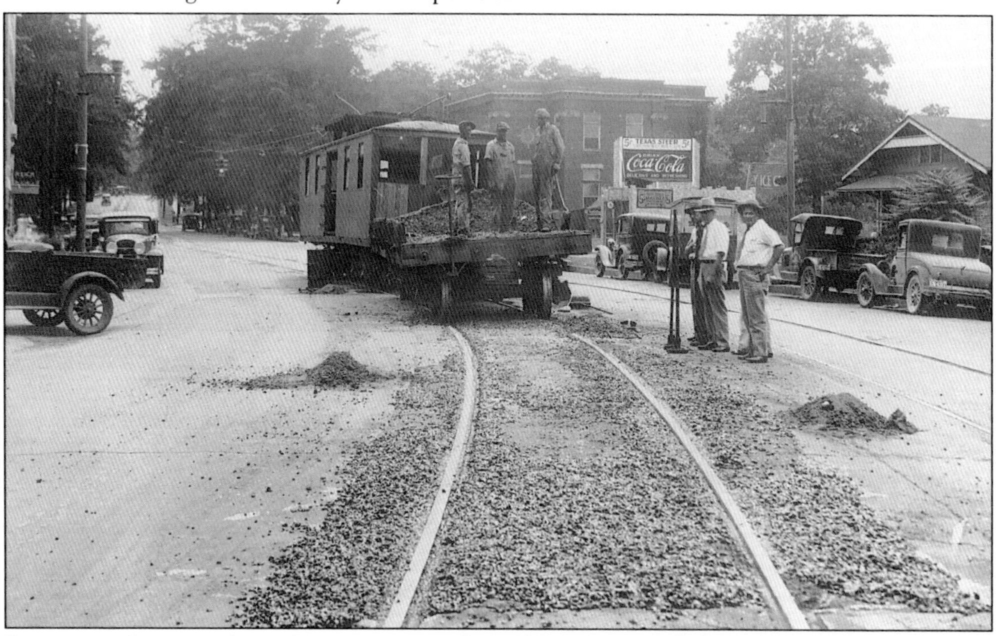

Repairs are being made to the streetcar tracks in downtown Gadsden in this photograph. The tracks have since been removed from the streets. Gadsden's early public library can be seen in the background, and a small cafe advertising a Texas Steer burger for 5¢.

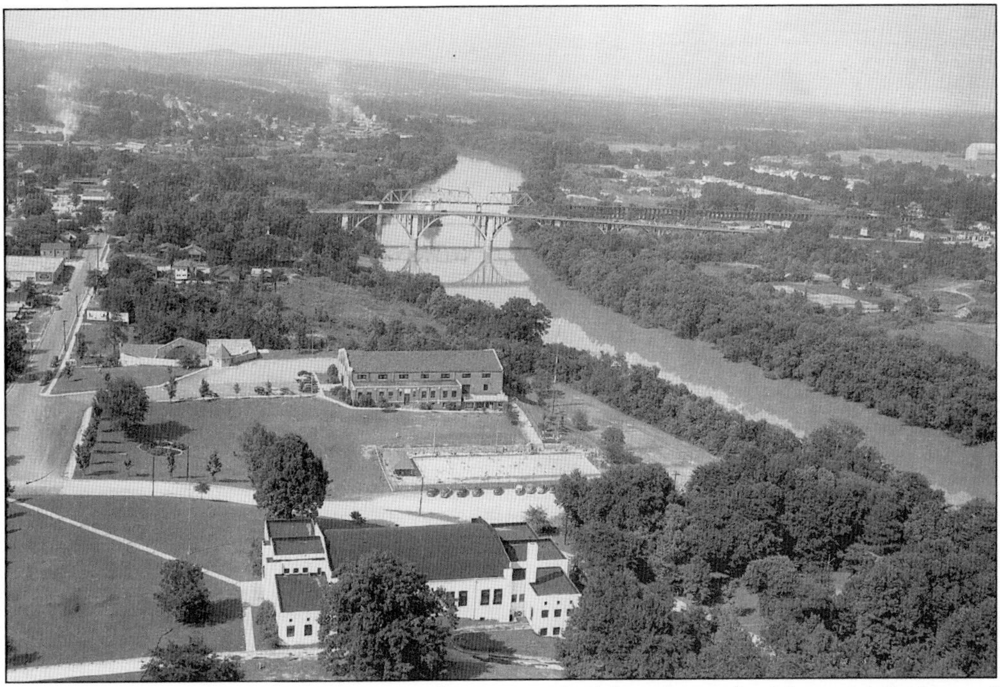

This aerial view of the Coosa River in downtown Gadsden shows the Memorial Bridge and the L&N Railroad trestle in the background. Gadsden's beautiful Convention Hall is also shown with the Municipal pool located nearby. The swimming pool and the armory are no longer in existence.

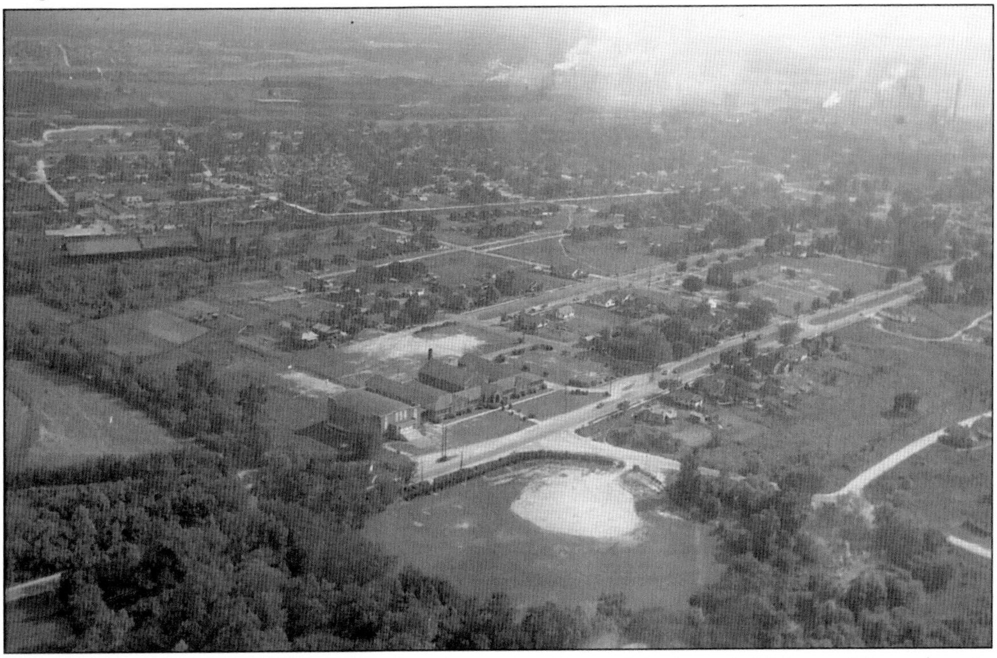

The old Emma Sansom High School is shown in this aerial view of Alabama City taken in November of 1951. The large field in front of the school was the former home of Dwight Park. General Forrest Middle School is presently located at this site.

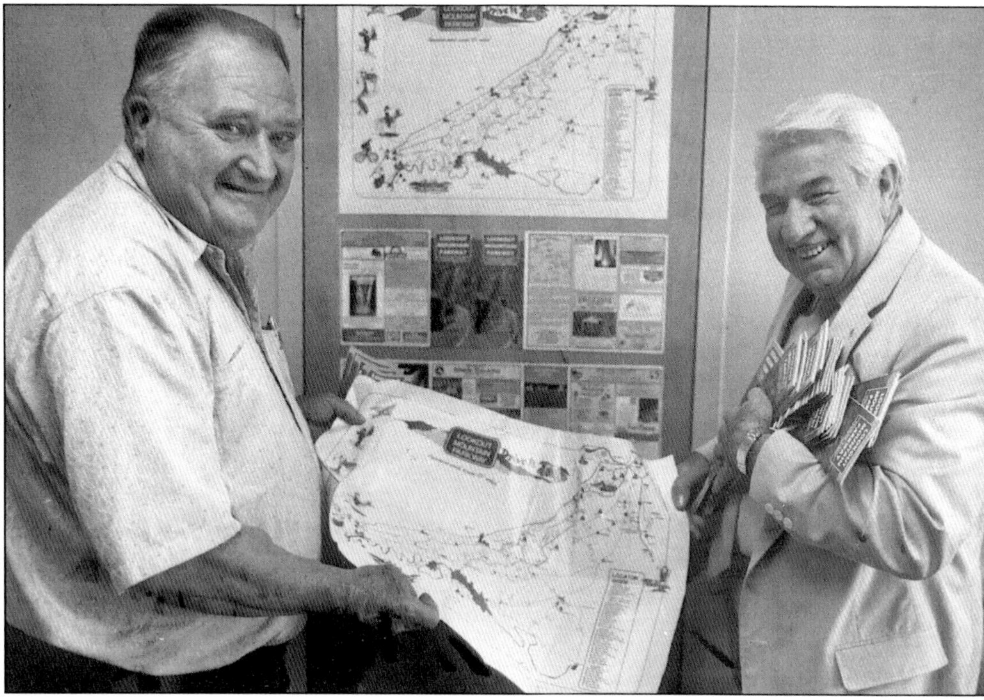

Local historian Joe Barnes on the left and Lloyd Wagnon, the director of the Etowah Tourism Board, are shown overlooking the route of the "world's largest yard sale." The yard sale begins at Noccalula Falls in Gadsden and continues north to near Cincinnati, Ohio. This event is held each summer and attracts thousands of tourists to the area.

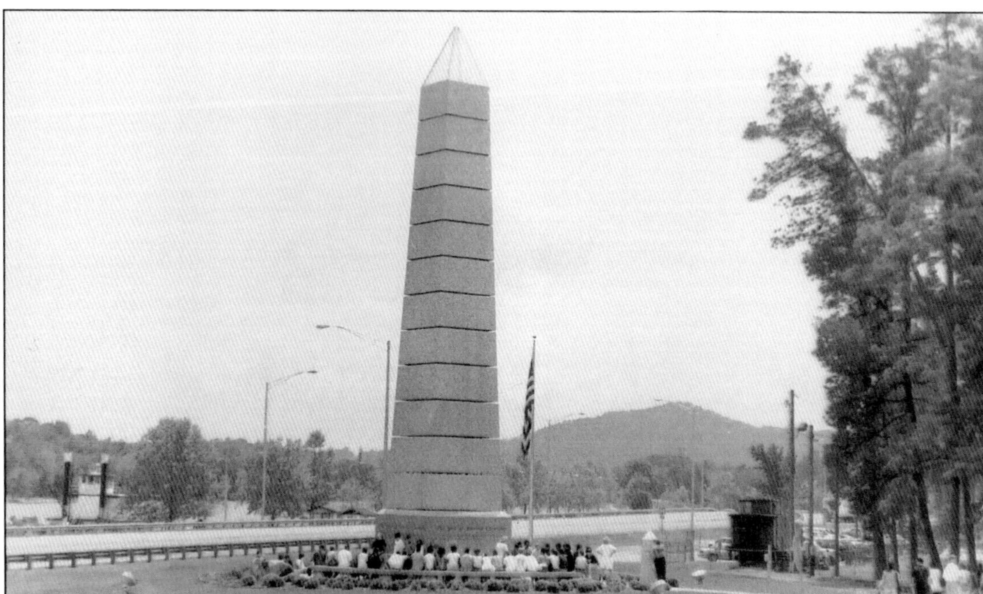

A group of school children are shown here at the Spirit of the American Citizenship Monument located near the banks of the Coosa River in downtown Gadsden. This beautiful monument was built to remind the citizens of Etowah County that each and everyone is important and that committed citizens can improve our nation.

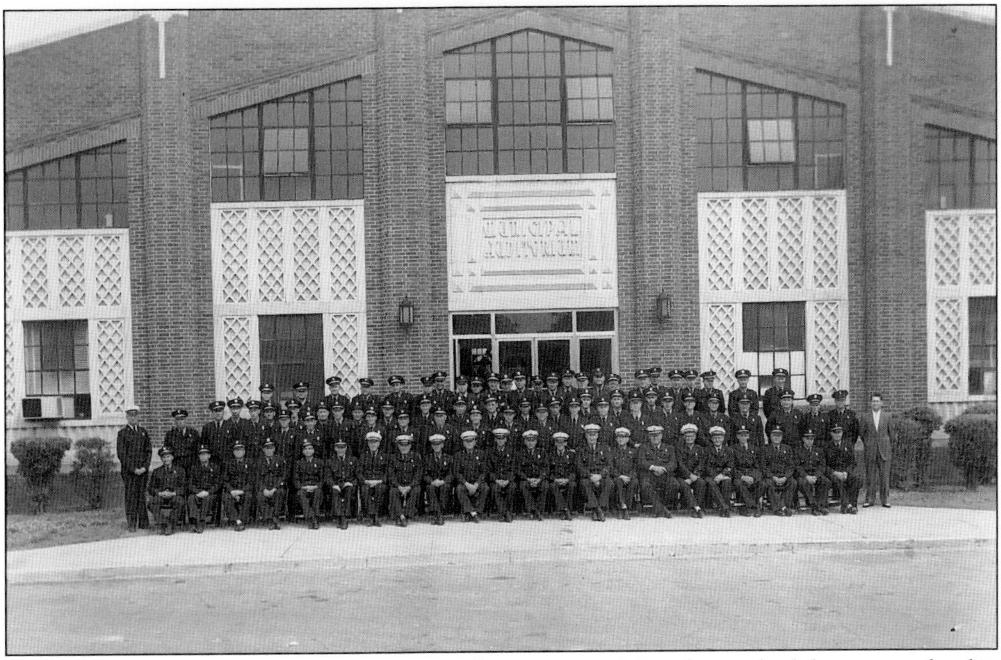

Members of the Gadsden Fire Department take time out of their busy schedules to pose for this photograph in June of 1958, taken in front of the Gadsden Municipal Auditorium. Gadsden has always taken pride in its fire department since its beginnings in the late 1800s.

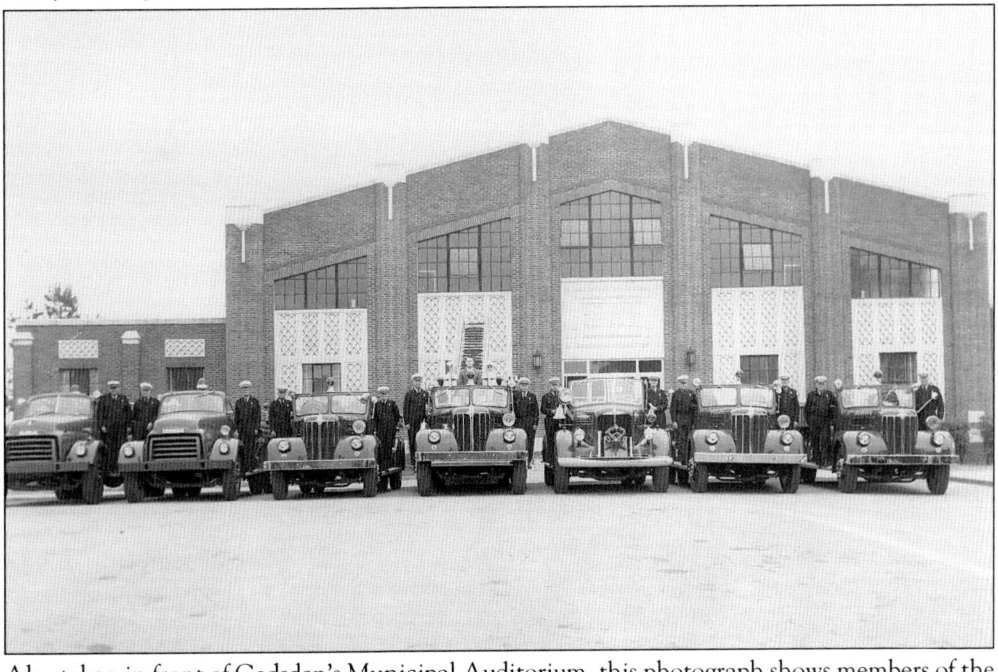

Also taken in front of Gadsden's Municipal Auditorium, this photograph shows members of the fire department posing with some of their engines in 1958. The Gadsden Fire Department has been updated and is now one of the best-equipped departments in the State of Alabama. The Municipal Auditorium, shown in this photograph, was later remodeled and is now known as Convention Hall.

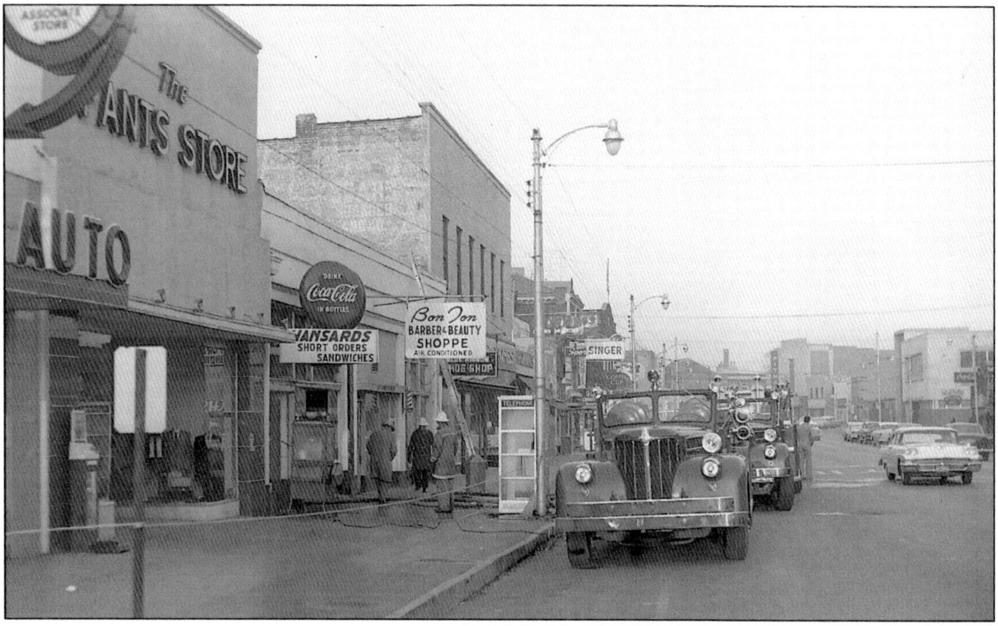

Broad Street in downtown Gadsden was a busy place during the early days of 1960. Firemen from the central fire station are shown here on the scene of a fire at the building that contained Hansard's Sandwich Shop and the Bon Ton Barber Shop. Hansard's was a popular place in downtown Gadsden for many years, and most older residents will tell you that they had the best hotdogs in town.

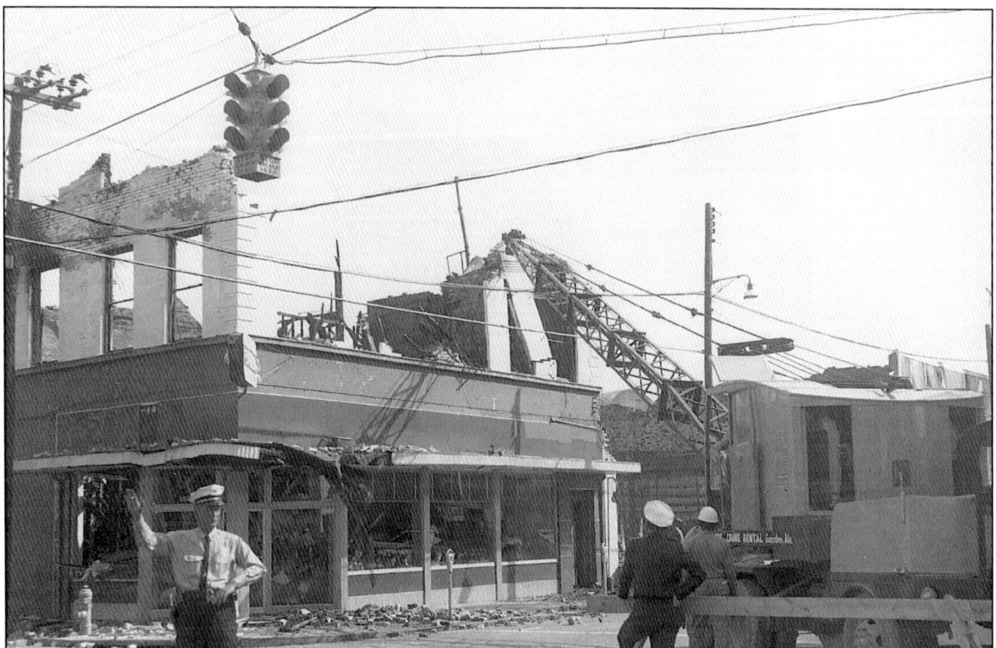

Demolition is underway at the corner of Third and Chestnut Streets where the Walthour Flowers and Sibert Hardware Buildings were located. These buildings burned in a large fire in 1966. Police directed traffic as a crane swung a large wrecking ball to bring the buildings down.

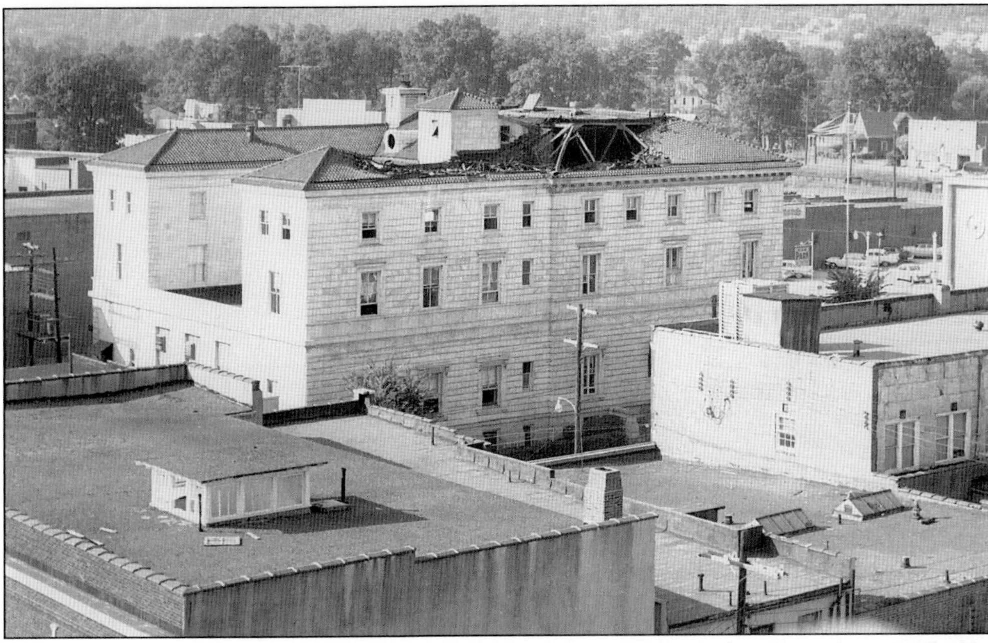

A large hole is seen in the roof of the United States Post Office in this photo from 1958. The post office was damaged heavily by a fire on the second and third floors. This building was later repaired and houses several federal offices; the post office moved to a new building on Walnut Street.

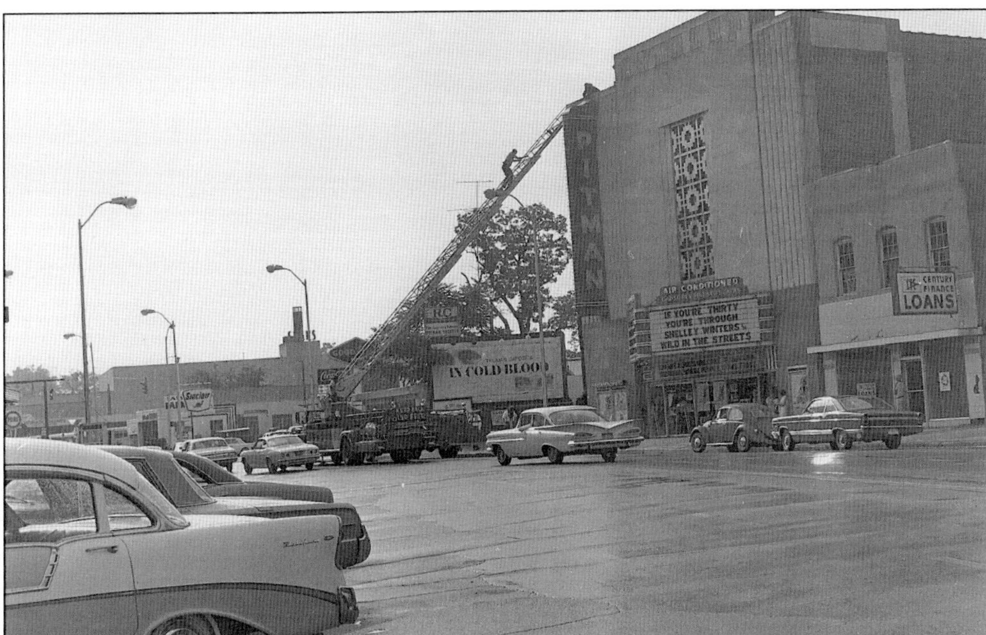

Members of the Gadsden Fire Department are shown here climbing the ladder from one of the fire trucks on the scene of a minor fire at the Pitman Theatre. The Theatre sustained little damage in the fire, but it created a lot of excitement in downtown Gadsden. The Theatre remained open for business until the 1980s.

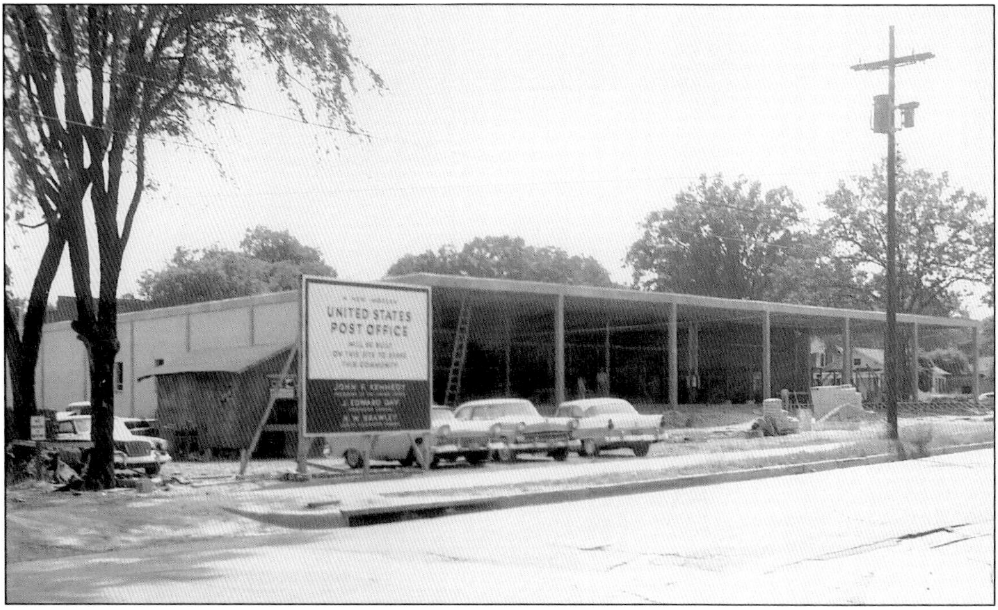

Gadsden's new United States Post Office is shown here under construction in August of 1962. The early post office located on the corner of Sixth and Broad Streets was damaged by fire in 1958, and the need was felt for a new post office. The new structure is located on the corner of Seventh and Chestnut Streets in downtown Gadsden. This was the original site of Disque High School.

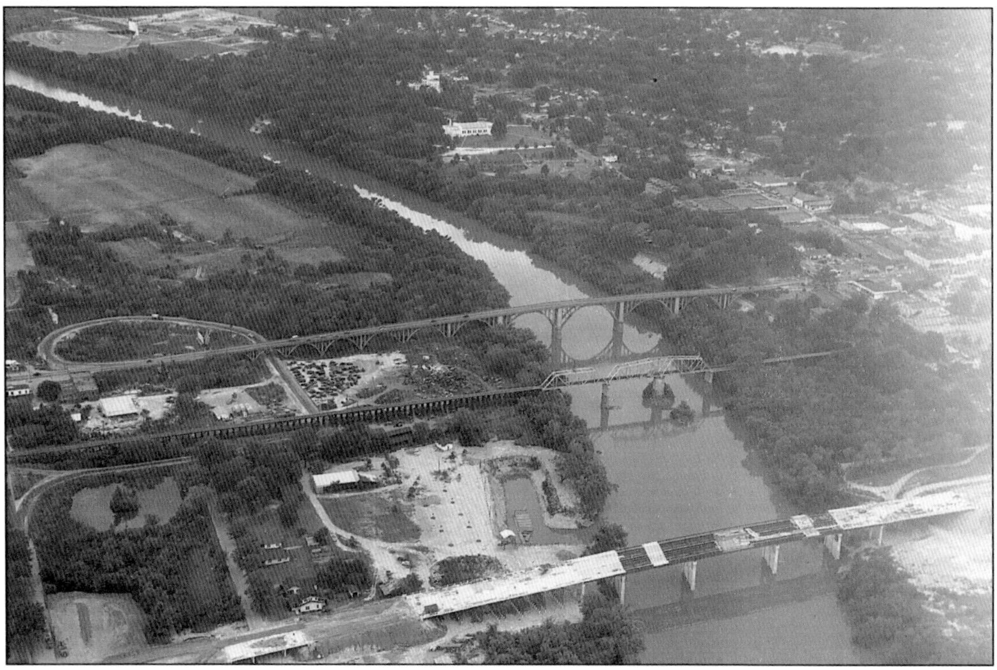

Named for Gadsden Mayor J. Herbert Meighan, the Meighan Bridge is shown under construction in this photograph from the late 1950s. This new bridge spanned the Coosa River and united downtown with East Gadsden. A welcome addition to the community, the bridge helped to eliminate the bumper-to-bumper traffic on the Memorial Bridge on Broad Street.

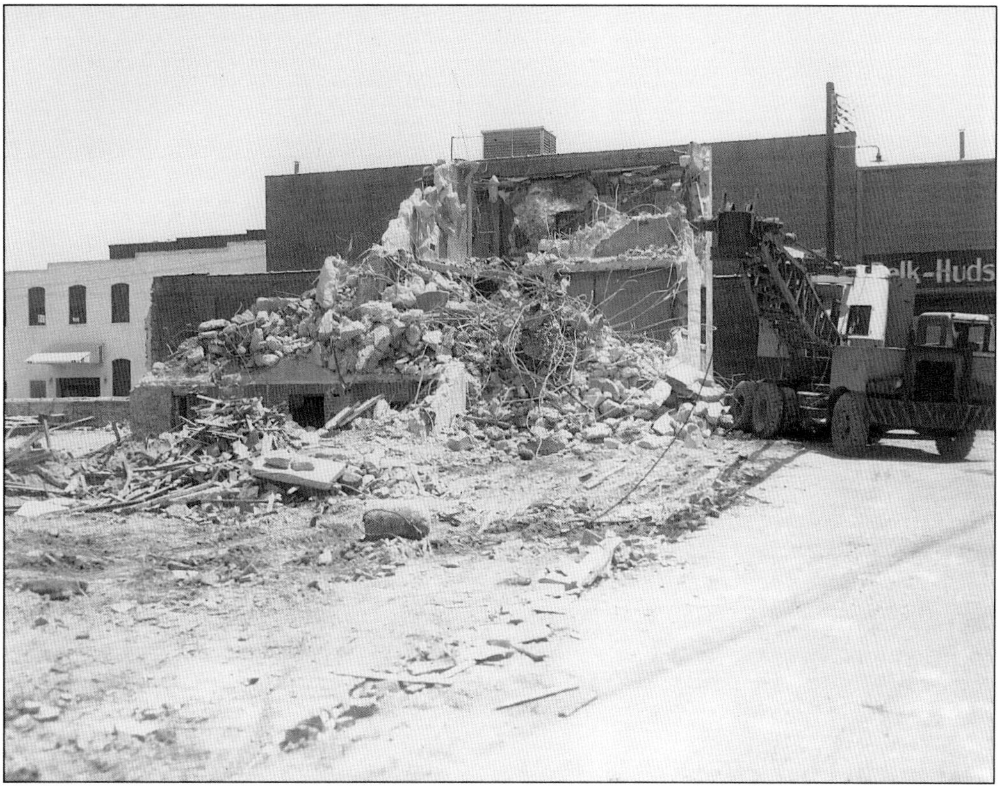

Demolition is underway at the old Gadsden city jail. Located at the rear of the early Gadsden city hall on North Fifth Street, the jail moved along with the city hall to a new facility on South First Street during the early 1960s. The old jail was torn down in 1965.

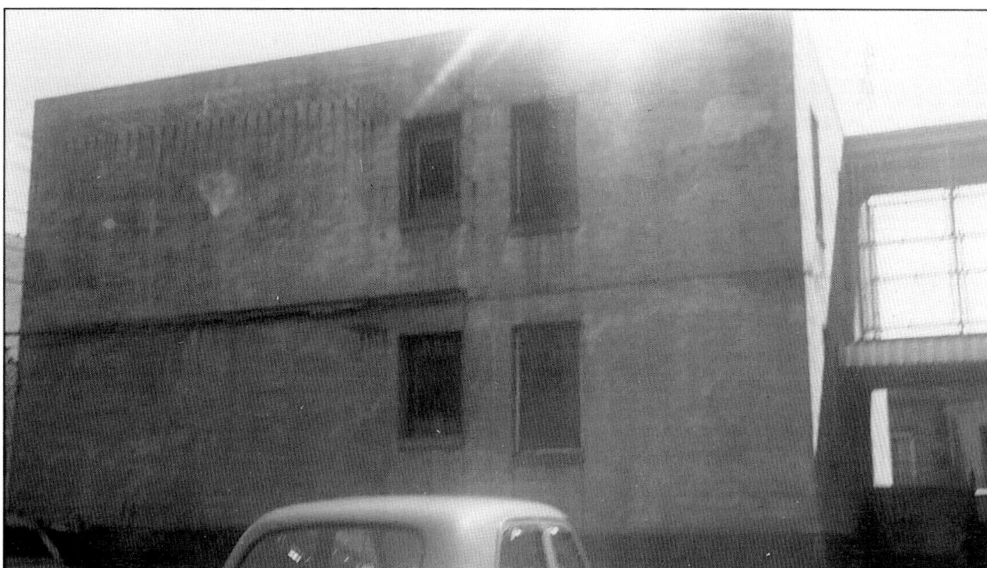

Another view of the old Gadsden city jail is seen in this photograph from the late 1950s. The old jail, fire department, police department, and city hall were torn down after standing vacant for quite some time.

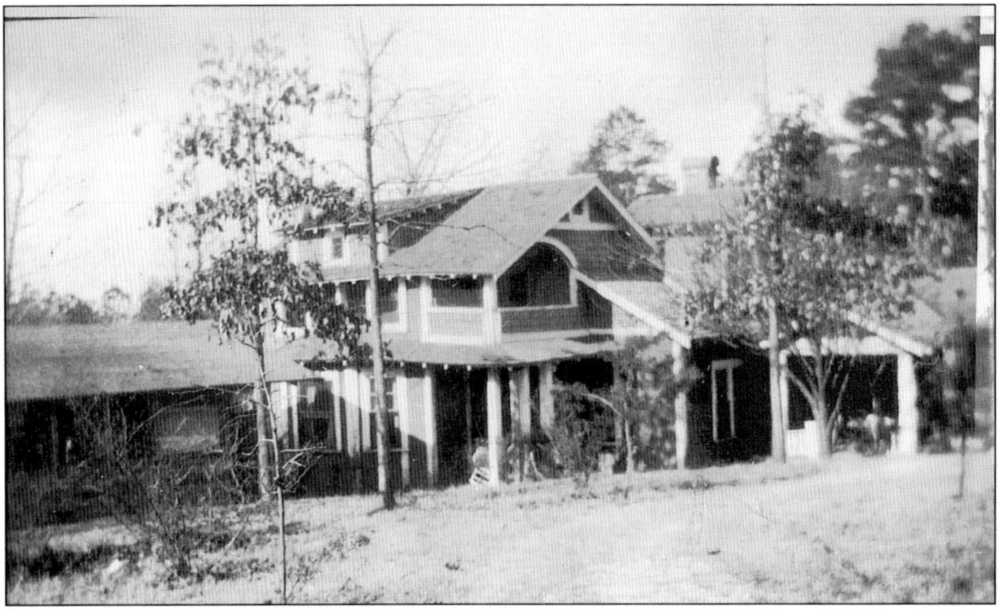

Shown here in a photograph from 1923 is the Fresh Air Camp that was located on Lookout Mountain, near the ruins of the beautiful Bellevue Hotel. At the time of this photograph, the hospital at the camp had 117 patients. This is a residential area today that looks out over the city of Gadsden over the brow of the mountain.

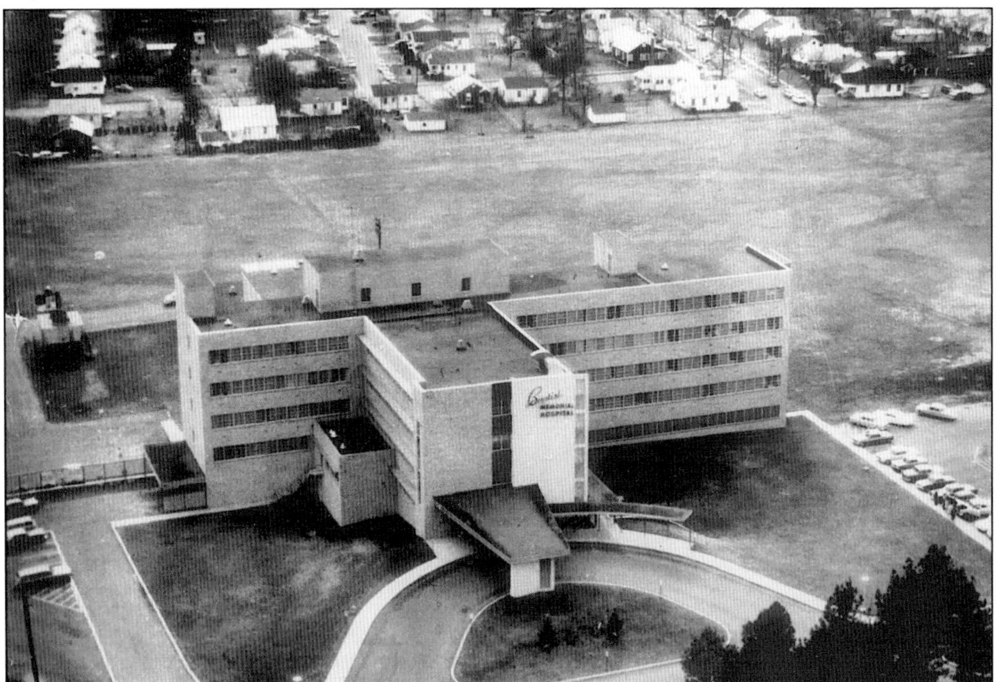

The Baptist Memorial Hospital is shown above, shortly after construction in 1963. Now known as the Gadsden Regional Medical Center, the hospital was owned for many years by the Etowah Baptist Association. Dedicated in 1963, it was located near the Goodyear Tire and Rubber Company.

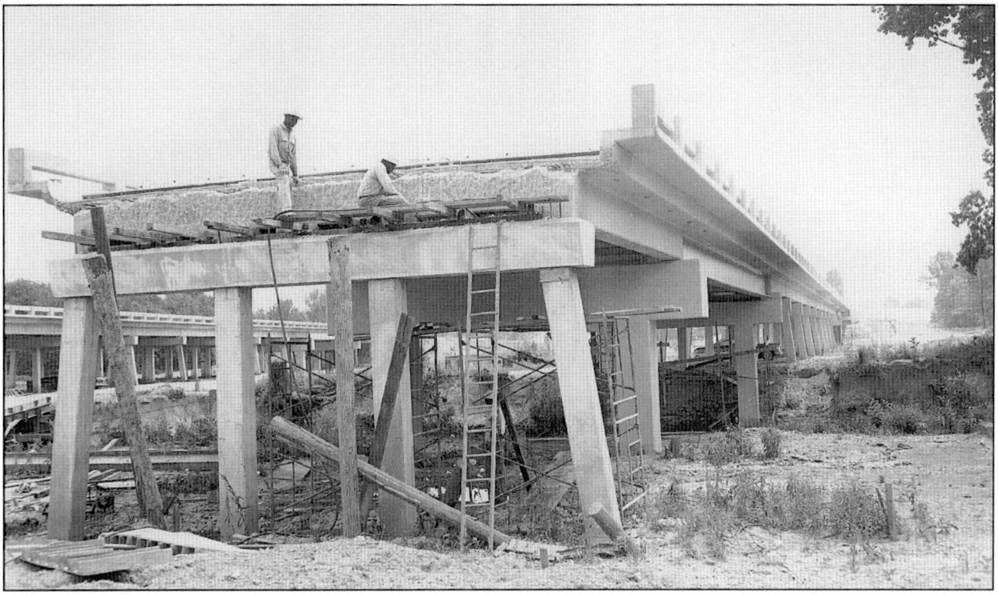

This group is seen hard at work on the construction of the bridges of Interstate 59. This large interstate was the first divided highway in the area and runs from Chattanooga to Birmingham, Tuscaloosa, and other southern points. It was built in 1962.

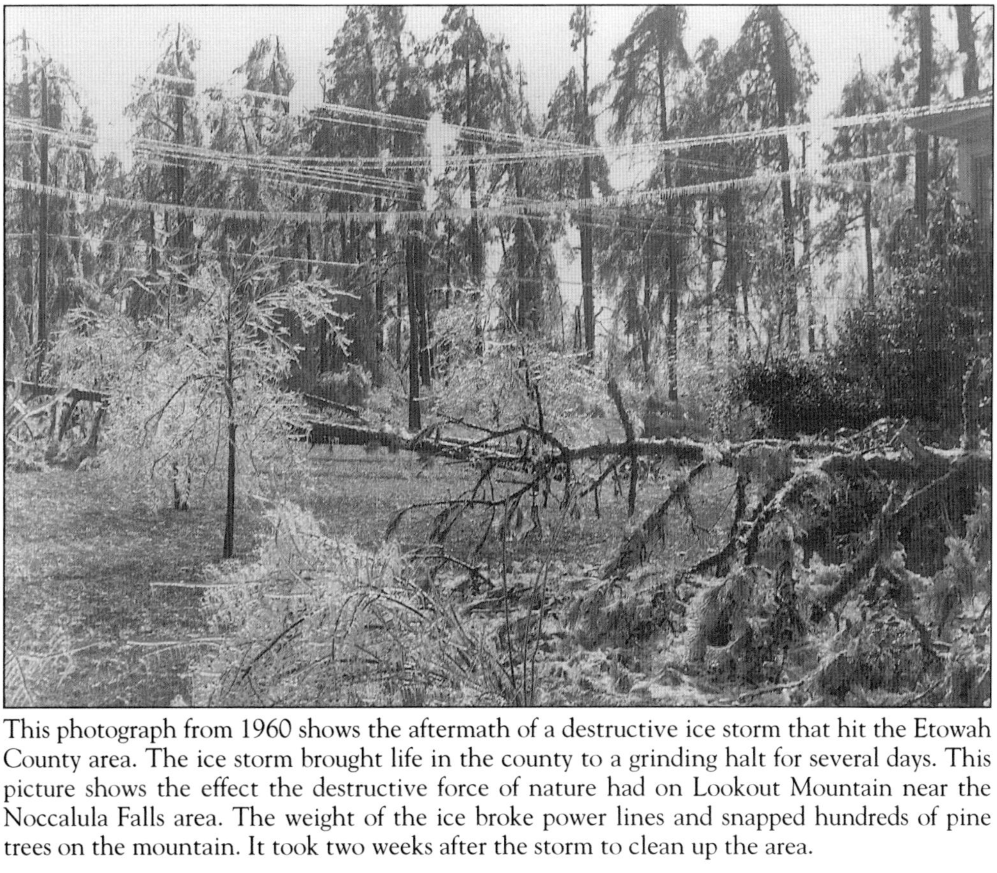

This photograph from 1960 shows the aftermath of a destructive ice storm that hit the Etowah County area. The ice storm brought life in the county to a grinding halt for several days. This picture shows the effect the destructive force of nature had on Lookout Mountain near the Noccalula Falls area. The weight of the ice broke power lines and snapped hundreds of pine trees on the mountain. It took two weeks after the storm to clean up the area.

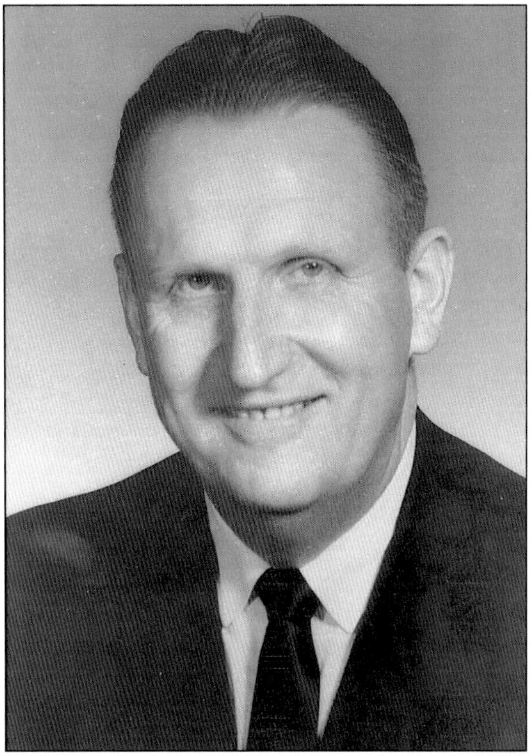

Born in Gadsden on December 8, 1912, to George Columbus and Mary Browning Allen, James Allen attended Gadsden Public Schools and the University of Alabama, where he received a law degree. He practiced law in Gadsden until 1942, and served Alabama in the House of Representatives in 1938, and as lieutenant governor in 1951 and 1963. Allen was elected to the United States Senate in 1968 where he served until his death in 1978.

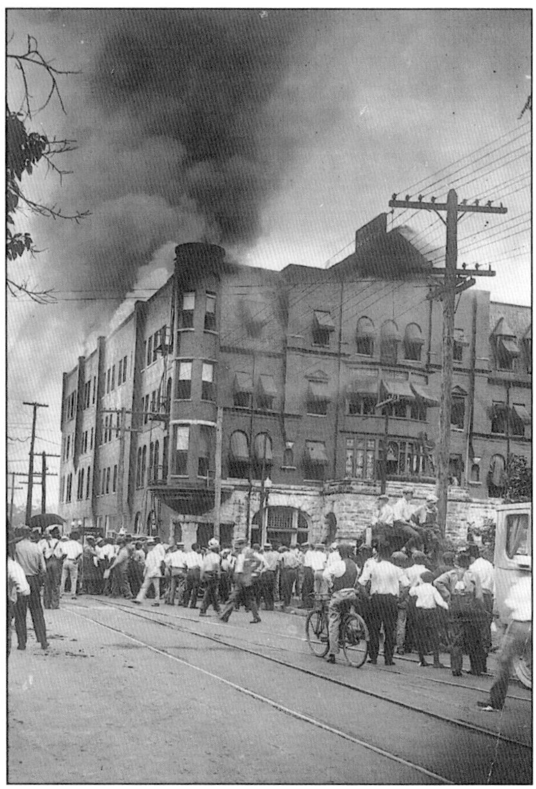

A group of curious onlookers watch the destructive fire that struck Gadsden's beautiful Printup Hotel. Built during the 1880s, the hotel was later managed by Adolph Reich, and was damaged heavily by two fires during the 1920s. Following this second fire, the hotel was totally remodeled with steel and concrete in an attempt to make it as fireproof as possible. During remodeling, the fourth floor was taken off.

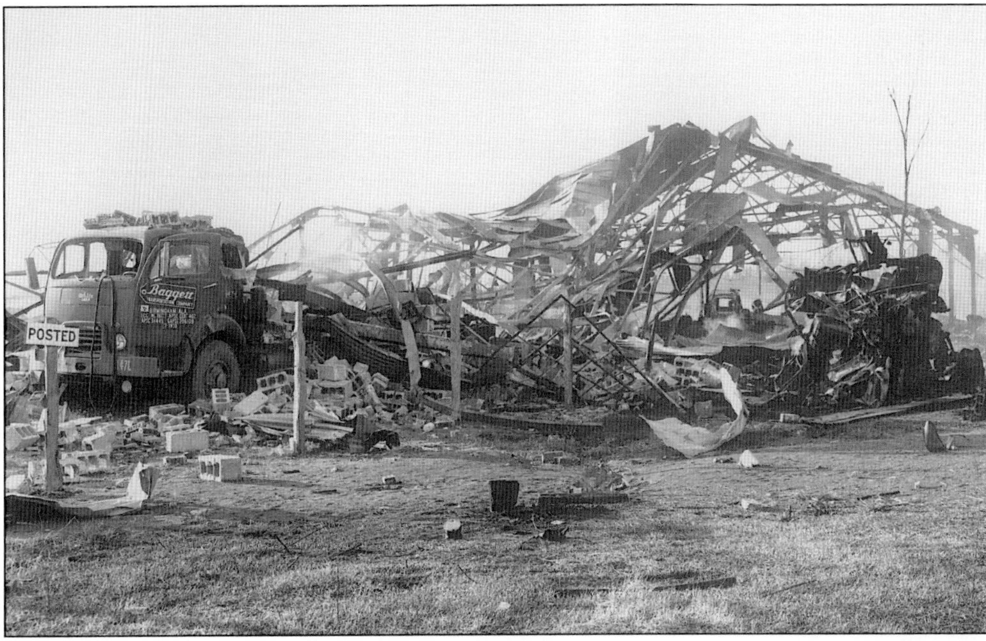

The charred remains of a local garage are shown in this photograph from Attalla. This spectacular fire totally ruined the garage, which was located at the present site of Wal-Mart at the intersection of Highway 11 and Highway 77. A Baggett Transportation truck is shown here in the ruins.

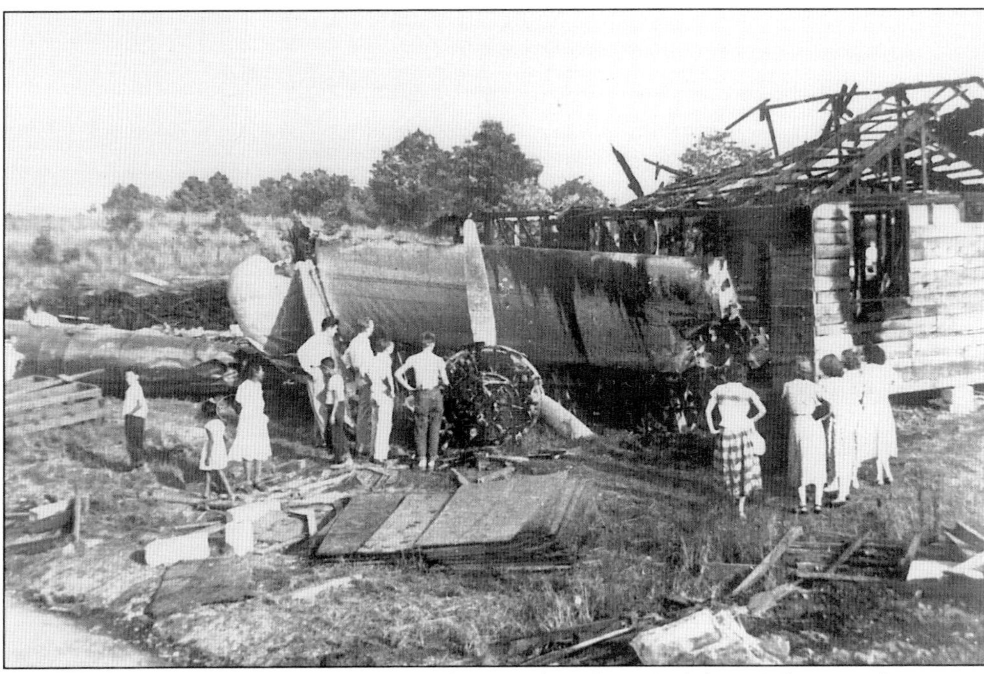

Depicted here is the aftermath of an airplane crash in East Gadsden. A large air force cargo plane went down near the site of what is now Highway 278. The plane crashed into two houses that were unoccupied at the time. Ironically, the people had refused to move in on this day because it was Friday the 13th.

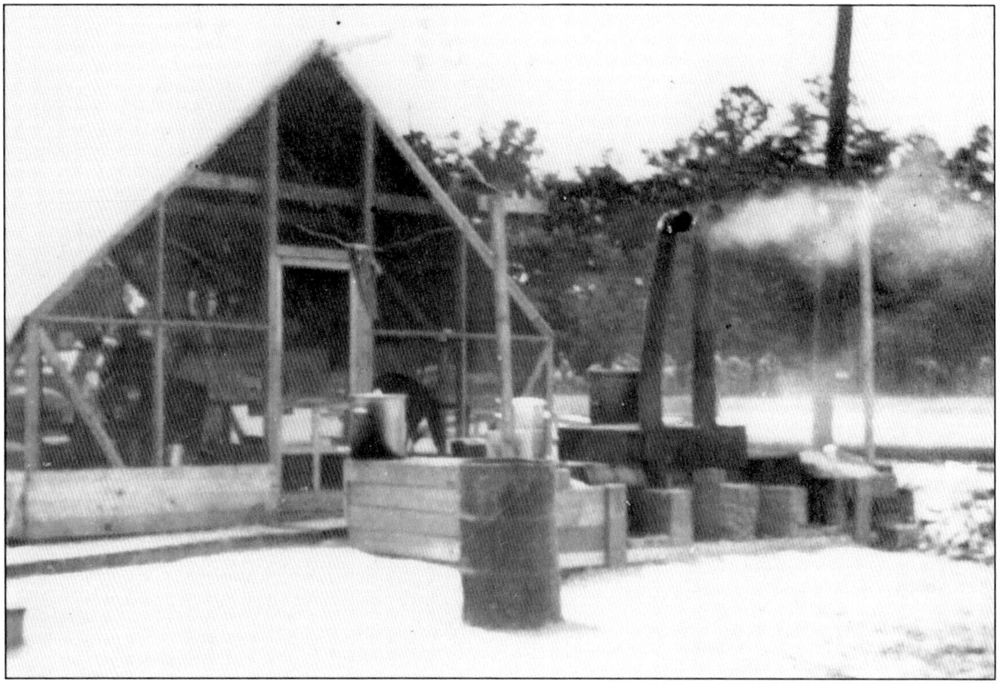

This photograph shows a mess tent at Camp Sibert. This large army installation was located in the Etowah County area during World War II. The installation was a chemical warfare training camp that also housed a large prisoner-of-war camp. The camp closed shortly after the end of the war, and little remains of it today.

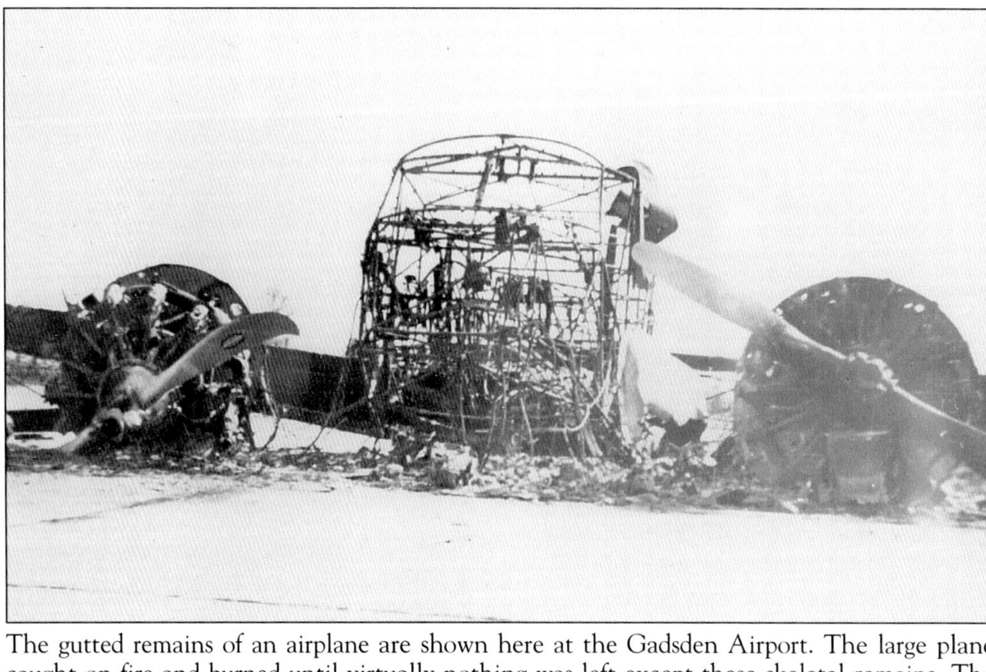

The gutted remains of an airplane are shown here at the Gadsden Airport. The large plane caught on fire and burned until virtually nothing was left except these skeletal remains. The fire also destroyed the hanger at the Gadsden Municipal Airport. The City took control of this airport when Camp Sibert closed.

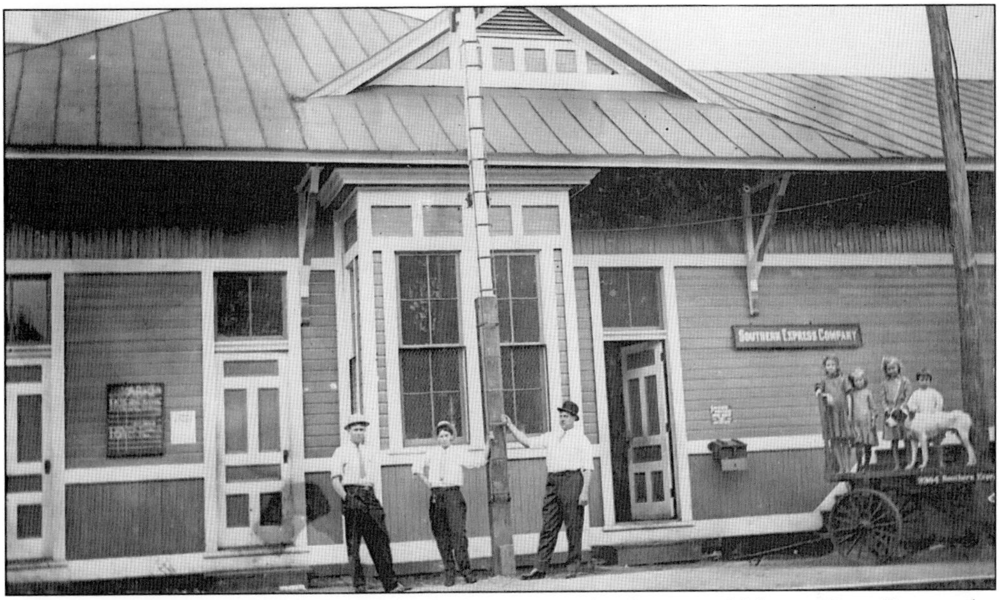

Several people are shown here waiting on the train at the depot in Alabama City. During the 1930s, rail service was very important to the residents of Etowah County. In the days before improved highways, goods were shipped by train and people would anxiously await the arrival of their packages at depots such as this one.

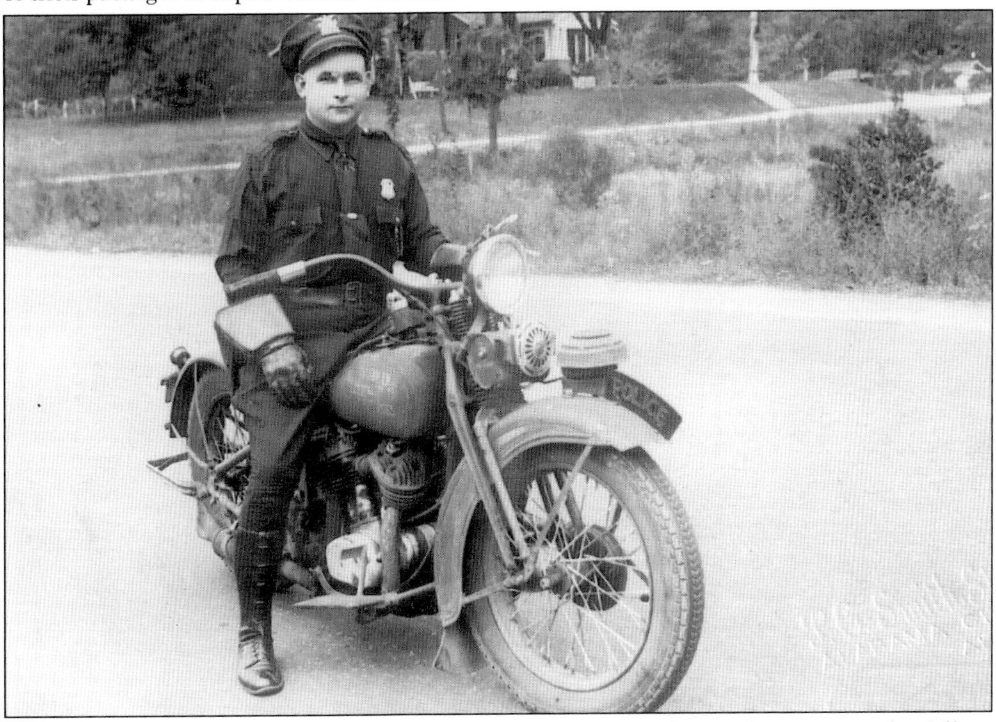

Officer Ben Stewart is shown here seated atop his Harley Davidson police motorcycle. Officer Stewart patrolled this area for many years, and along with the other officers of the Gadsden Police Department, he worked to ensure that crime rates in Gadsden were below the average each year. (Courtesy of P.C. Smith.)

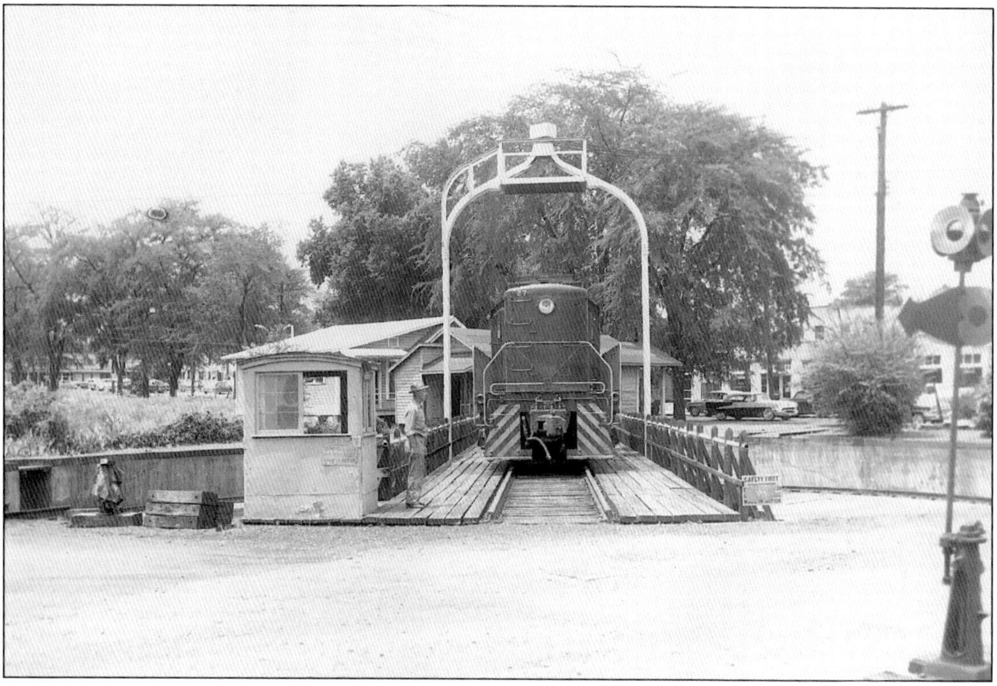

A train engine is shown here in one of the two turntables located in the Gadsden area. These L&N turntables were used to turn the steam engines around before the days of diesel engines and trains that could run in forward or reverse. There were two turntables, a small one located near Fourth Street and a larger one seen here located near North Ninth Street. These turntables were removed in 1958.

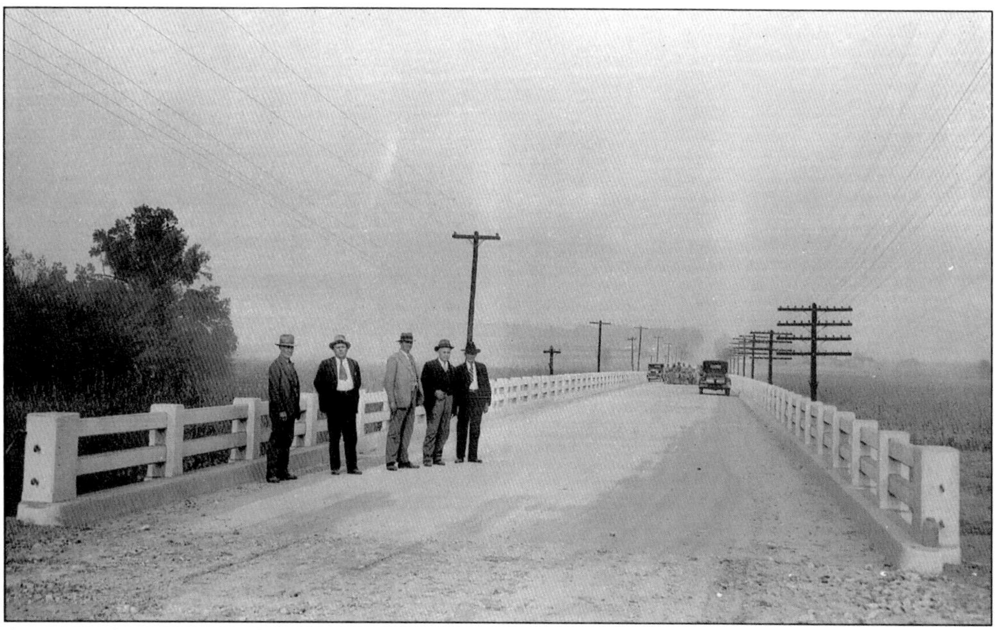

A group of men are standing on the bridge on US11 just south of Attalla. This photo was taken in 1928 near the present site of the Wal-Mart Store. Pictured here, from left to right, are Will Smith, W.T. Jeffers, Milton Durham, W.T. Chumley, and Joe Tinsley.

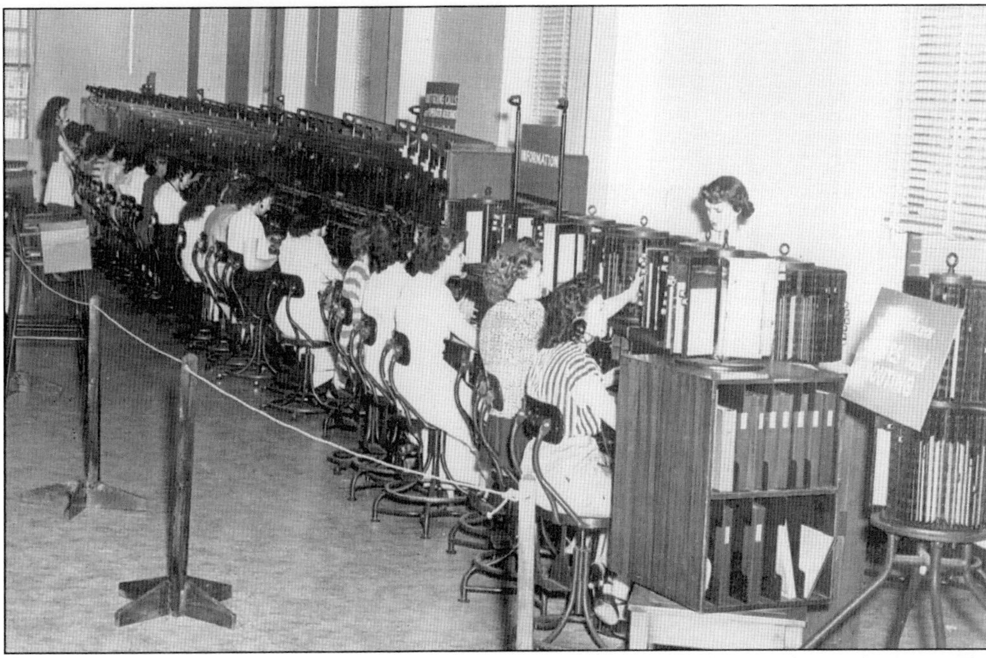

Local telephone operators are busy at work at the switchboard during the mid-1940s. The telephone switchboard was located on Broad Street just above the Alabama Power Company. A large work force of telephone operators were required to man the switchboard to handle the huge volume of calls in the Etowah County area.

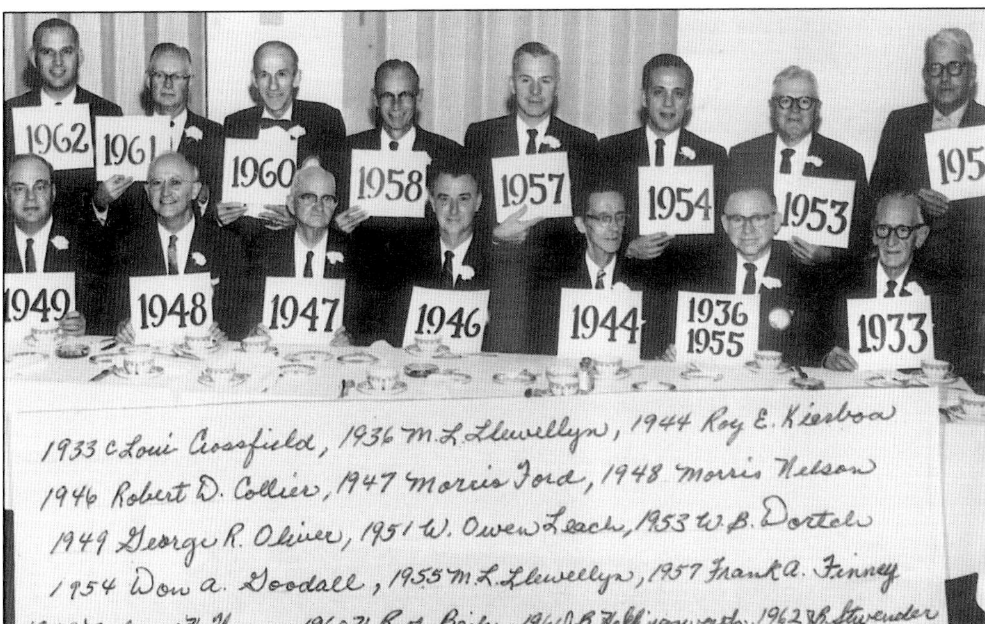

Pictured above are several past presidents of the Gadsden Kiwanis Club. This organization is very active and supports many local charities. Pancake Day, held annually at the Convention Hall and attended by hundreds each year, has provided thousands of dollars to local charities over the years.

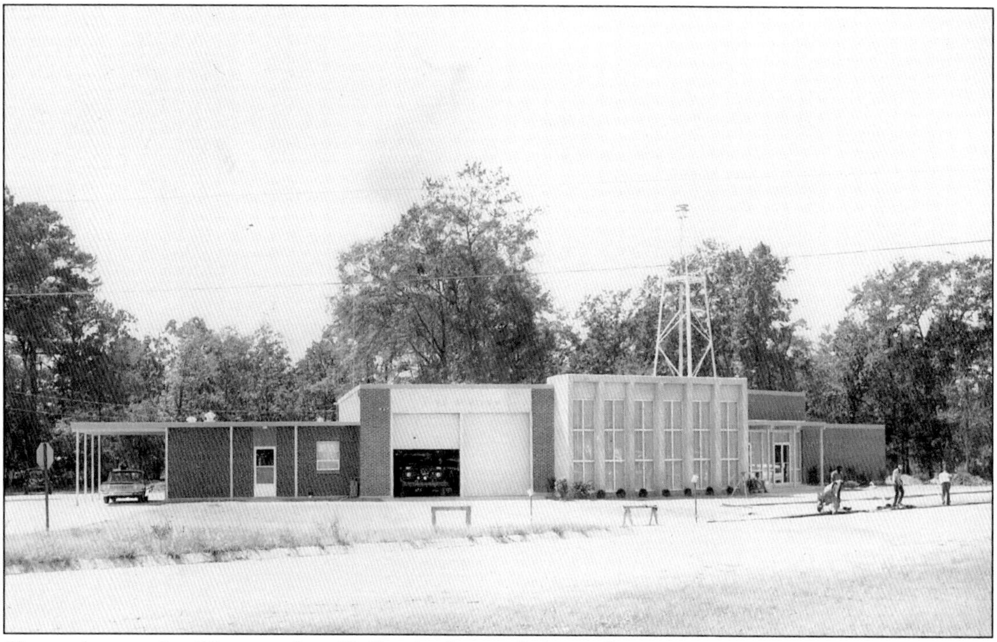

Shown here is the Glencoe City Hall, which was dedicated on September 6, 1964. Gov. George C. Wallace was the main speaker at the dedication of this beautiful structure. The town of Glencoe was incorporated on September 9, 1939, with A.J. Chastain as its first mayor. This municipal building houses the city hall, police department, and one of the city's fire stations.

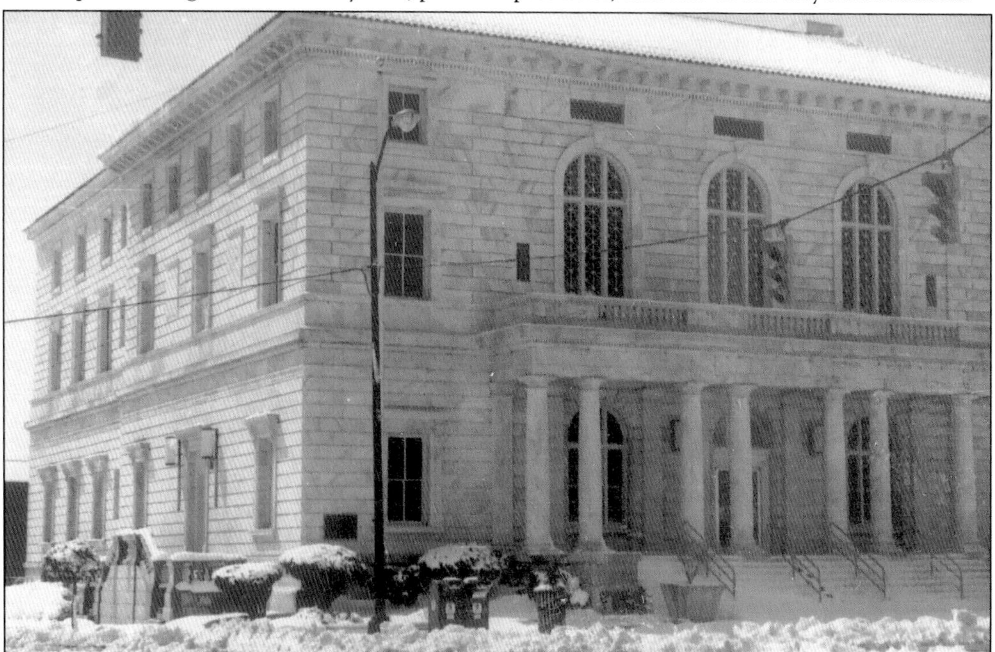

Gadsden's beautiful Federal Building is shown here in a photograph from 1993. Several inches of snow had fallen the day before, practically bringing the city to a standstill. This building originally housed the United States Post Office, and was damaged in a fire in 1958. It was later restored to house several federal agencies.

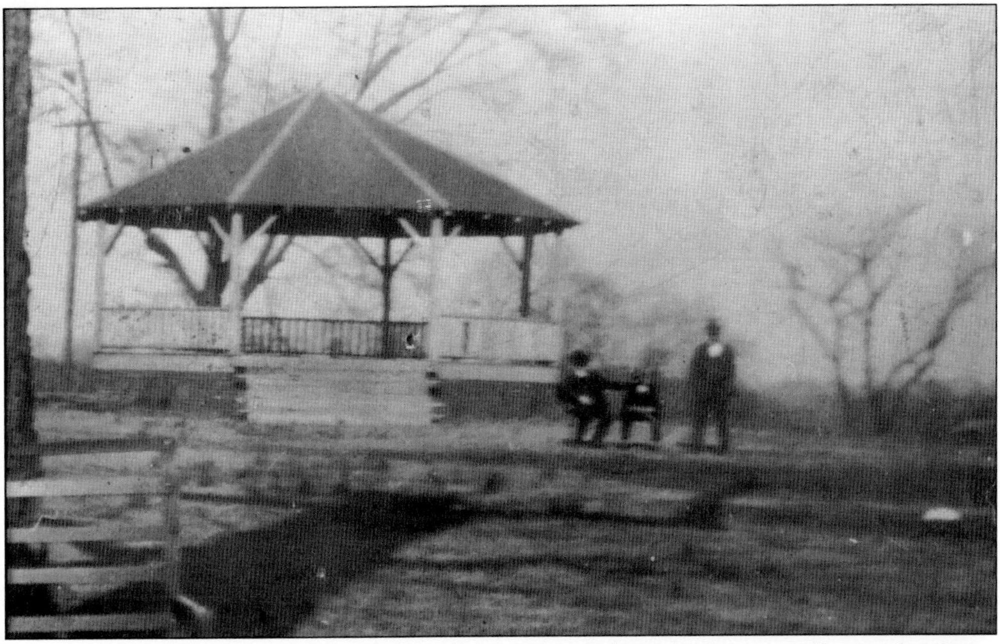

This photograph shows the early gazebo that was located on the "commons" near the Coosa River in downtown Gadsden, near the present site of Gadsden's City Hall. This area was also known as Emma Sansom Park because of its location near the Emma Sansom Monument. A gazebo was later rebuilt on the same spot by students of the Alabama Technical Trade School.

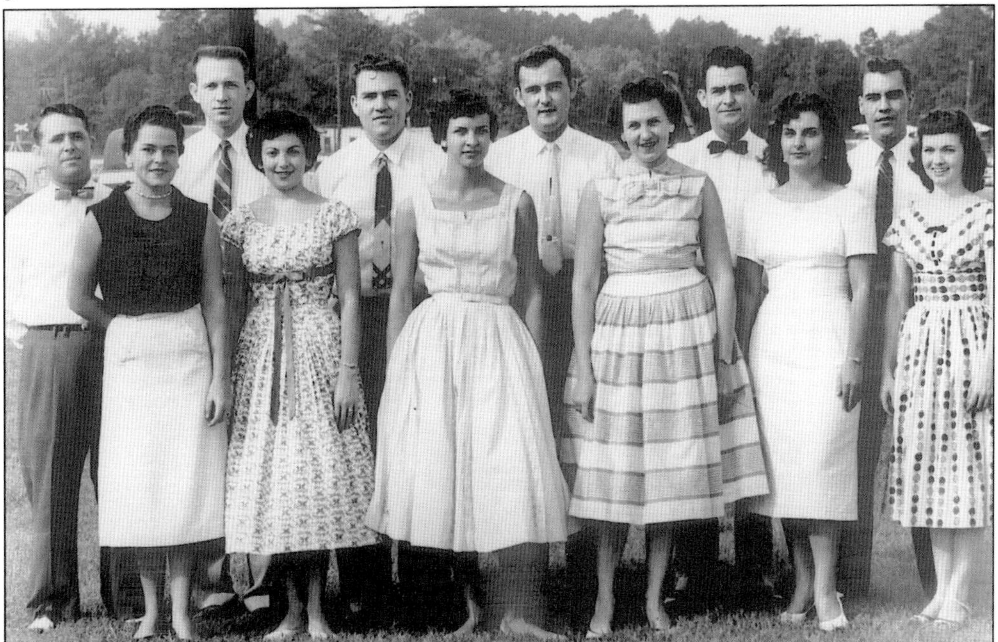

Pictured here, from left to right, are the contestants of the Gadsden Air Freight Depot King and Queen Contest: (front row) Anne Burttram, Cecile Woodham, Betty Gilbreath, Mary Frances McCoy, Joyce Swan, and Gwendolyn Gregory; (back row) George Roebuck, Robert Kell, Preston Compton, Ralph Sewell, Roscoe Alexander, and Johnny Cox.

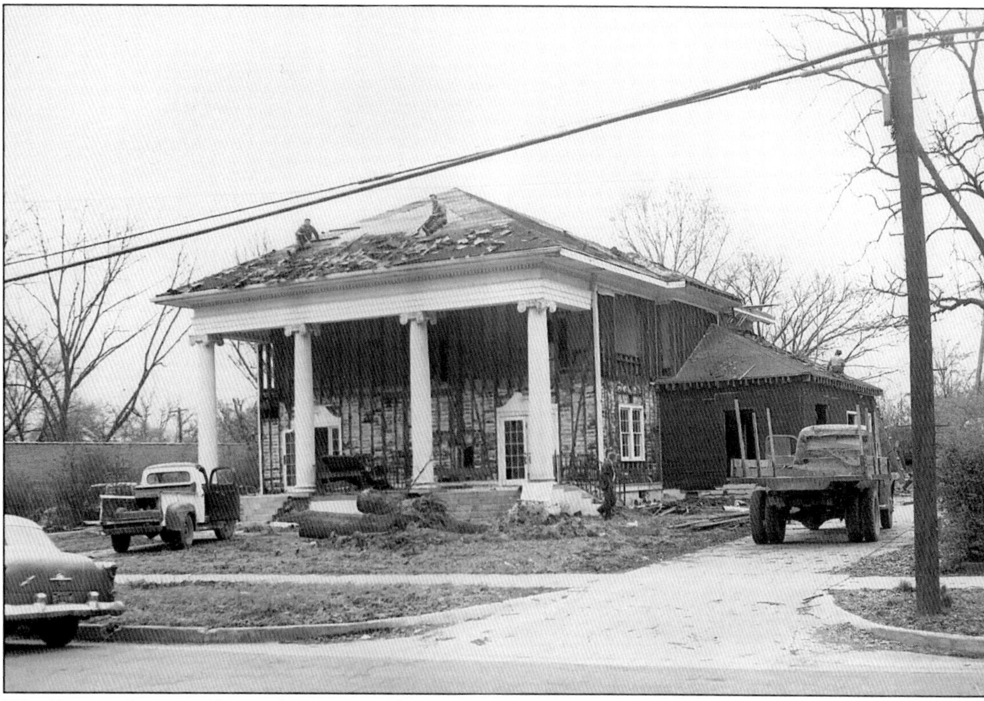

The Brown Service Funeral Home in downtown Gadsden is being torn down in this photograph from 1961. Located at 320 South Fourth Street, this was one of the many funeral homes in Etowah County over the years.

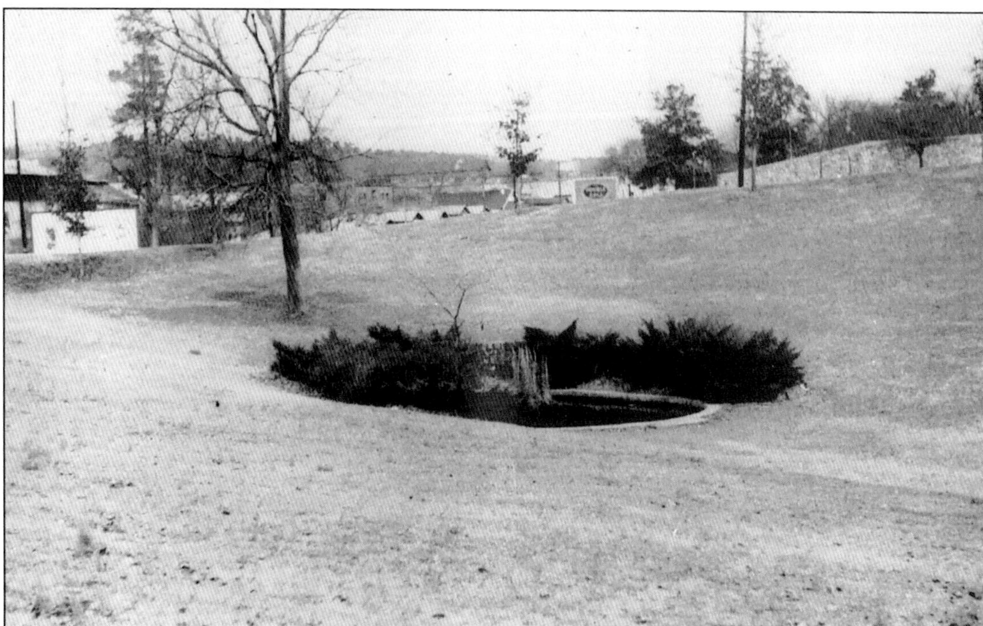

A small spring-fed pond is shown in front of Gadsden's Convention Hall in this 1950 photograph. The spring was later capped off and the pond was filled in. The pink sandstone wall of the Gadsden Amphitheatre can be seen in the background. Both the Amphitheatre and the Convention Hall were built during 1935. (Courtesy of Hugh Hall.)

Six

RESTAURANTS

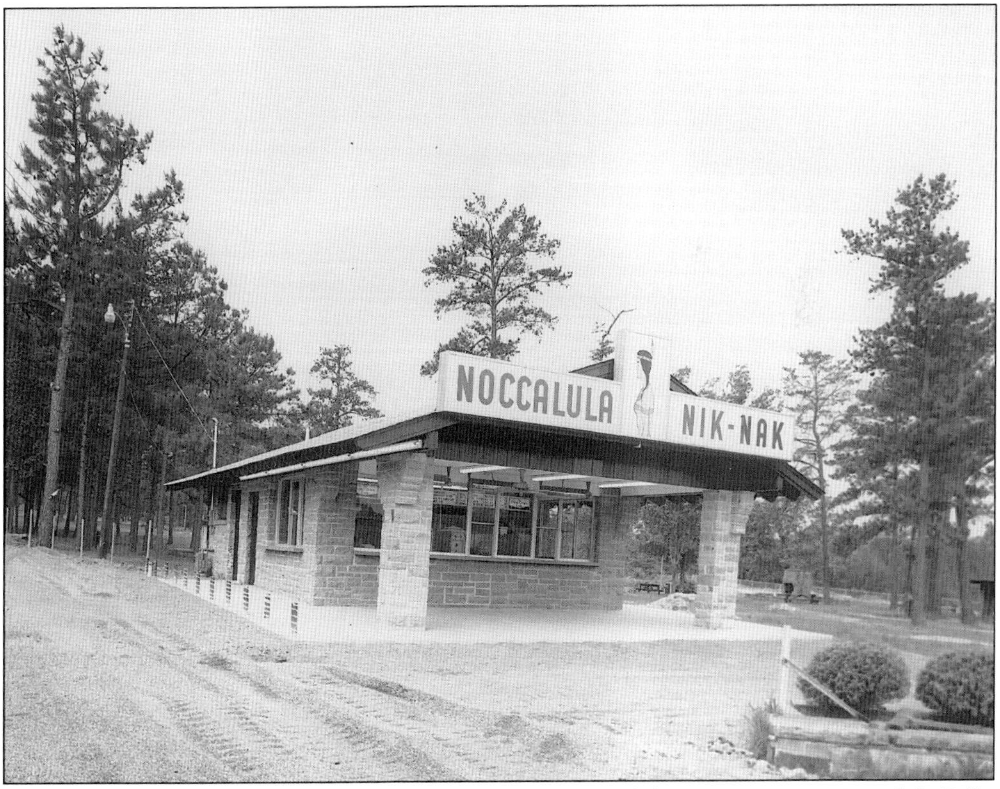

The Noccalula Nik-Nak was located at the entrance to Gadsden's picturesque Noccalula Falls. This photo from 1964 shows the fast food restaurant at the time of its opening. Sandwiches of all types were available as well as soft drinks and ice cream. A local favorite was the brown derby—vanilla ice cream dipped in chocolate.

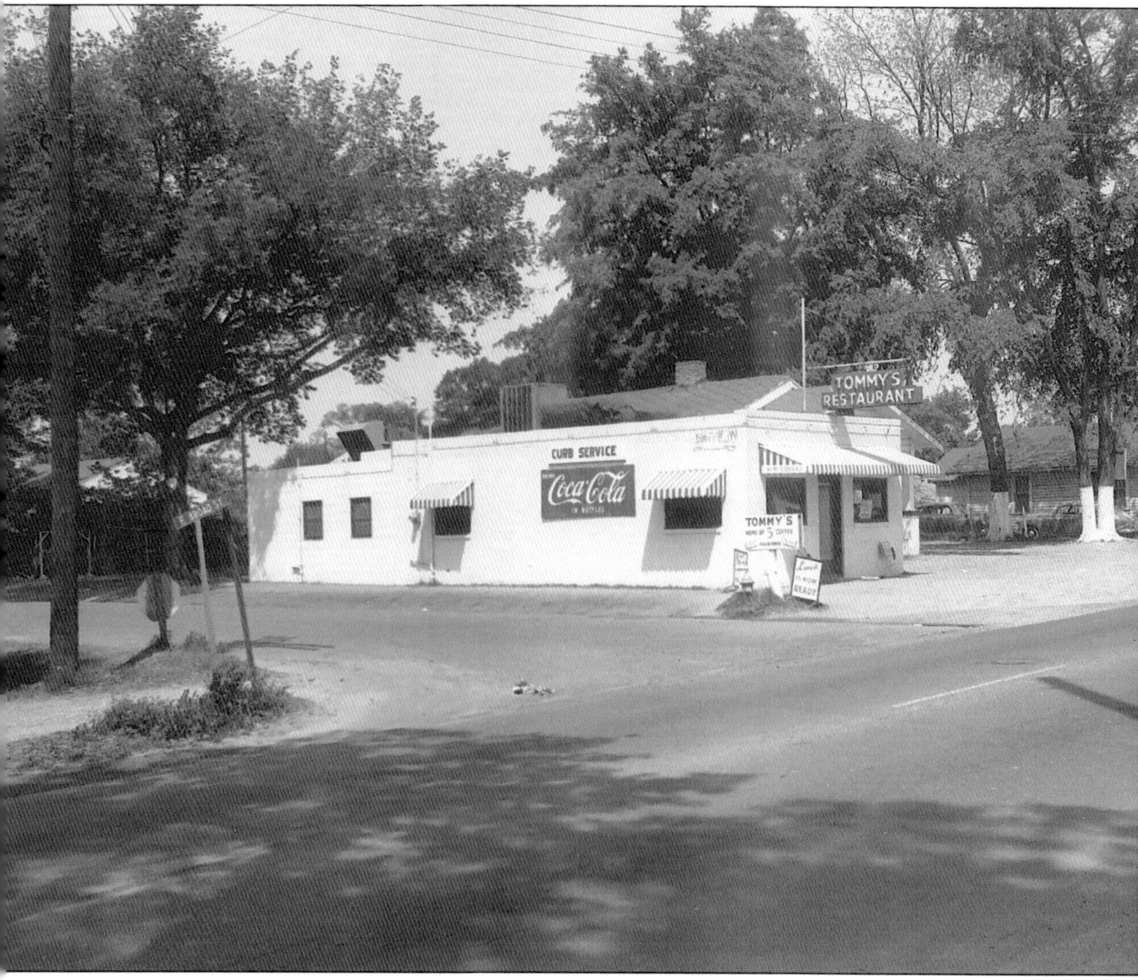

Located on East Broad Street next to the Trade School, Tommy's Restaurant was typical of the locally owned and operated restaurants throughout Etowah County. Such eateries were famous for homemade hamburgers and blue plate lunches. Tommy's advertised coffee for a nickel a cup and curbside service.

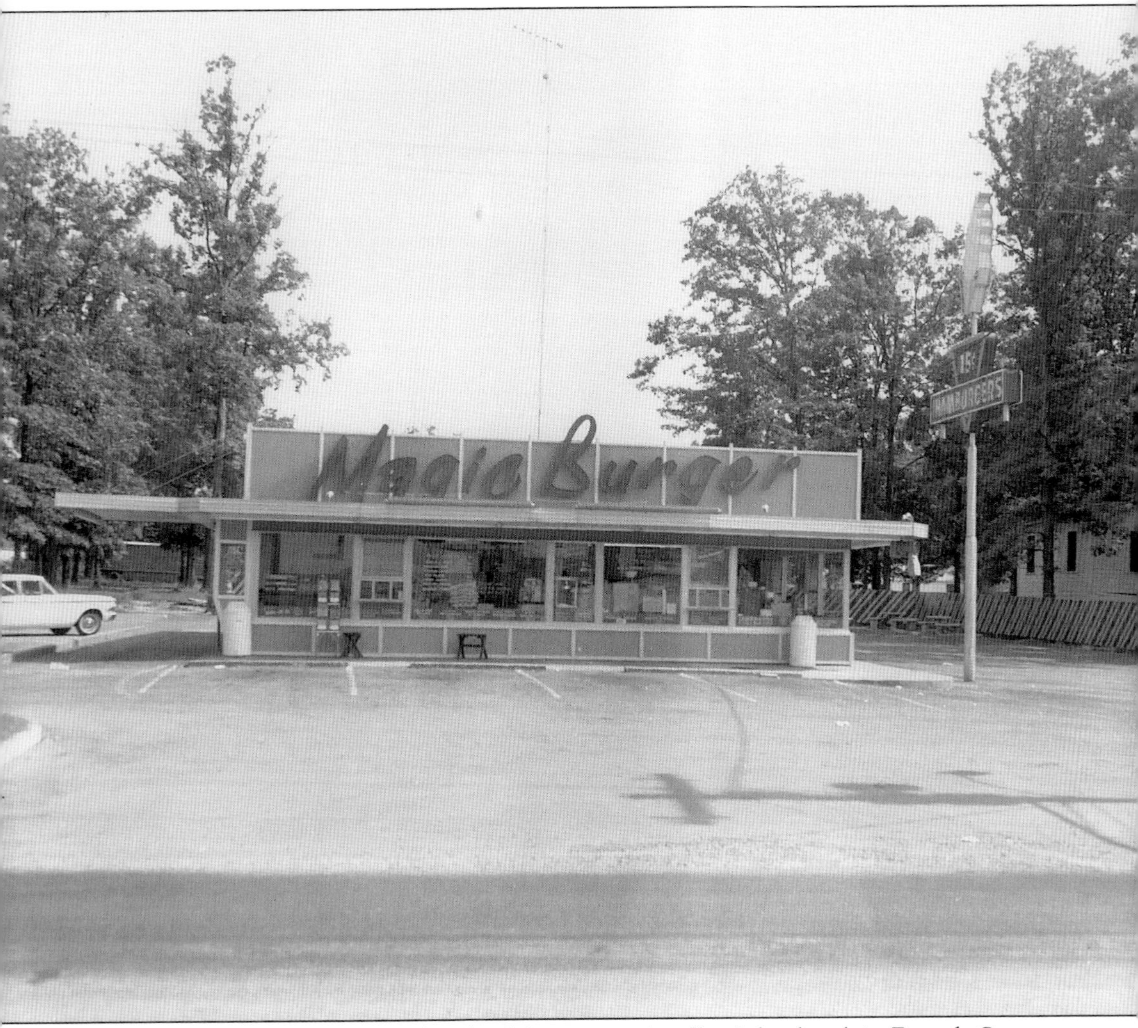

The Magic Burger is located on Cleveland Avenue in Attalla. A landmark in Etowah County since 1960, the Magic Burger was owned by Art May. He also owned Arts Number Two on Rainbow Drive near the present site of the Gadsden Mall. The Magic Burger advertised hamburgers for 15¢ during the early 1960s.

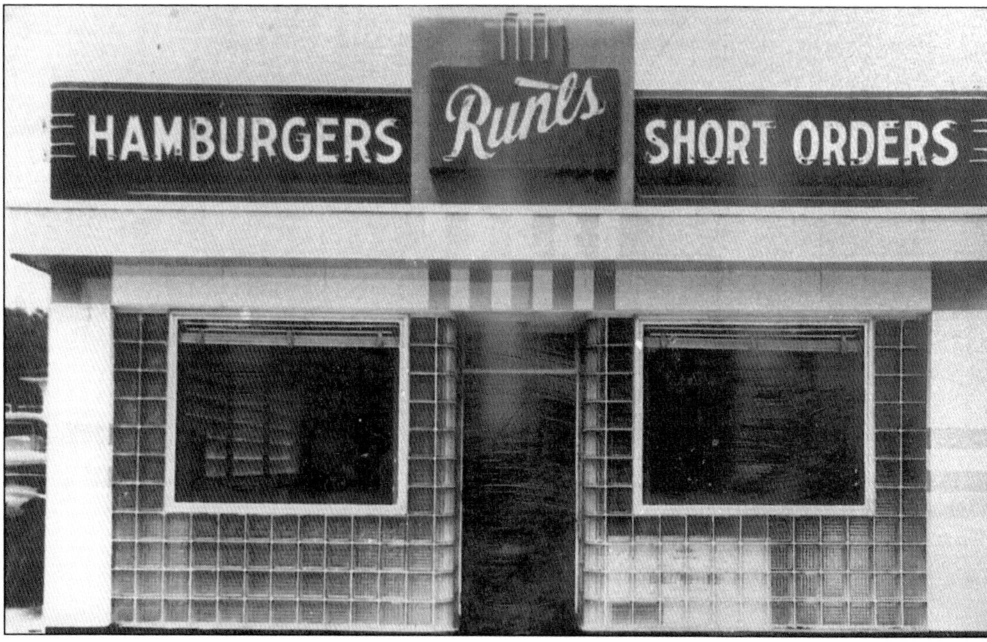

Runts Place, a downtown landmark for many years, was owned and operated by Runt Denson for much of its existence on Broad Street. Runts offered breakfast and lunch to the working people of the downtown area, and was also a favorite spot for movie-goers from the Pitman Theatre next door.

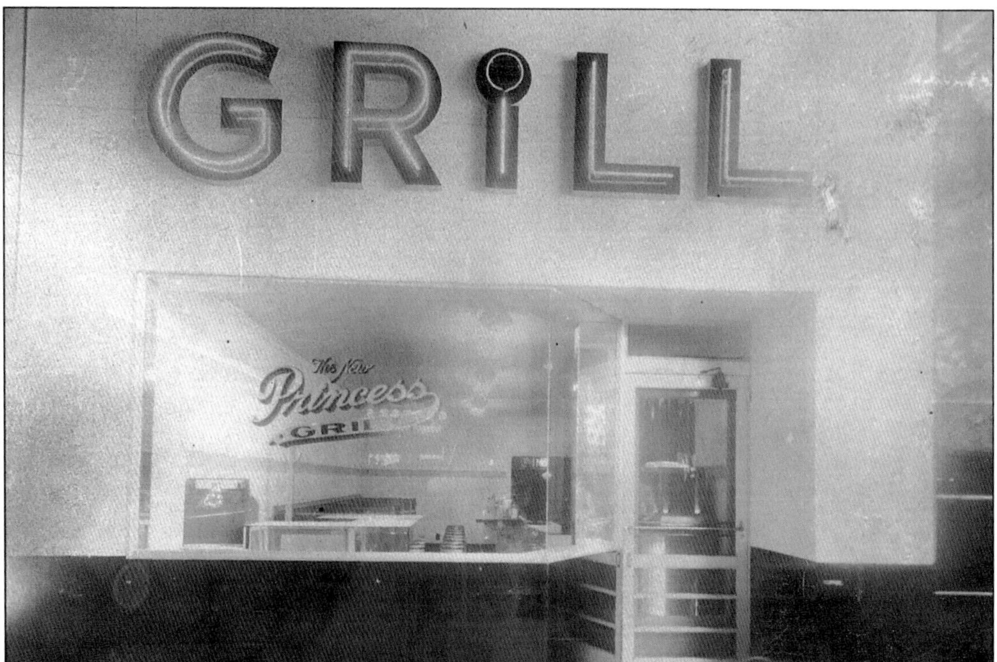

The Princess Grill was located next to the Princess Theatre in downtown Gadsden. A favorite place for short orders and sandwiches, the Grill was never reopened after a destructive fire in the mid-1950s.

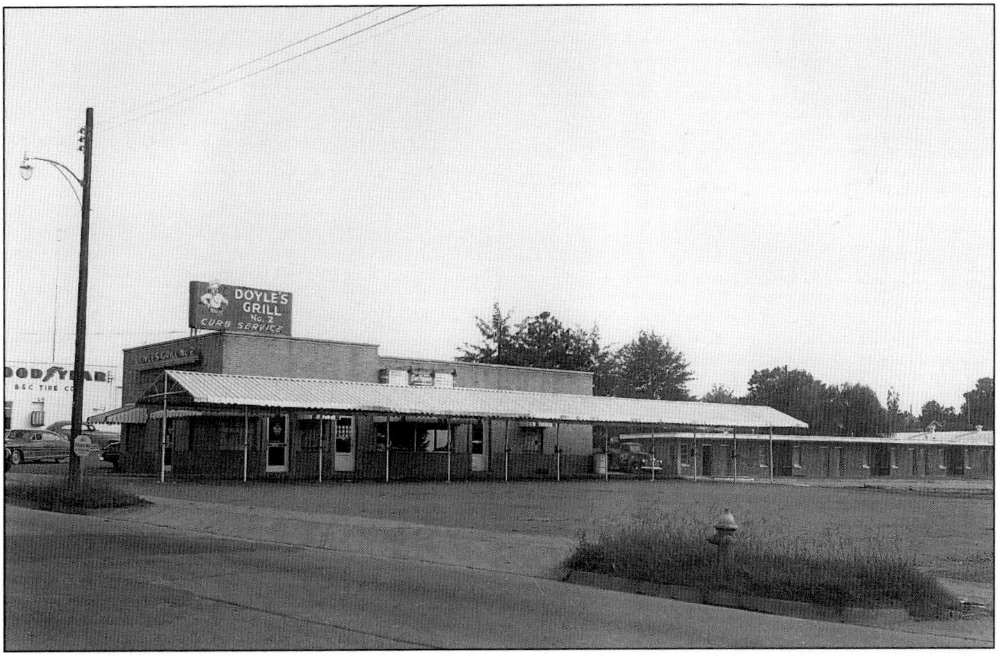

Doyle's Grill was another popular spot for the young people of Etowah County during the 1950s. Pictured here is Doyle's Grill Number Two on East Broad Street, with Doyle's Motel located at the rear. Another Doyle's Grill was located on North Twelfth Street. Note that curb service was offered at this eatery.

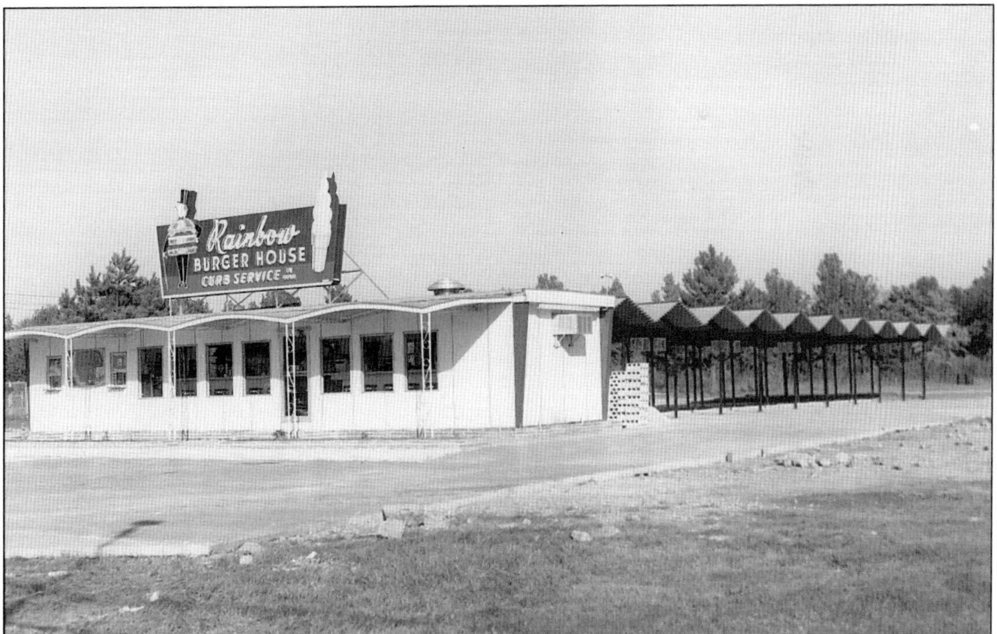

The Rainbow Burger House was located on Rainbow Drive in the early 1960s. Owned by Jack Mynatt, this early drive-in offered curbside service as well. Because the Burger House was located near the banks of the Coosa River, it was prone to flooding during the spring months. Many businesses have been forced to relocate over the years due to this flooding.

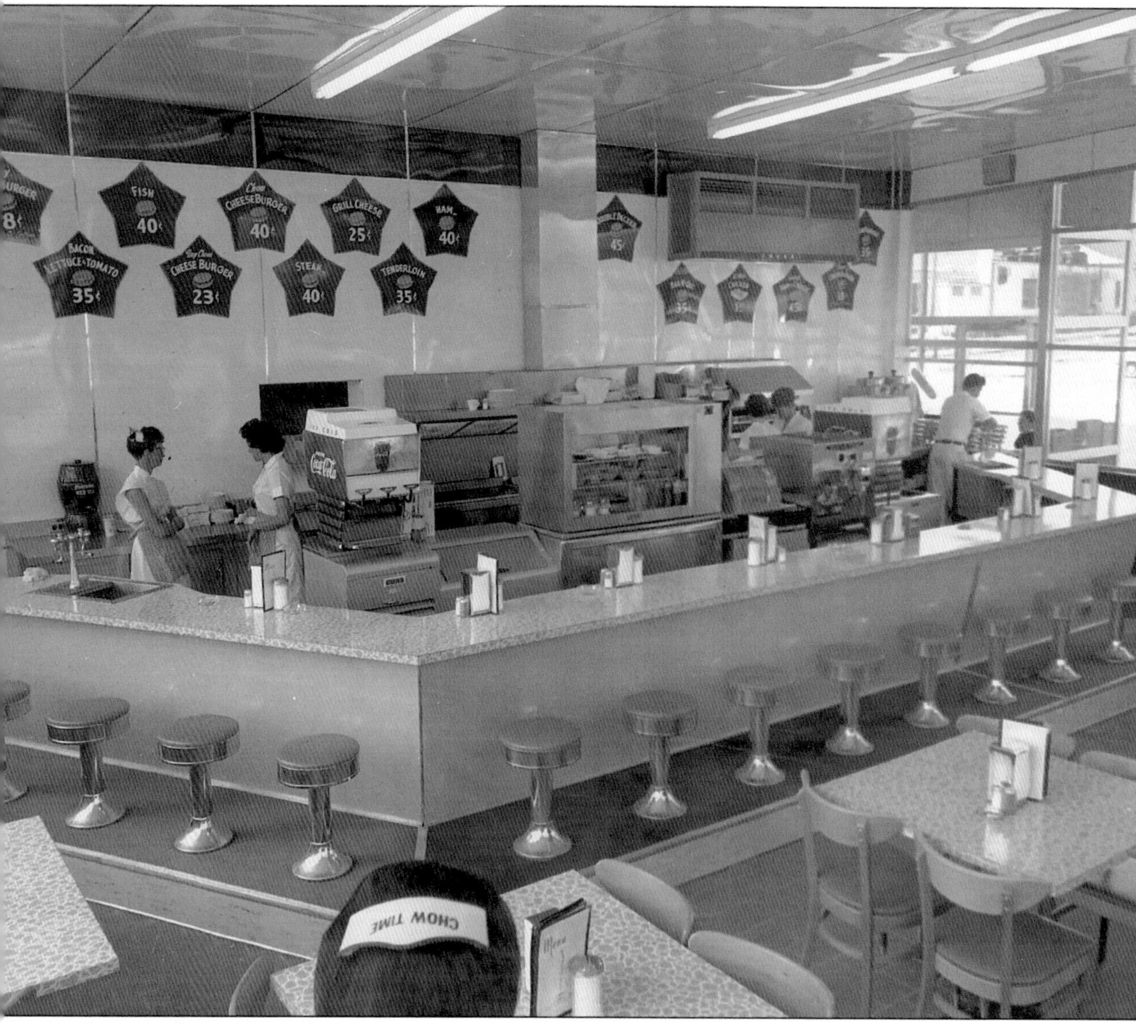

A great place to get a hamburger during the 1960s, the Chow Time offered a tiny chow burger for 18¢ and a steak sandwich for 40¢. Over the years, this property has been the home of several businesses, most recently Thee Grill, a restaurant with a back-to-the-50s theme.

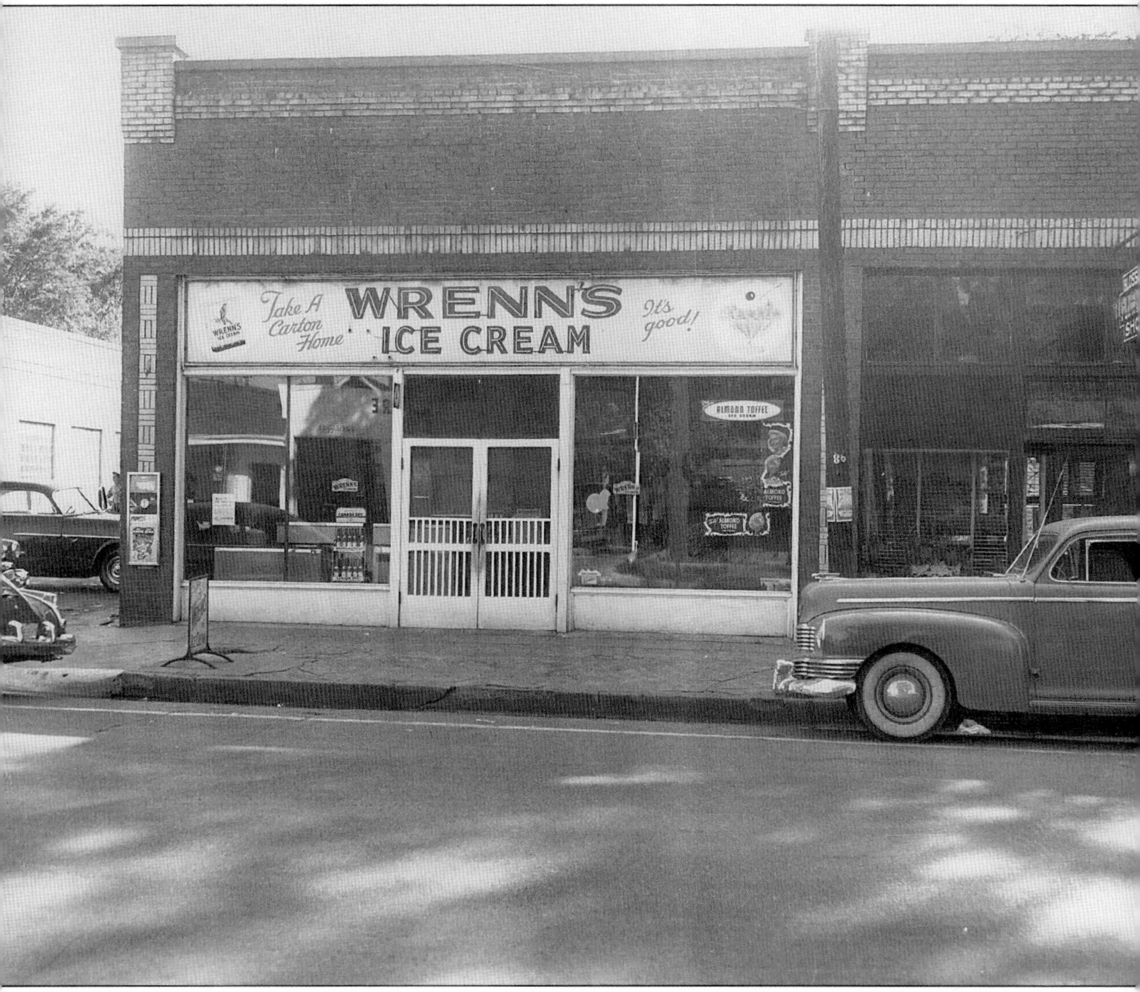

Wrenn's Ice Cream was a locally owned and operated ice cream shop in Gadsden and famous throughout Etowah County. Situated on the 1100 block of Forrest Avenue in West Gadsden, Wrenn's offered a large milkshake for 25¢ during the 1950s.

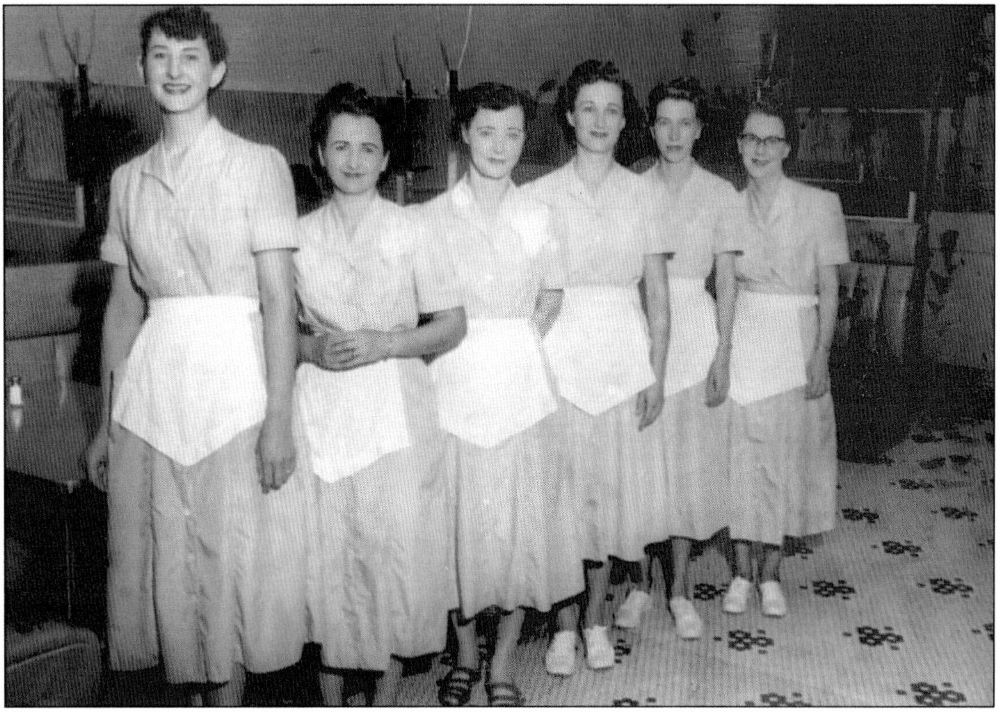

Shown here are the waitresses form the White Palace Cafe in 1940. A longtime Gadsden landmark, the cafe has changed very little over the years. The beautiful art-deco entrance and the interior remain very close to the original.

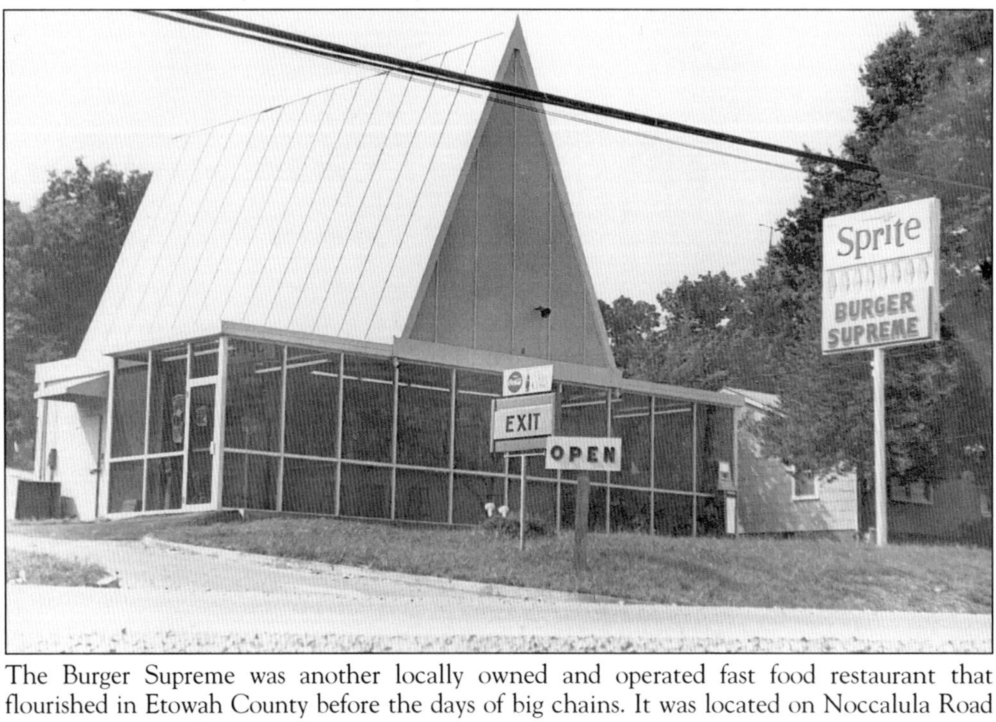

The Burger Supreme was another locally owned and operated fast food restaurant that flourished in Etowah County before the days of big chains. It was located on Noccalula Road near Noccalula Falls on Lookout Mountain.

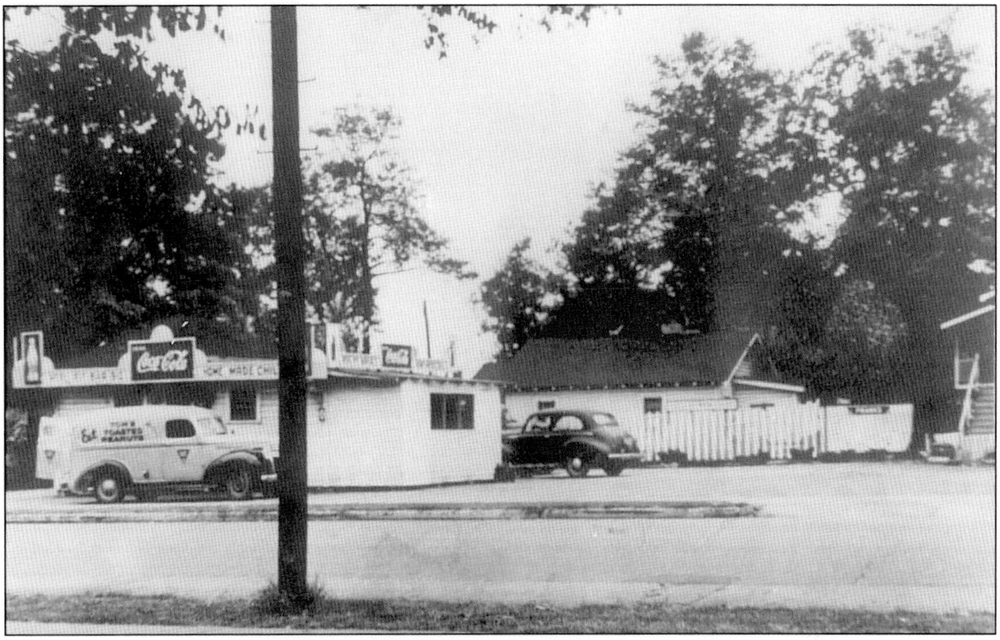

This photograph shows the first building that housed Frank's Bar-B-Q, located for many years on Forrest Avenue. In later years, the restaurant was housed in a brick building. Frank's was famous for their cheeseburgers and barbecue sandwiches, and delivered lunches to the steel plant nearby.

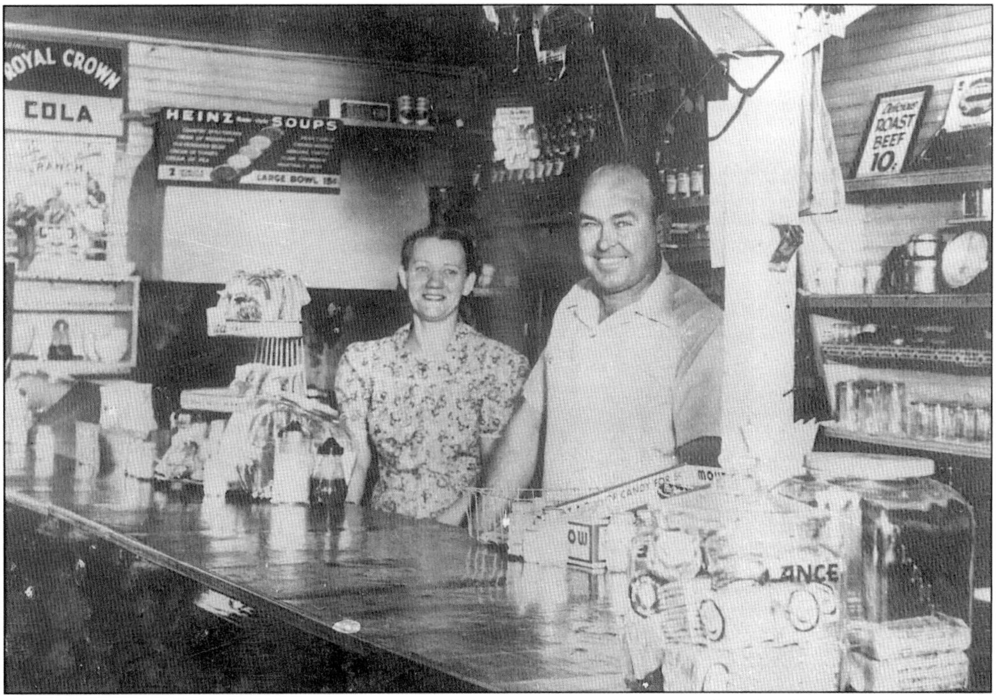

Frank Jarvis is shown here at the counter of the restaurant he opened in 1937 in the 2500 block of Forrest Avenue in Alabama City. Frank's was a popular place to eat, especially among the employees of the steel plant.

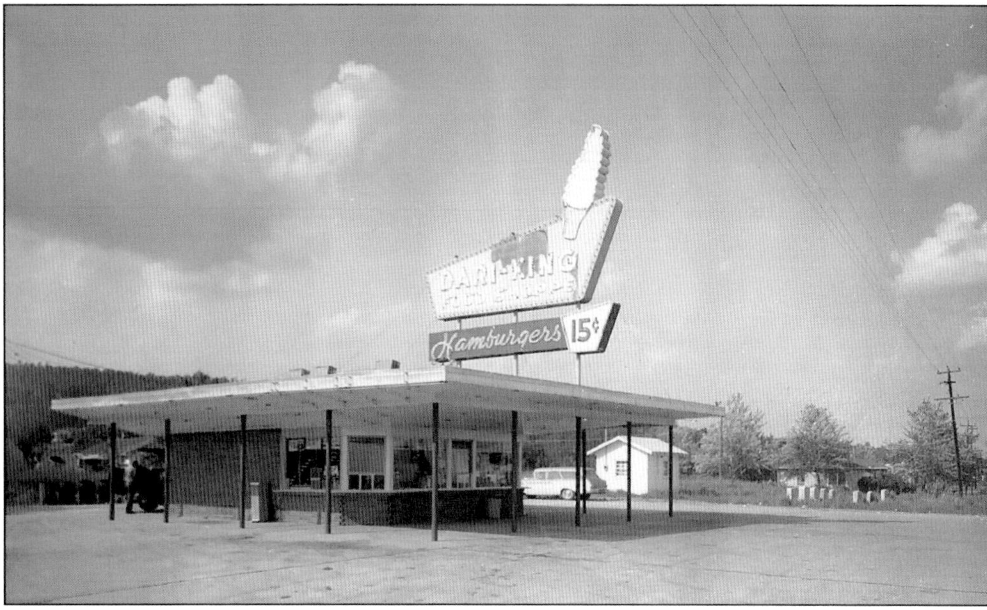

The Dari-King, still in operation in North Gadsden, is located on Ewing Avenue. Shown here in a photograph from 1964, the Dari-King is a popular place for sandwiches and short orders, as well as ice cream, milkshakes, and soft drinks.

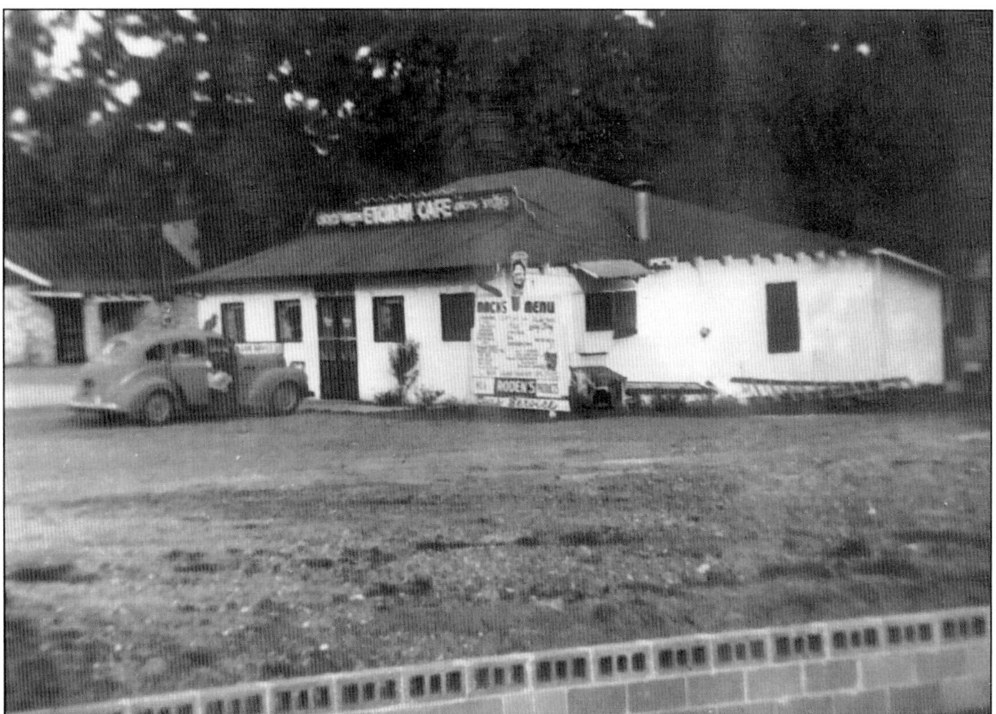

The Etowah Cafe is shown here in a photograph from early 1950. Small cafes such as this one were popular throughout the area during the early 20th century. The perfect stop for a hungry traveler to have a cheeseburger or a complete meal, these cafes offered curbside service and paved the way for modern fast food restaurants.

Seven

INDUSTRY

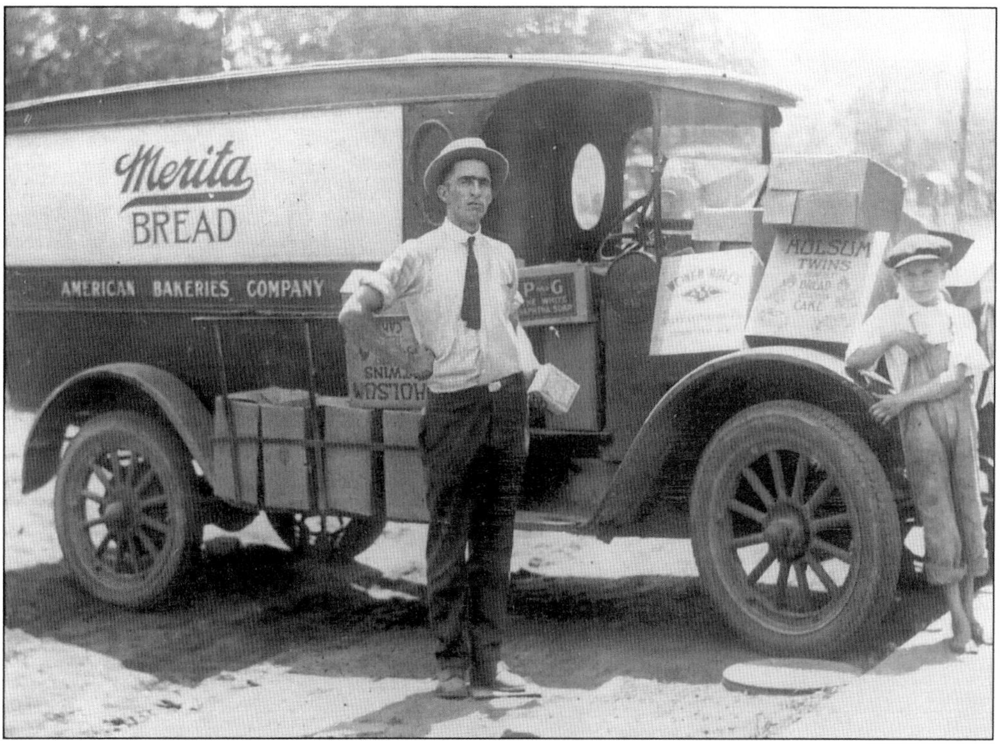

This photograph shows one of the early American Bakeries bread trucks. Later known as Merita Bakery, the American Bakery was located in the 500 block of Broad Street before moving to First Avenue, and was a part of Etowah County for more than 60 years. The original site of the American Bakery is the current home of Fuller Medical Supply.

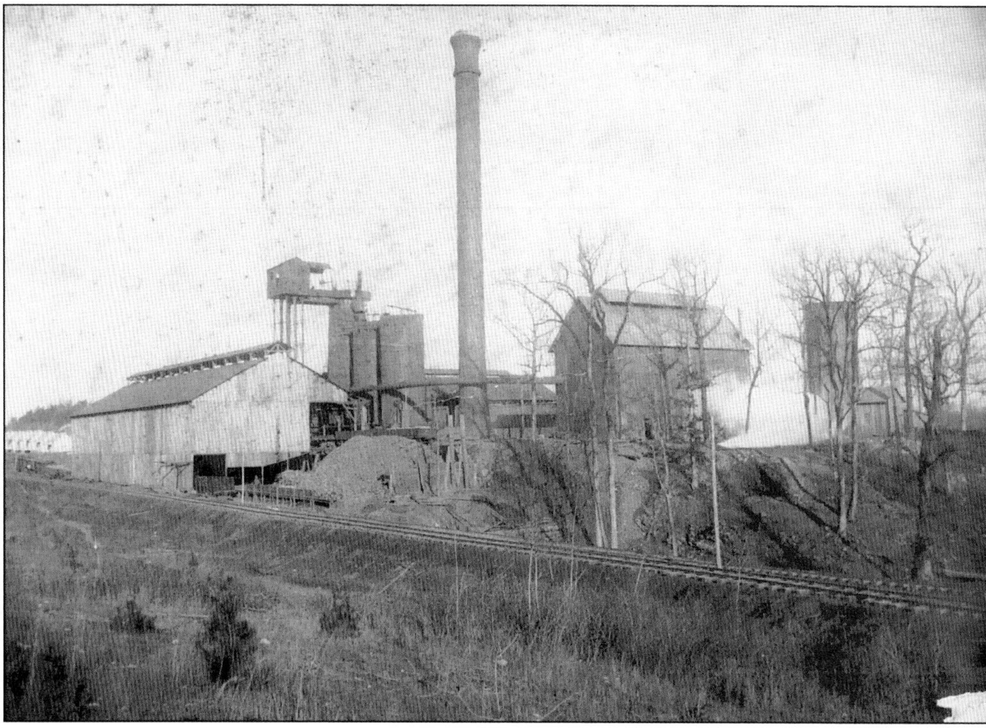

This picture was taken at the Alabama Furnace Company in North Gadsden in 1880. Several pig-iron furnaces such as this one were found in the surrounding area in the days before modern steel production. Tons of iron ore were shipped to these furnaces by railroad and processed daily. Very little remains of this furnace today.

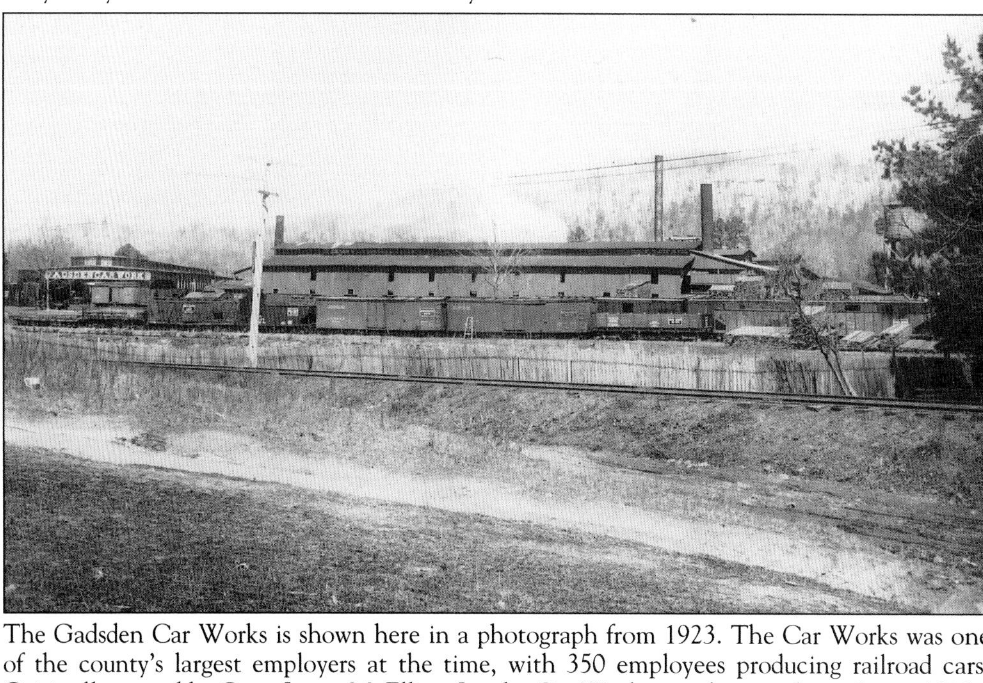

The Gadsden Car Works is shown here in a photograph from 1923. The Car Works was one of the county's largest employers at the time, with 350 employees producing railroad cars. Originally owned by Capt. James M. Elliott Jr., the Car Works was destroyed in a fire in 1923.

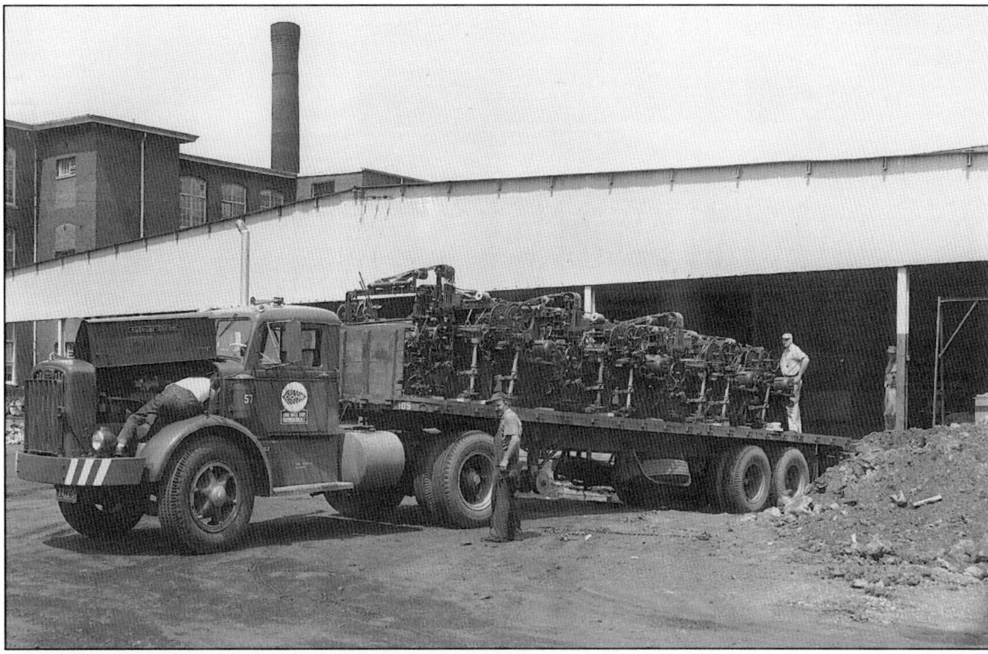

Machinery is being removed out of the Cone Mill in Alabama City. This giant cotton mill was built by Dwight Manufacturing Company in 1895. The mill was later sold to a company from North Carolina that operated it until a labor dispute interrupted operation at the giant textile plant. The company closed the mill and turned it into a warehouse.

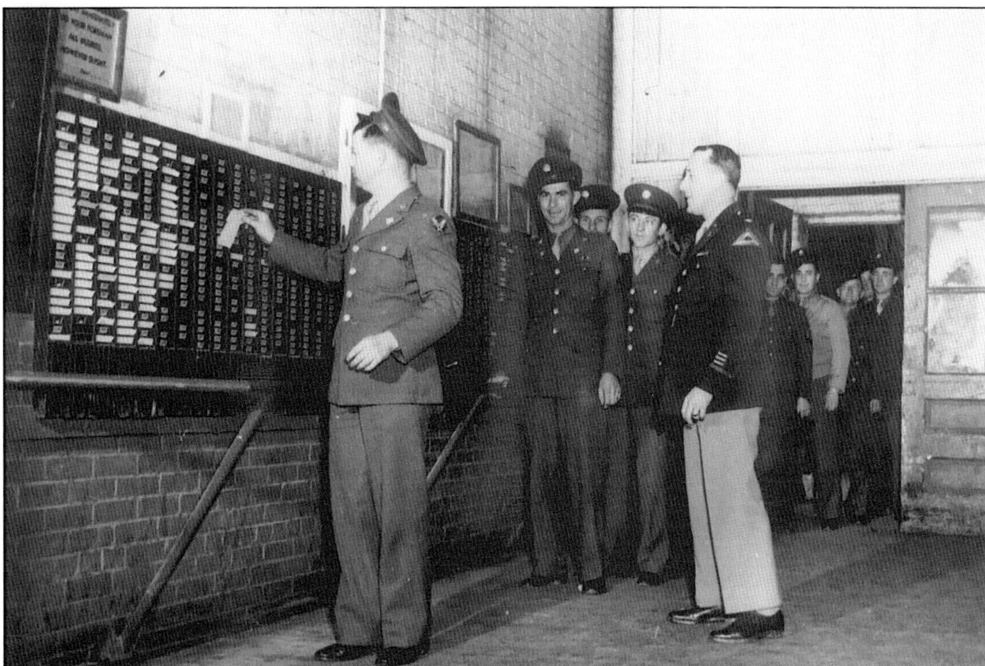

Returning servicemen are shown here clocking into work at the Dwight Manufacturing Company in Alabama City. After World War II, many young men returned to the work force in Gadsden, Attalla, and Alabama City.

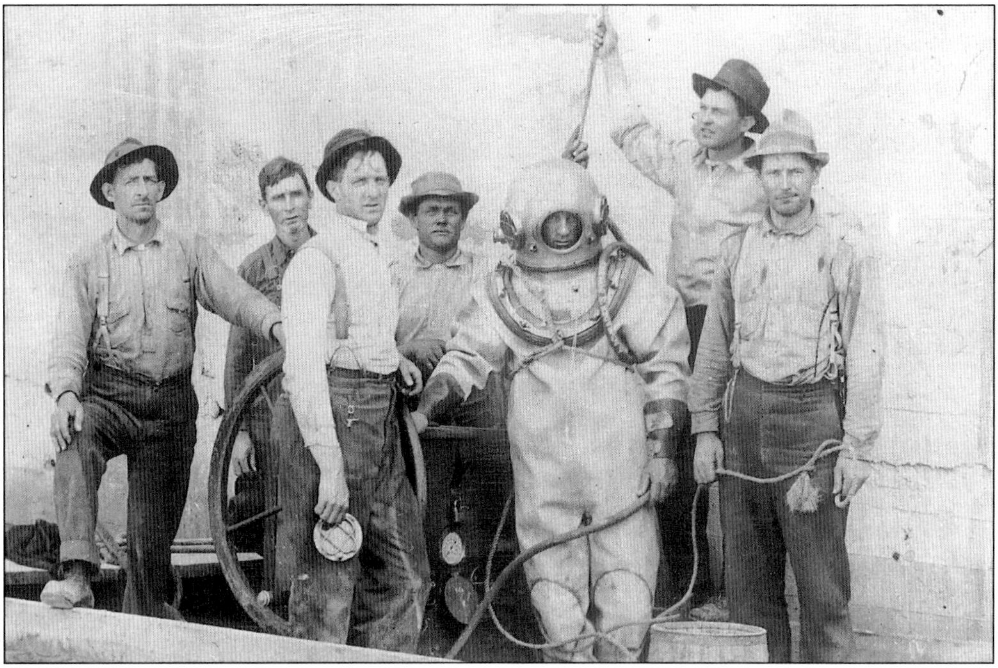

This early photograph shows a group of workers on the Coosa River. Lock construction on the river was important for opening the waterway to trade. Many of the divers who worked on the river told stories of huge catfish that lined the river's bottom.

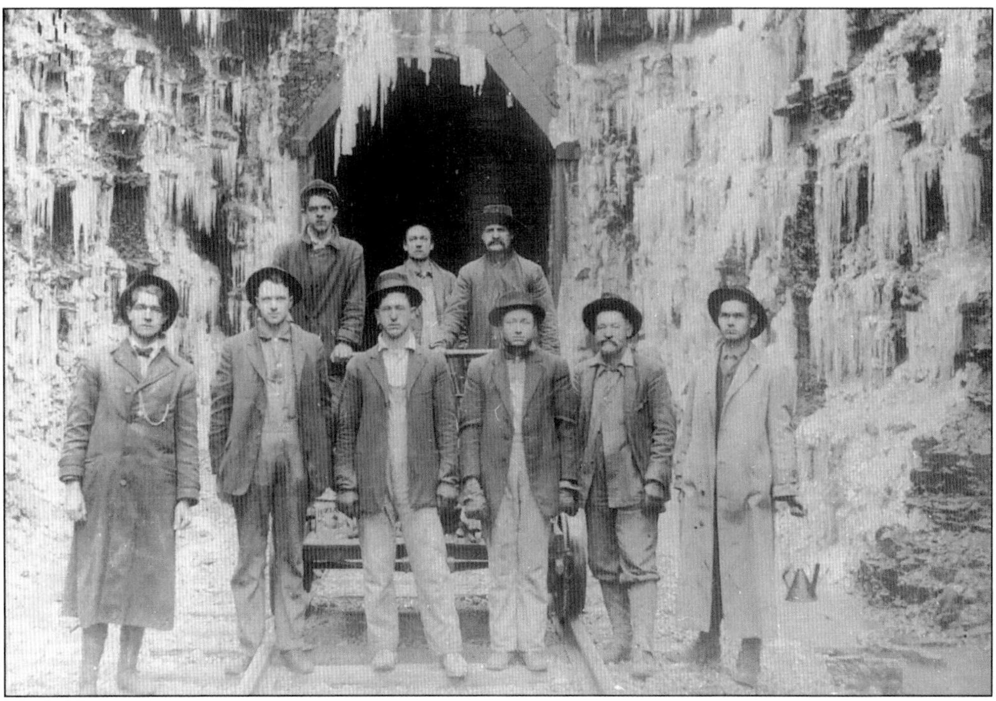

A group of workmen are pictured at the entrance to the railroad tunnel near Altoona. Taken during the height of winter, this photo shows large amounts of ice hanging on the walls and the entrance to the tunnel, which was located near the Blount and Etowah County lines.

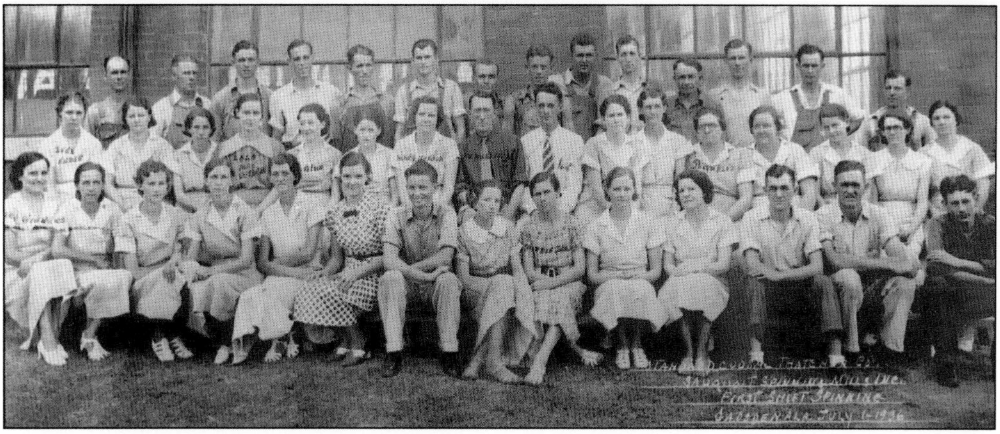

Members of the first shift spinning department at the Standard Coosa Thatcher Company take time out to pose for this photograph in July of 1936. These employees were part of the work force of the Sauquoit Spinning Mill, a large textile mill located on North Eighth Street in Gadsden near the foot of Lookout Mountain.

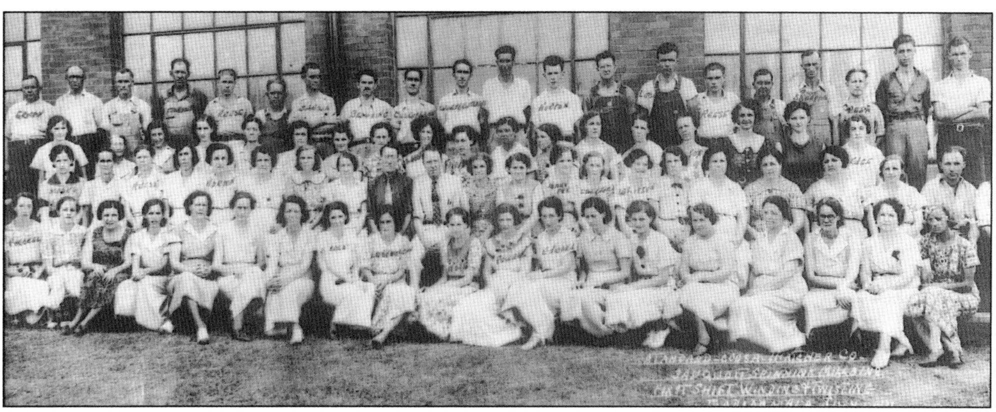

Shown here is another view of the Sauquoit Spinning Mill employees in July of 1936. The mill is now closed and the building is vacant.

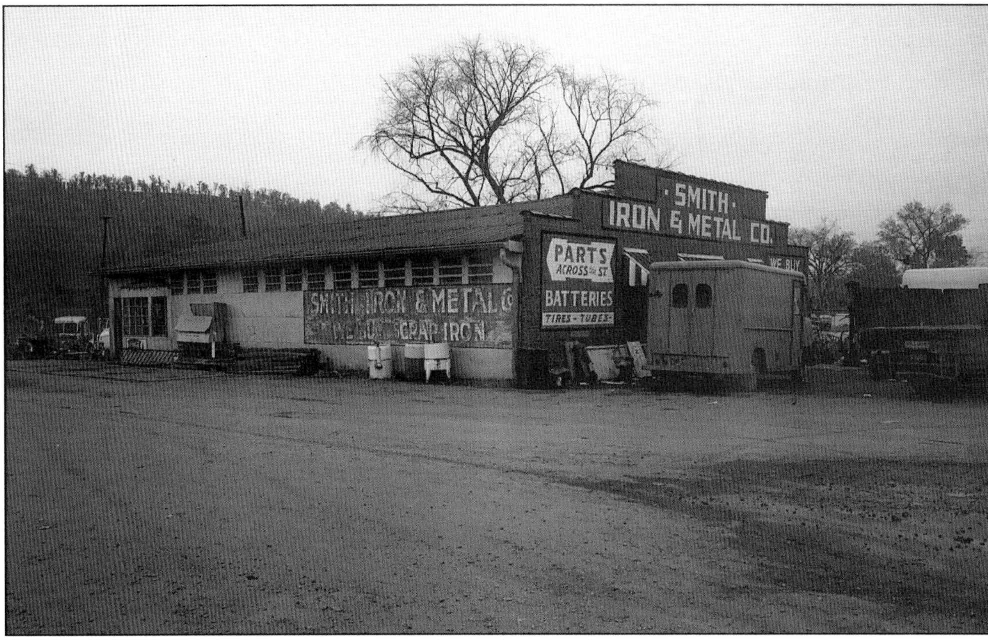

The Smith Iron and Metal Company was located in Attalla on Cleveland Avenue at the present site of the entrance and exit ramps to Interstate 59. The interstate highway was constructed during the early 1960s, and several fast food restaurants and service stations are located in the area today.

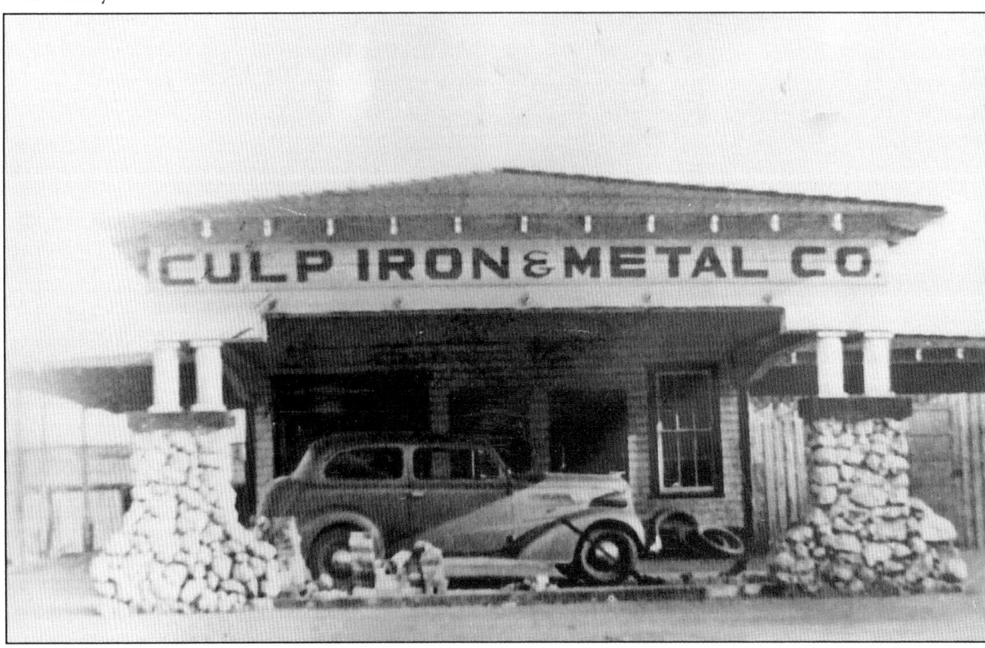

Pictured here is the original home of the Culp Iron and Metal Company that was located in the Attalla area. Henry Culp Sr. founded this company in the early 1930s to recycle scrap metal. This original location is the present site of Johnson's Giant Foods. The business was later moved to Lake Rhea Road. The Iron and Metal business was later sold, although the family owns several other business interests, which are run by Henry Culp Jr. and Ralph Culp.

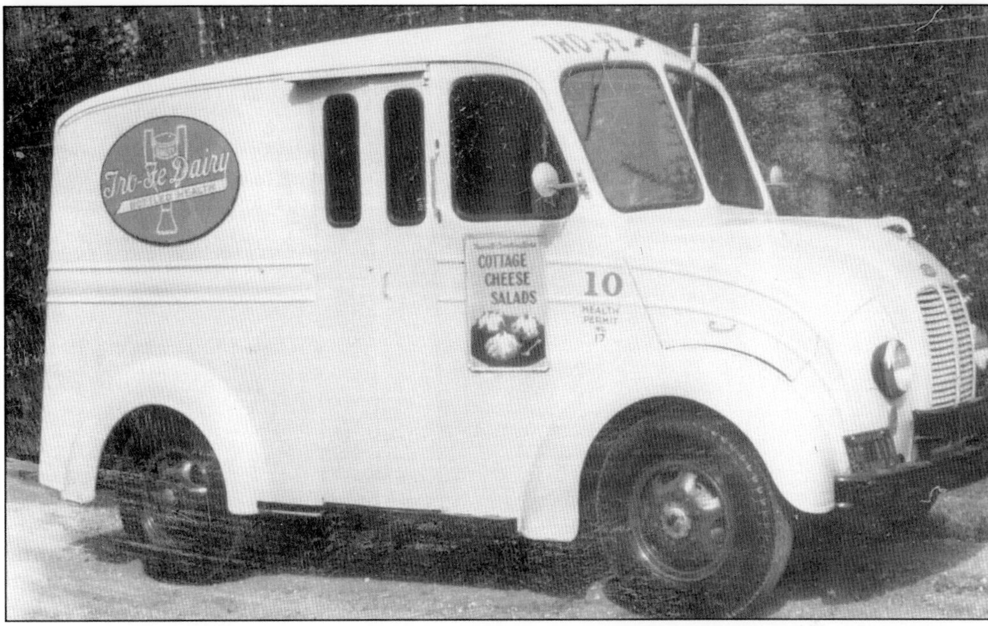

Milk was delivered throughout rural Etowah County in a small delivery truck such as the one pictured above. Home delivery was very popular in the area, and was offered by such companies as Tro-Fe Dairy. Vern Troutman and Fred Feger founded the company, and it went on to become an Etowah County landmark. Troutman later purchased Feger's interest in the company.

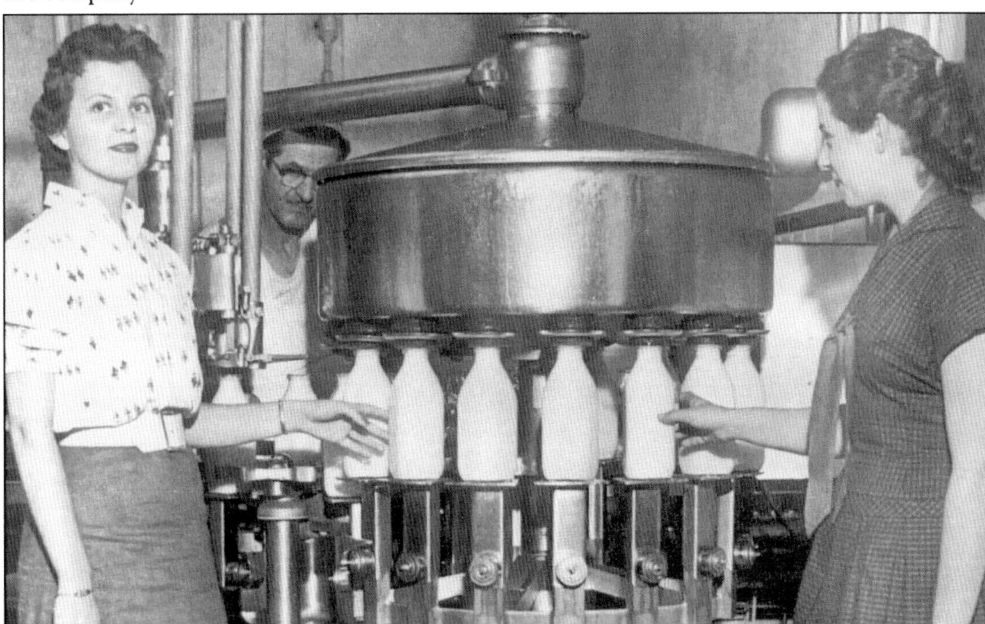

Pictured here are workers bottling milk at the Tro-Fe Dairy, an important industry in the Gadsden area for many years. The first local dairy to offer pasteurized milk and homogenized milk, it was later bought out by Meadow Gold and eventually closed. This building was recently torn down.

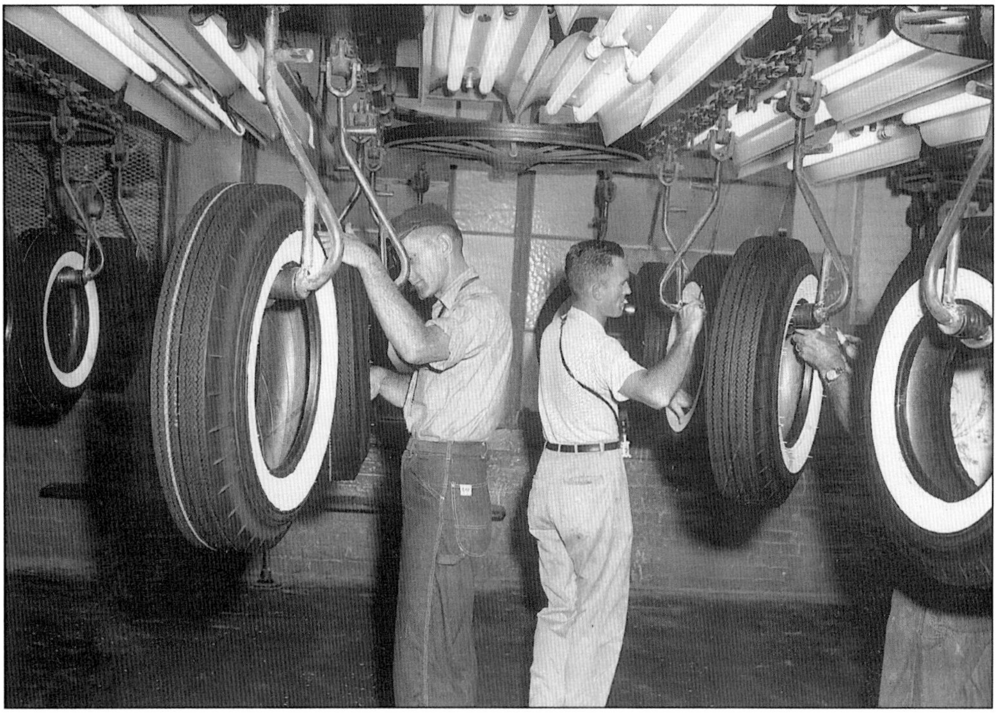

Shown here are workers at the Goodyear Tire and Rubber Company in East Gadsden. Goodyear established a plant here in 1928 and was one of Etowah County's largest employers for 70 years. Recent cutbacks have affected many in the Gadsden area.

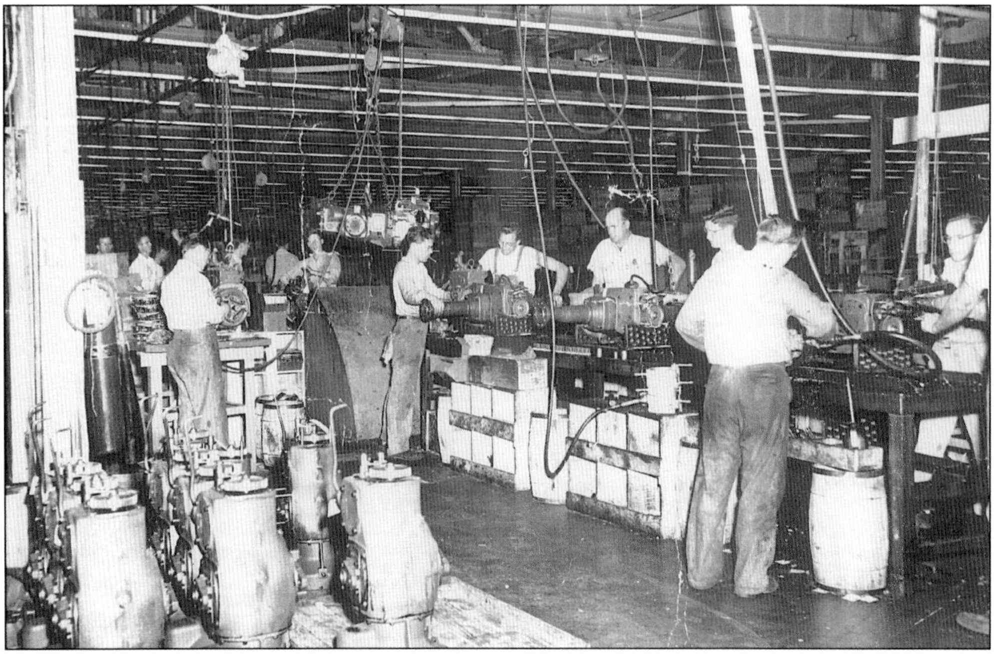

Employees of Gadsden's Allis Chalmers Plant are hard at work on the Model G tractor assembly line. Allis Chambers was a large employer in the Gadsden area from the 1950s to the 1970s and is now closed.

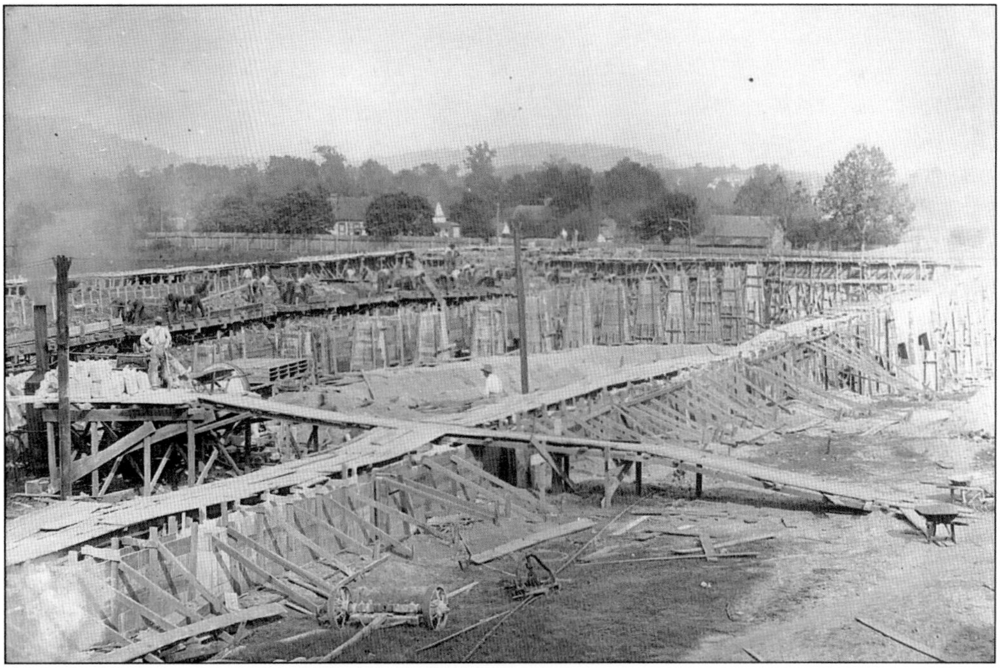

This early photograph shows Gadsden's steel plant. Growing from a small mill to a giant steel producer, the plant has had many owners in its over 90 years of existence in Etowah County.

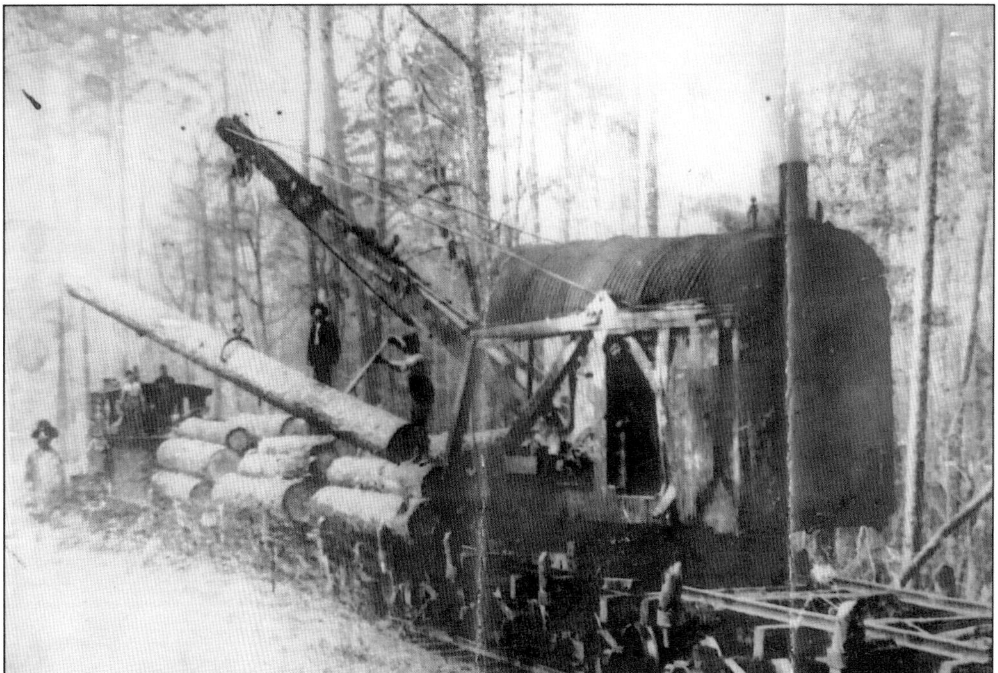

Logging has for many years been an important industry in rural Etowah County that continues to this day. Thousands of feet of timber were cut in the Ball Play and Hokes Bluff area and then transported on the Coosa River to the sawmills in Gadsden. In later years, the logs were hauled by trucks.

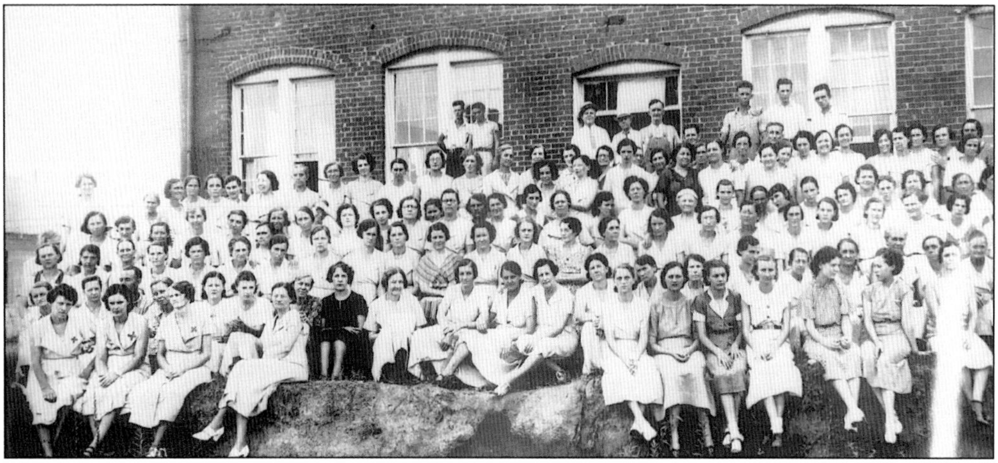

Located on North Tenth Street just off of Gardner Street on the east side, the United Overall Company was typical of many of the industries located in Etowah County. This overall producer was located in the area during a time when many mills were in operation.

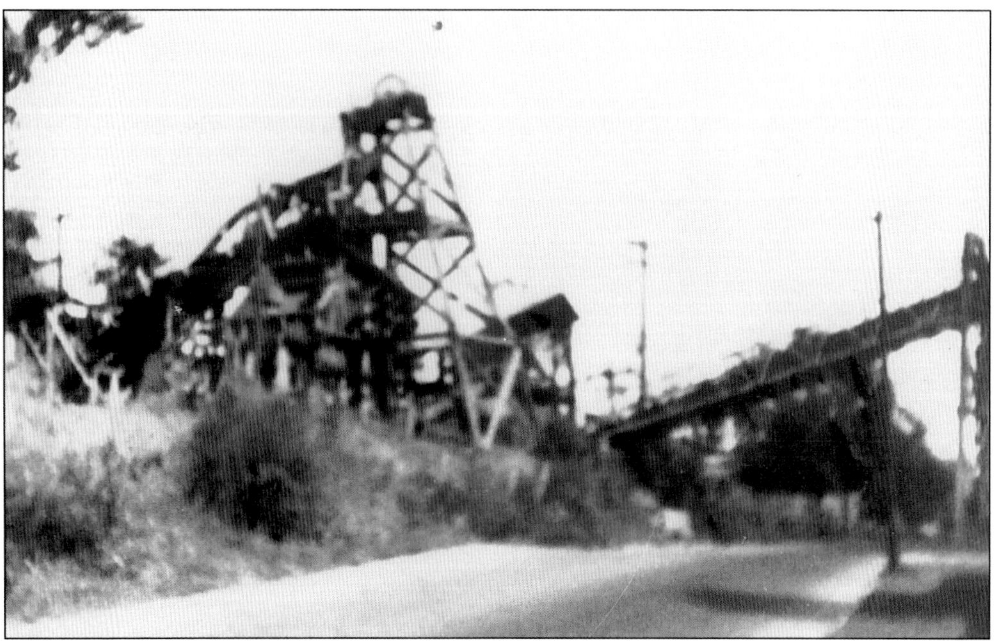

This "Jap" mine was located on Tuscaloosa Avenue east of Owls Hollow Road, just outside of the Gadsden city limits. Several types of mines were located in the area, ranging from iron ore to sandstone and granite.

Eight

HOMES

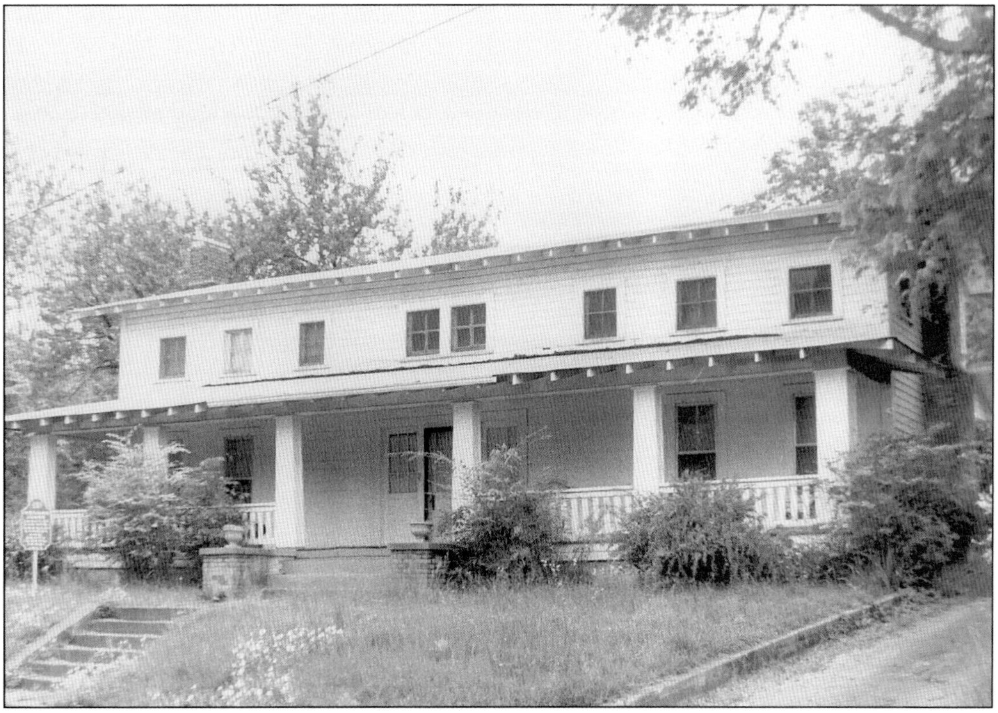

Pictured above is the first house built in the settlement of Double Springs, which would later grow into the city of Gadsden. This structure, originally built of logs, was a stop on the stagecoach route as well as the early Pony Express route. It is still standing today at the corner of Third Street and Tuscaloosa Avenue.

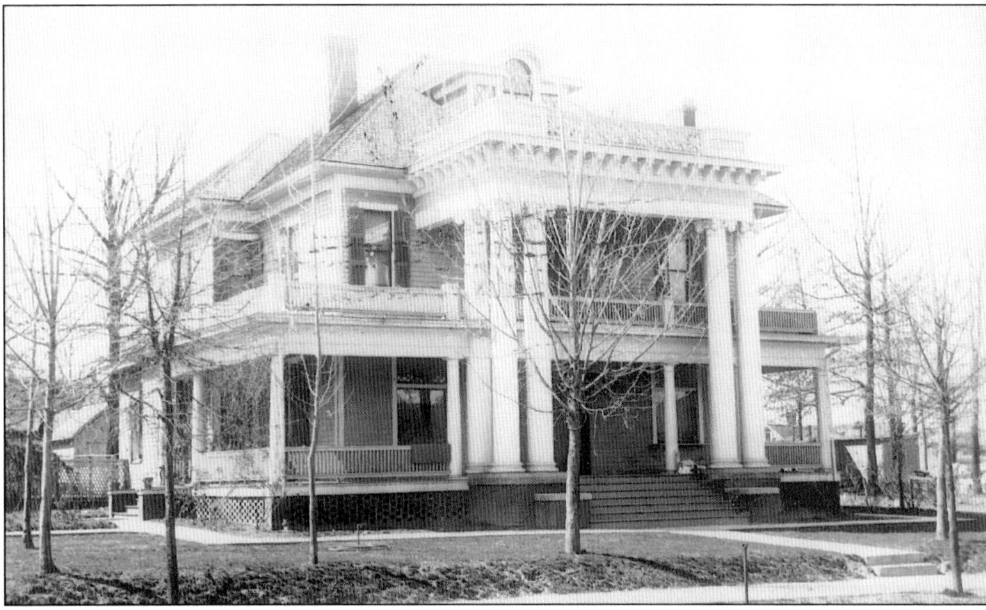

The Cottle home, one of the beautiful residences formerly located in the area of Forrest Avenue from Twelfth Street to Seventh Street, was completely destroyed in a fire. This lot stands vacant today.

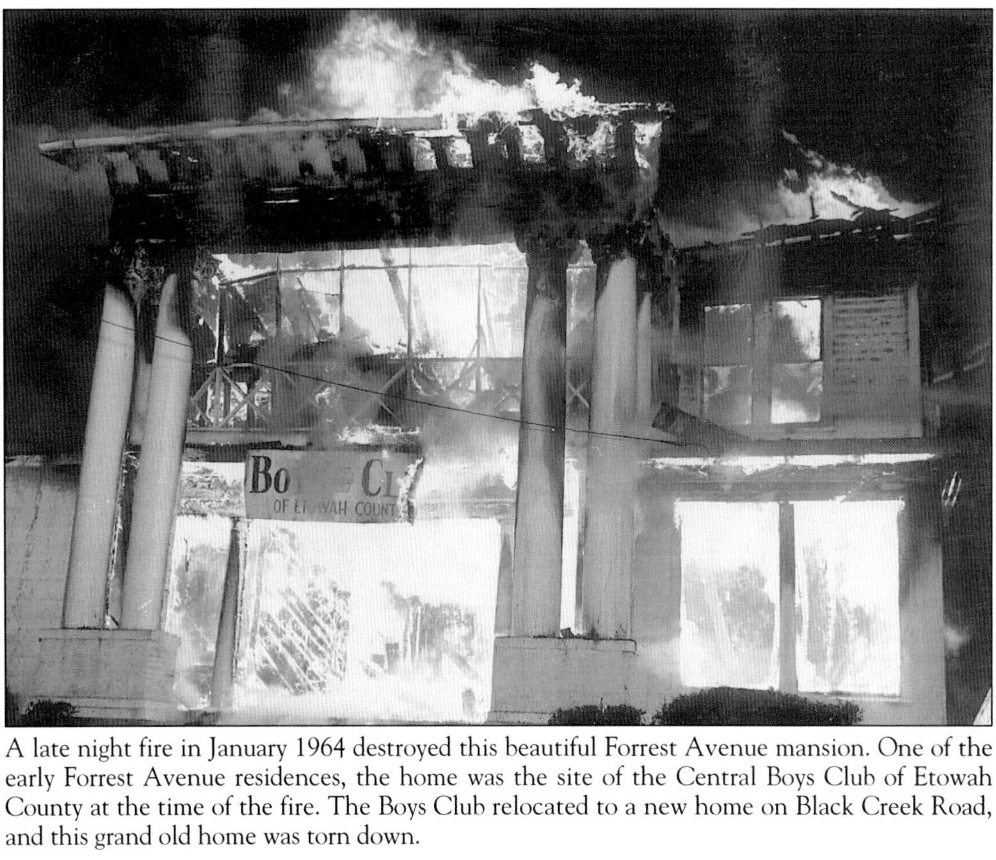

A late night fire in January 1964 destroyed this beautiful Forrest Avenue mansion. One of the early Forrest Avenue residences, the home was the site of the Central Boys Club of Etowah County at the time of the fire. The Boys Club relocated to a new home on Black Creek Road, and this grand old home was torn down.

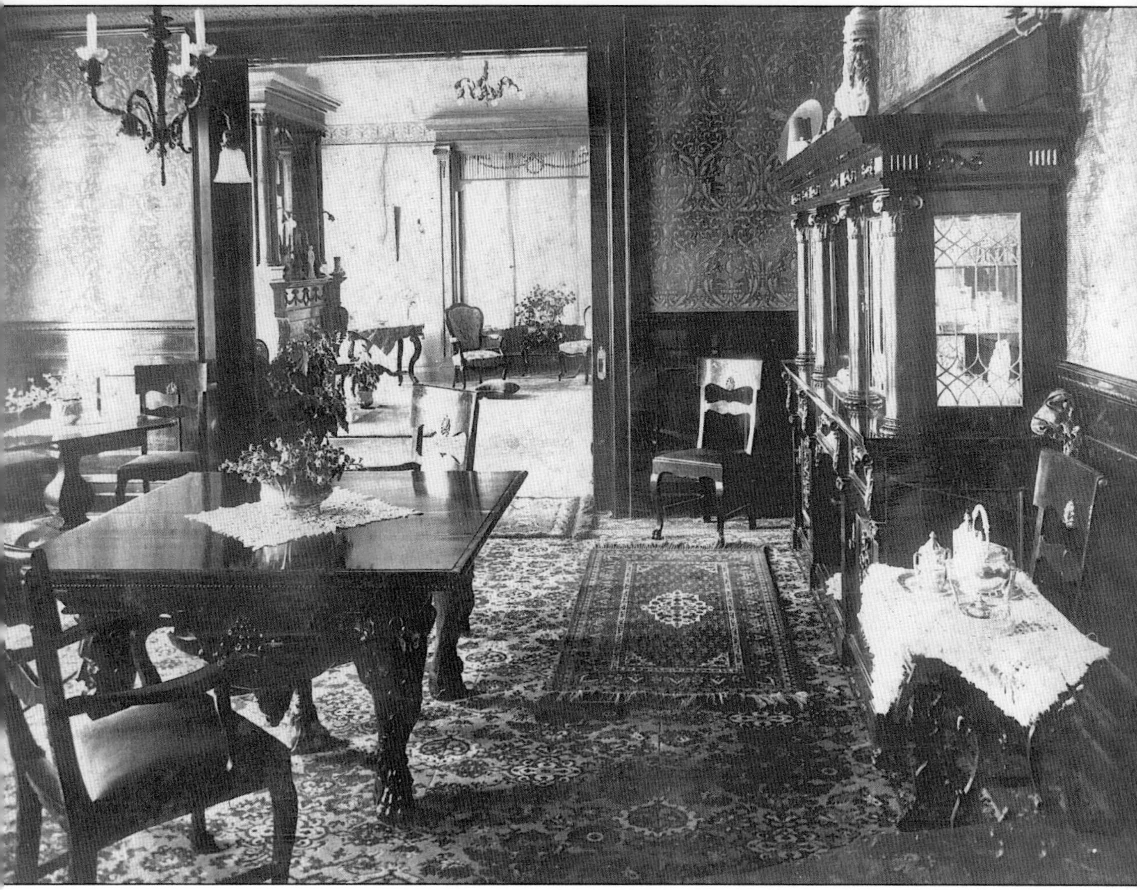

This interior view was taken in the Elliott home, which was located at the present site of the Etowah County Courthouse. It was the residence of Capt. James M. Elliott Jr. and Nena Kyle Elliott, the oldest daughter of Col. R.B. Kyle. Undoubtedly the most recognizable home in Etowah County at that time, the house boasted beautiful furnishings, such as the hand-carved table shown here. It was probably made at the Alabama City Furniture Works.

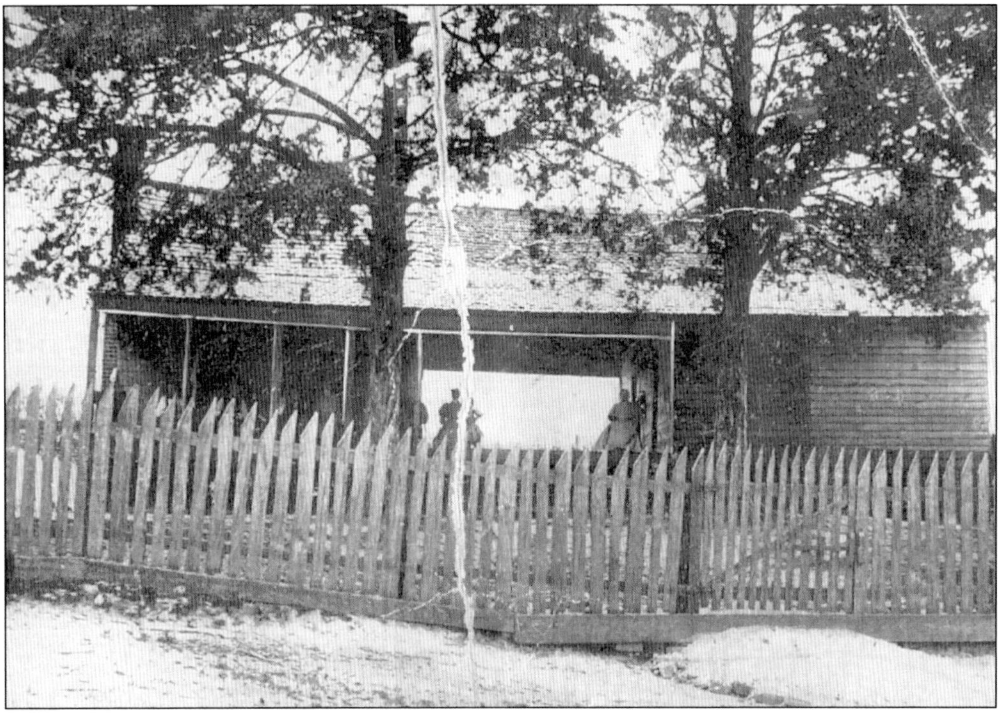

The homeplace of Emma Sansom is shown in this photograph from 1920. At 16 years old, Emma Sansom showed extreme bravery while leading General Nathan Bedford Forrest across Black Creek in the face of Union sniper fire during the War Between the States. The Sansom homeplace was located near the present site of Emma Sansom High School.

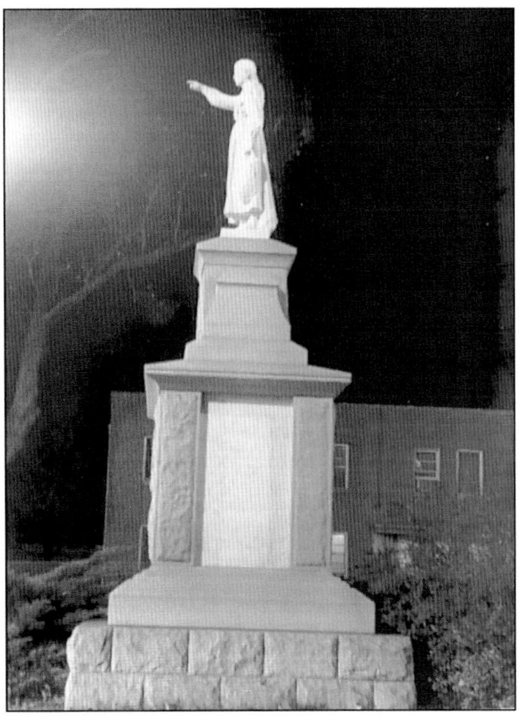

Erected in 1907, the Emma Sansom Monument is shown here at night. It was erected to honor the 16 year old's bravery in aiding General Nathan Bedford Forrest in his pursuit of Union Colonel Abel Straight. Forrest later overtook the Union troops near Cedar Bluff and forced them to surrender.

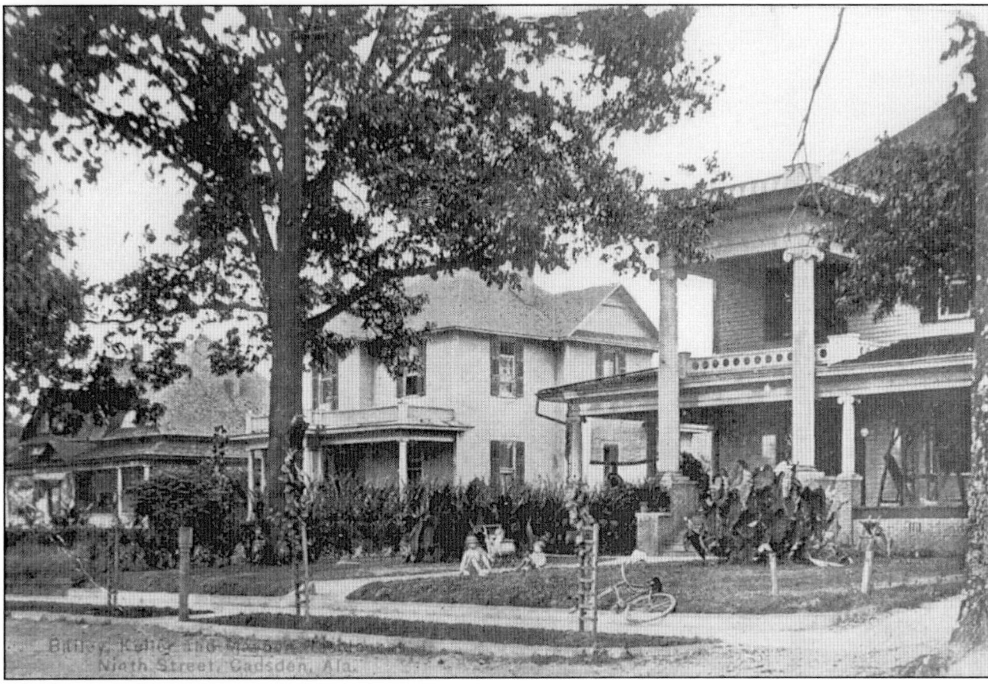

These beautiful homes are located on Ninth Street near downtown Gadsden. These homes appear very similar today as they did in this 1925 photograph; very little has been changed and they have kept their identities intact.

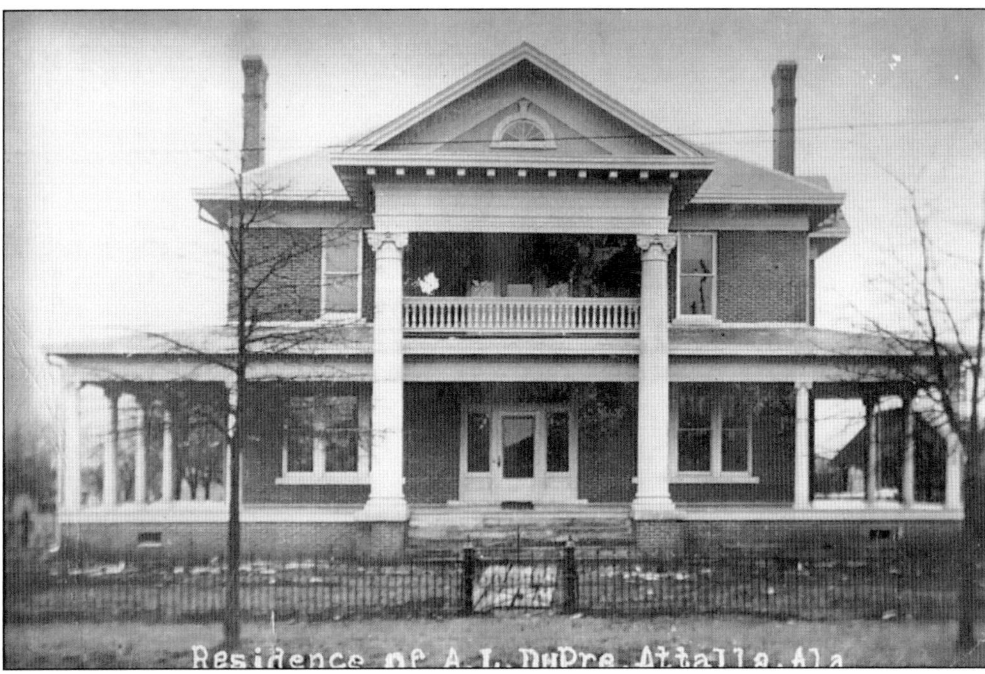

Located in Attalla, the former residence of A.L. DuPre is typical of the many elegant homes located throughout Etowah County. The DuPre family owned a large hardware business in the downtown Attalla. The house is still standing.

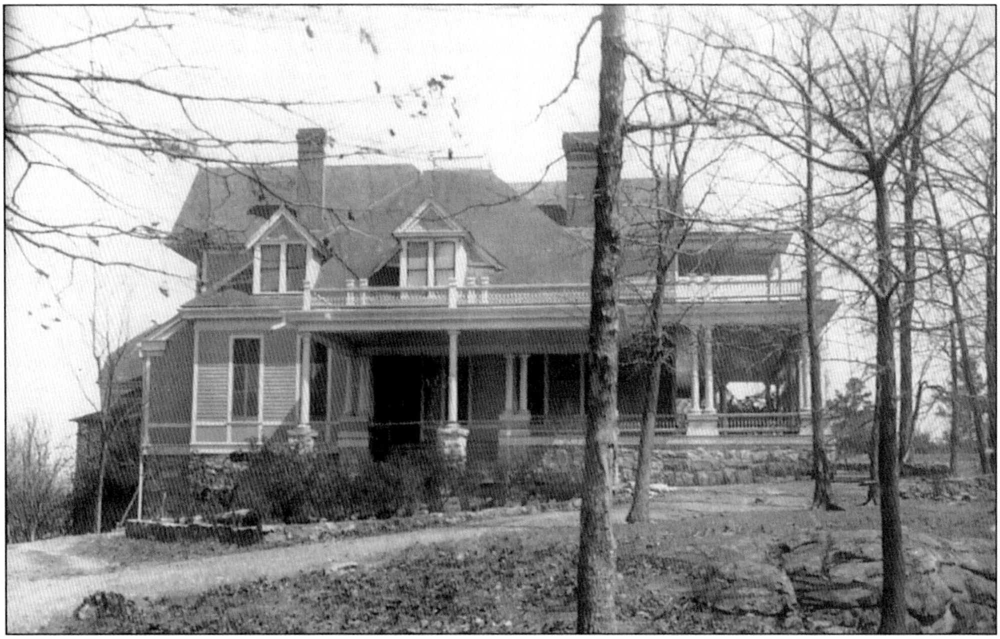

Whitehurst was the final home of Col. R.B. Kyle. Located on Lookout Mountain, this elegant home overlooks Gadsden below. Colonel Kyle was Gadsden's first mayor and one of the town's most respected citizens. This home has been completely restored and is currently the residence of Mr. and Mrs. Lewis Fuller.

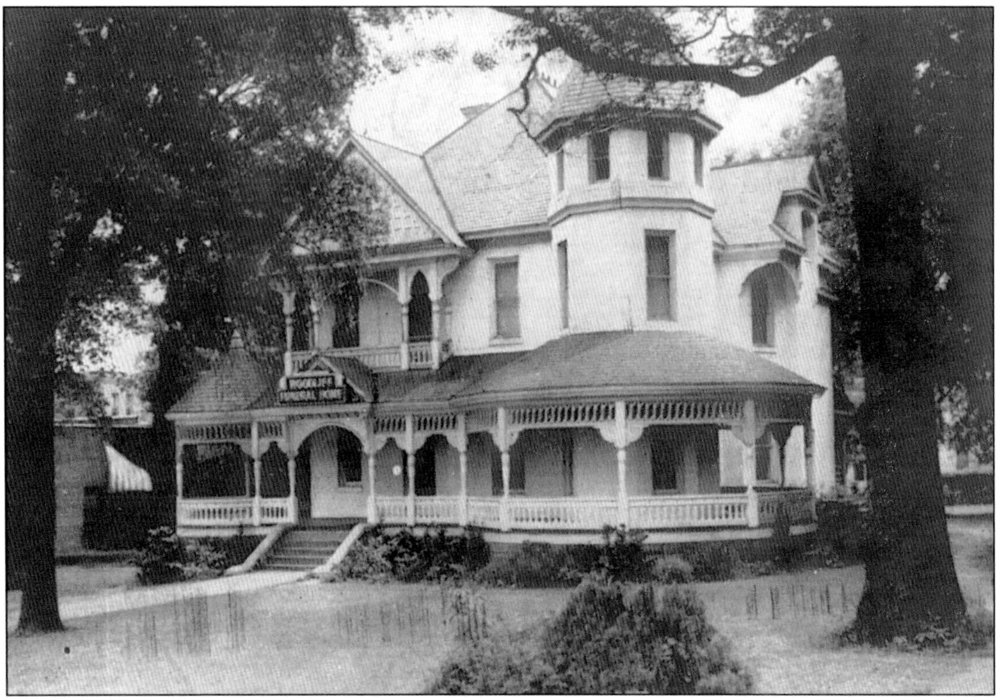

A stately residence on Forrest Avenue during the early 20th century, the Bellenger home was located between Seventh and Eighth Streets near the present site of Baker Tire Company. This was later the site of the Woodliff Funeral Home, which burned during the late 1940s.

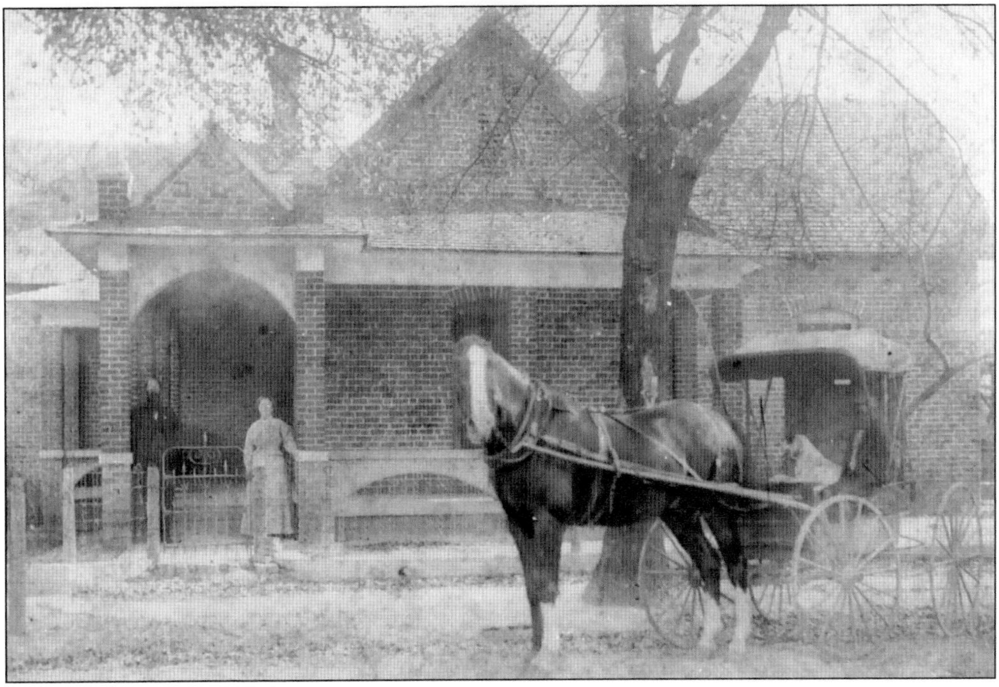

The Chadwick home is located on South Fifth Street in downtown Gadsden. The Chadwick family operated several brickyards in the area, and theirs was the first brick home built in Gadsden. Still standing today, this unique home features a well on its porch.

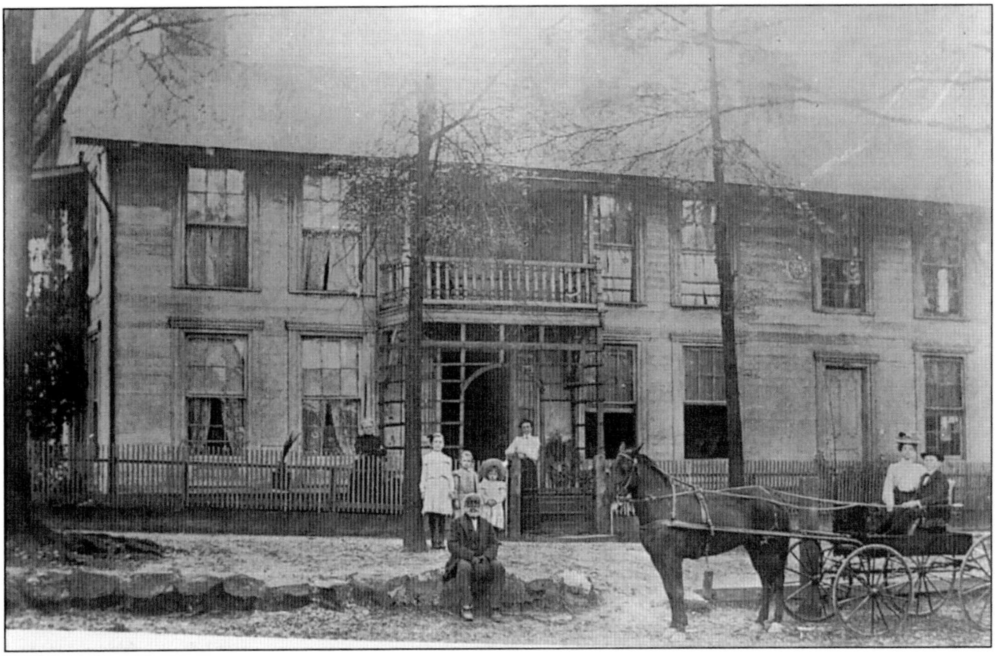

This wooden structure was probably the first hotel built in the Gadsden area. Originally known as the Turrentine Inn, it was owned and operated by Gen. D.C. Turrentine. The Inn was located at the present site of First and Broad Streets near the riverboat landing, and was also known as the Barrett House.

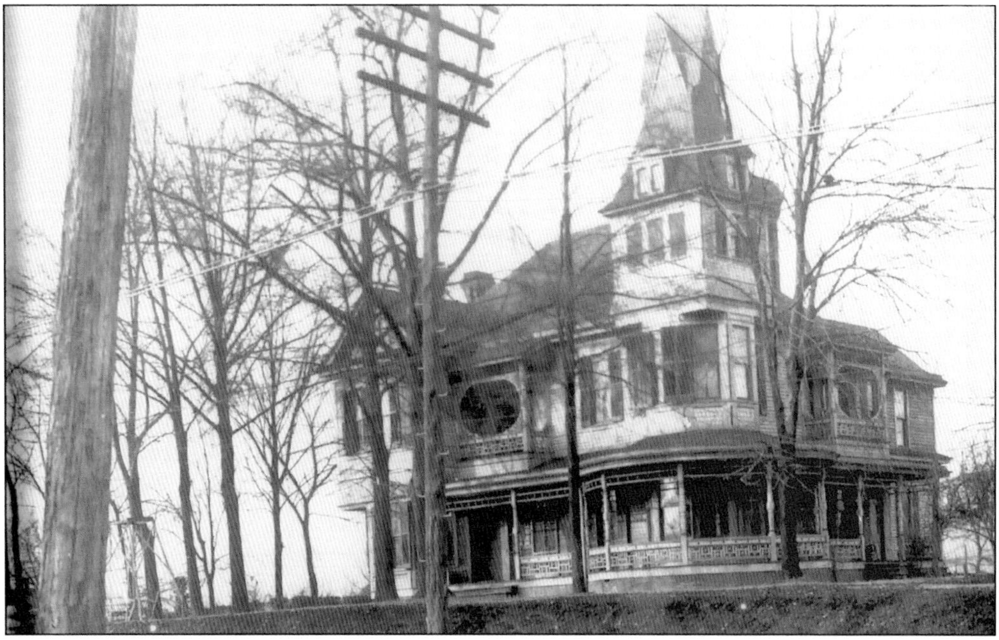

Pictured here is the W.P. Lay home, another of the stately mansions of Forrest Avenue. William Patrick Lay was the founder of the Alabama Power Company and lived much of his life in the Gadsden area. The Lay home is the present site of the Alabama Power Company offices in Gadsden.

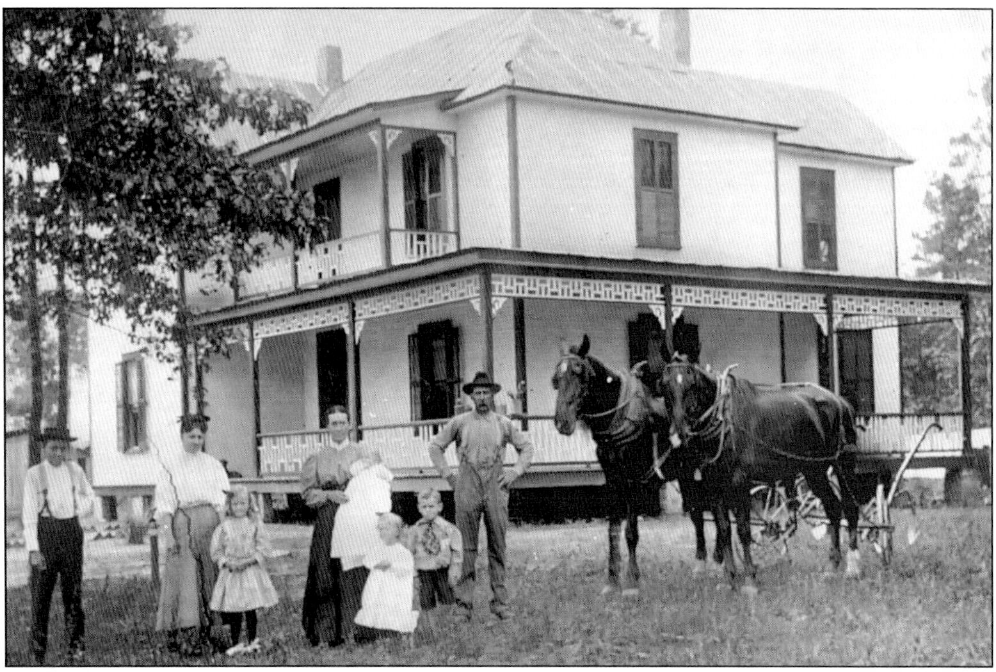

The Erwin family is pictured outside of their home in East Gadsden during the early 1900s. This beautiful home was typical of the early homes in the Etowah County area. East Gadsden did not become a part of the Gadsden city limits until the mid-1920s. Note the two large horses and the plow in the picture.

Nine

Pastimes

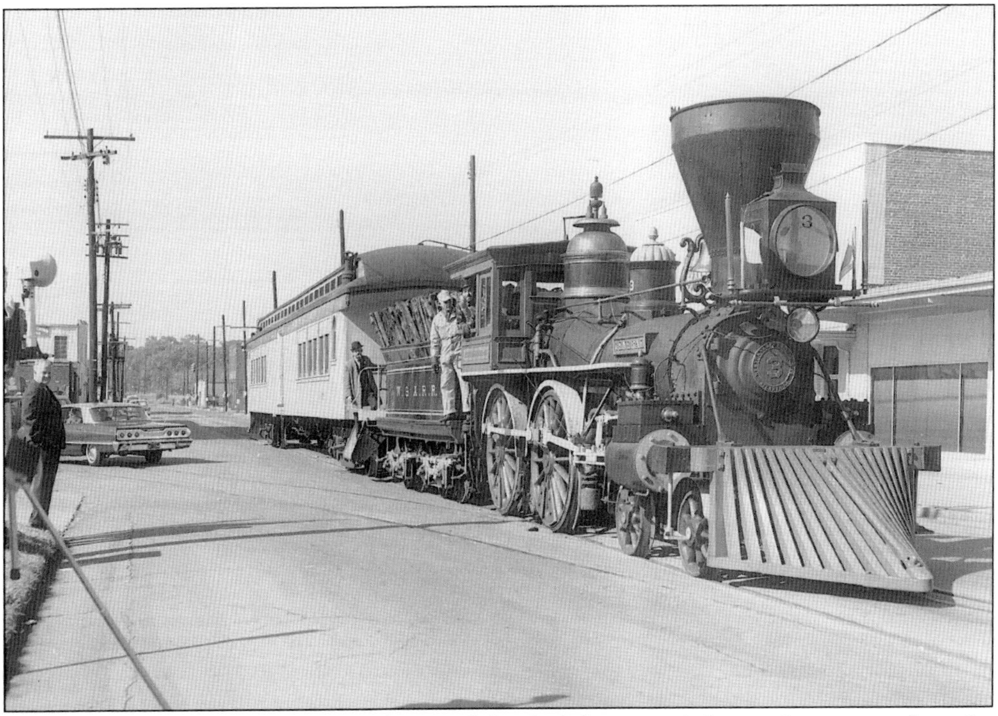

During the early 1960s, the "General" visited the Gadsden area. A famous locomotive from the days of the Civil War, the train is shown here on the L&N tracks on Locust Street in front of the *Gadsden Times* office. Many local citizens turned out to see this famous engine as it made its way through Etowah County.

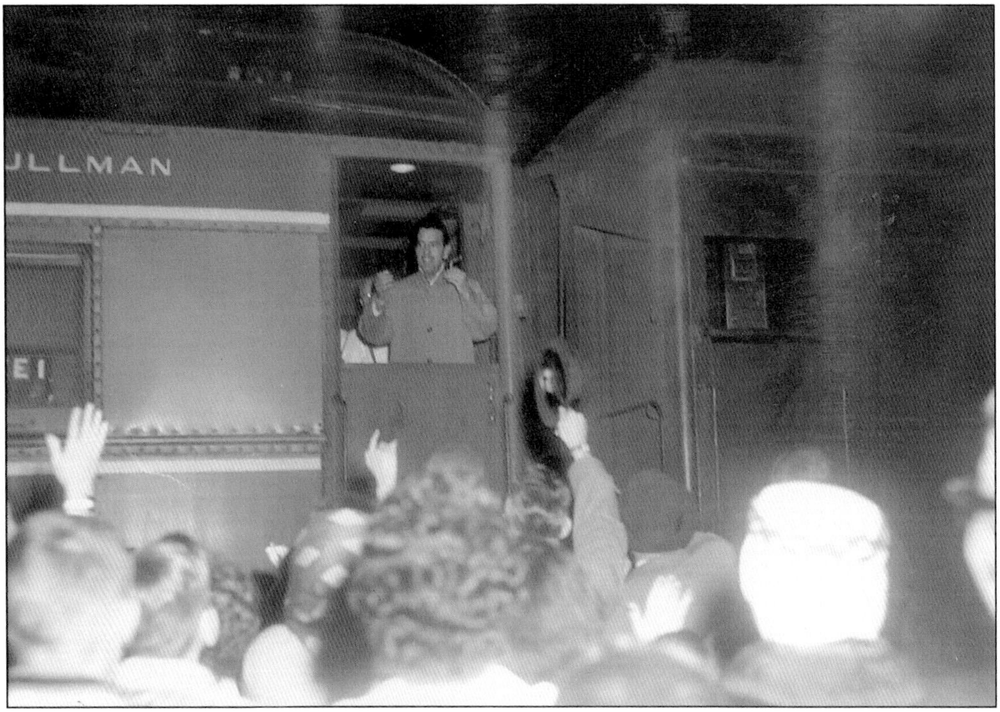

Tennessee Ernie Ford is shown here at the train station in Attalla. A large group of fans and well-wishers came to the Union Terminal to greet the star as his train passed through in December of 1960.

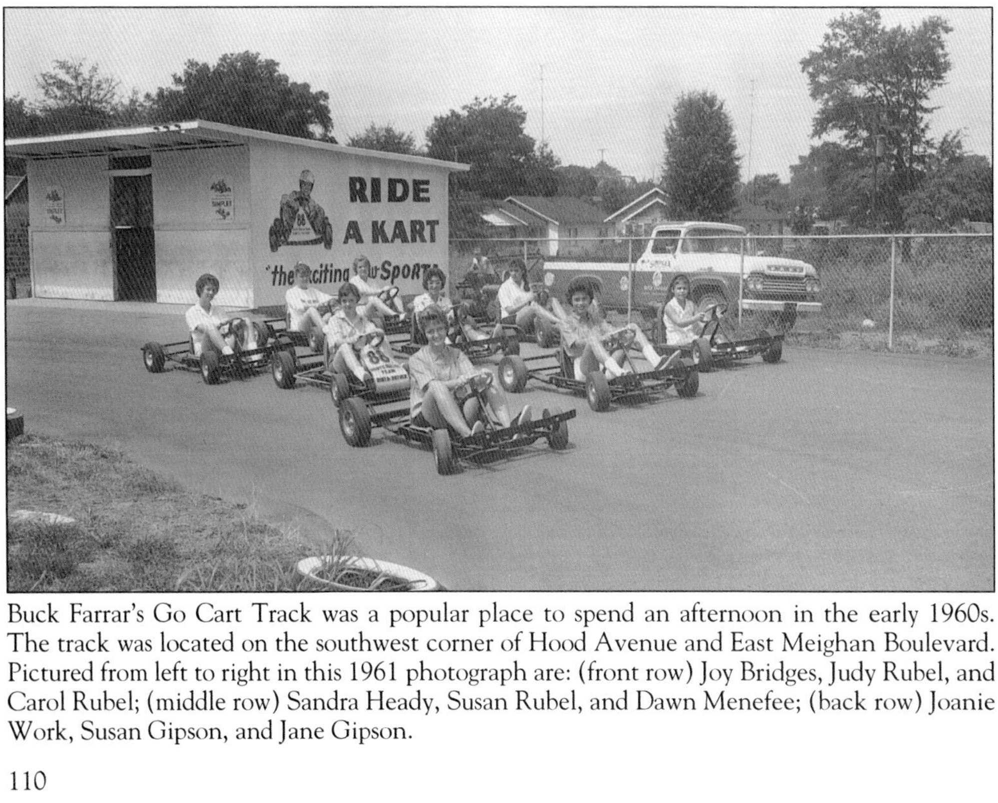

Buck Farrar's Go Cart Track was a popular place to spend an afternoon in the early 1960s. The track was located on the southwest corner of Hood Avenue and East Meighan Boulevard. Pictured from left to right in this 1961 photograph are: (front row) Joy Bridges, Judy Rubel, and Carol Rubel; (middle row) Sandra Heady, Susan Rubel, and Dawn Menefee; (back row) Joanie Work, Susan Gipson, and Jane Gipson.

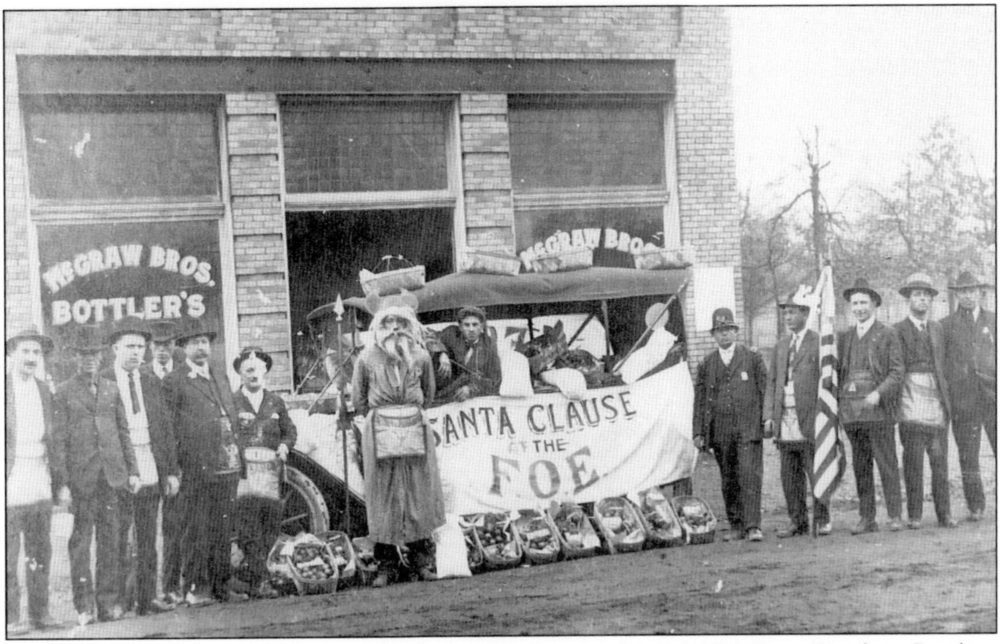

Members of the Fraternal Order of Eagles are shown outside of the McGraw Brothers Bottling Works in Alabama City. Located on Twenty-fourth Street, this building was home to the Fraternal Order of Eagles and later became a funeral home. It is presently the home of Dwight Lodge #550 F&AM.

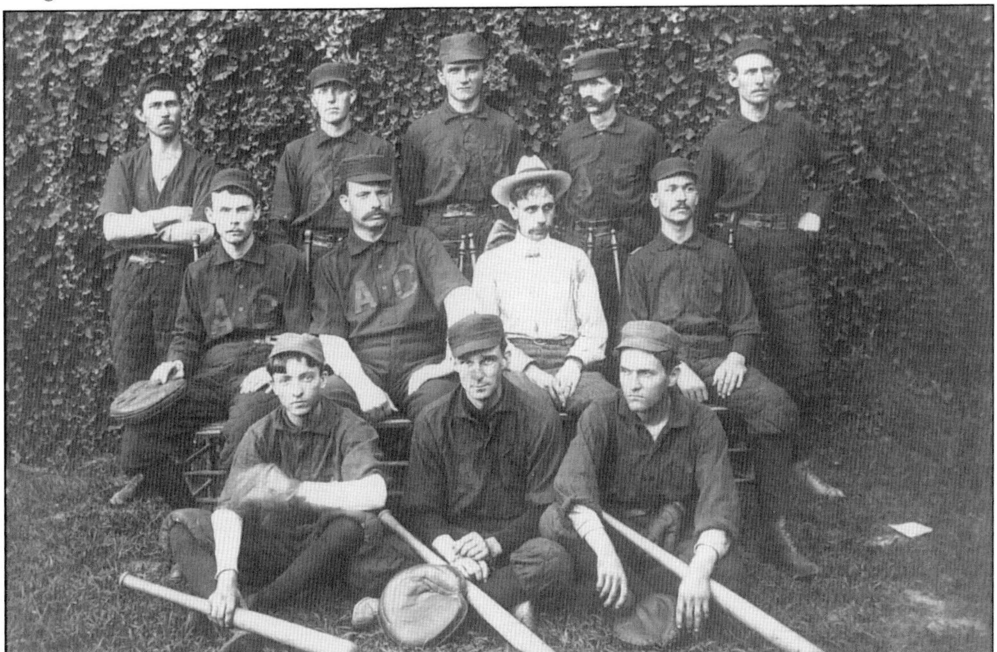

Members of the "Dwights" take time out to pose for a picture before a game at Dwight Park. The local industrial team from Dwight Manufacturing Company was well-known throughout the southeast. C.H. Moody, the mill superintendent and one of Alabama City's early mayors, is shown here posing with his team.

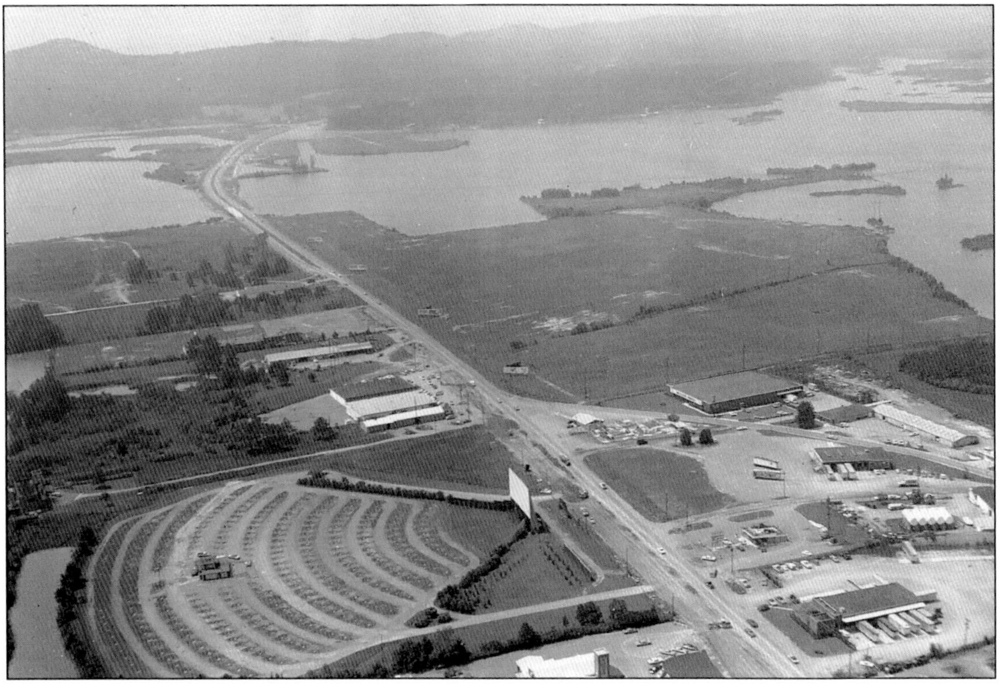

Gadsden's Rainbow Drive is pictured in this photo from 1971. The Rainbow Drive-In Theatre was a popular place for many years until the screen was destroyed in a wind storm. This photo was taken before the Gadsden Mall and Interstate 759 were constructed.

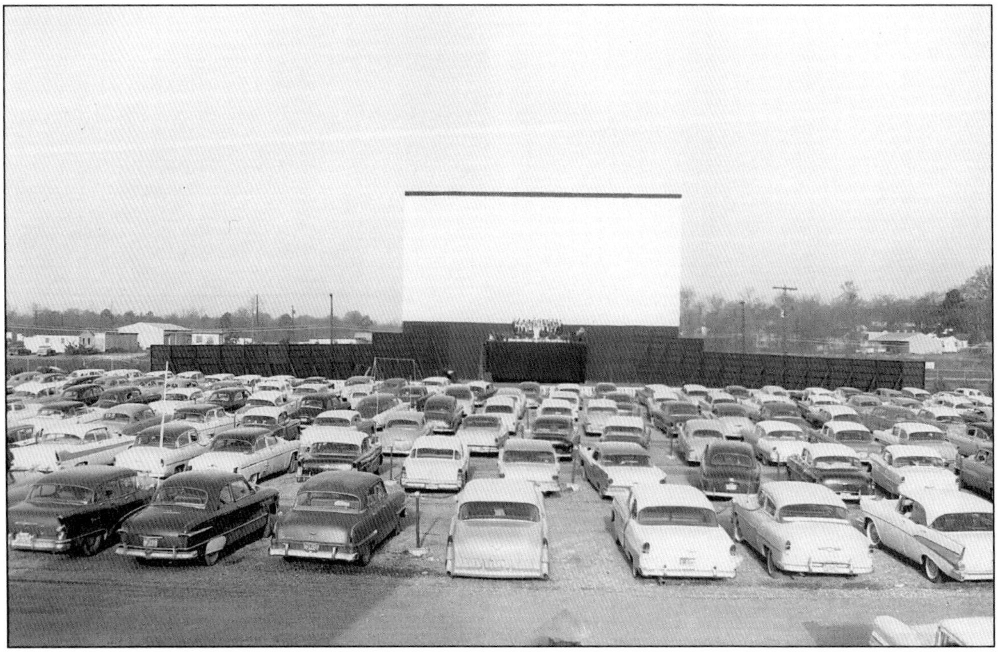

The Rainbow Drive-In Theatre would host a sunrise service each year on Easter Sunday. This inter-denominational service was well attended as evident by the number of automobiles pictured. The drive-in offered this service to the residents of Etowah County until it closed in the late 1970s.

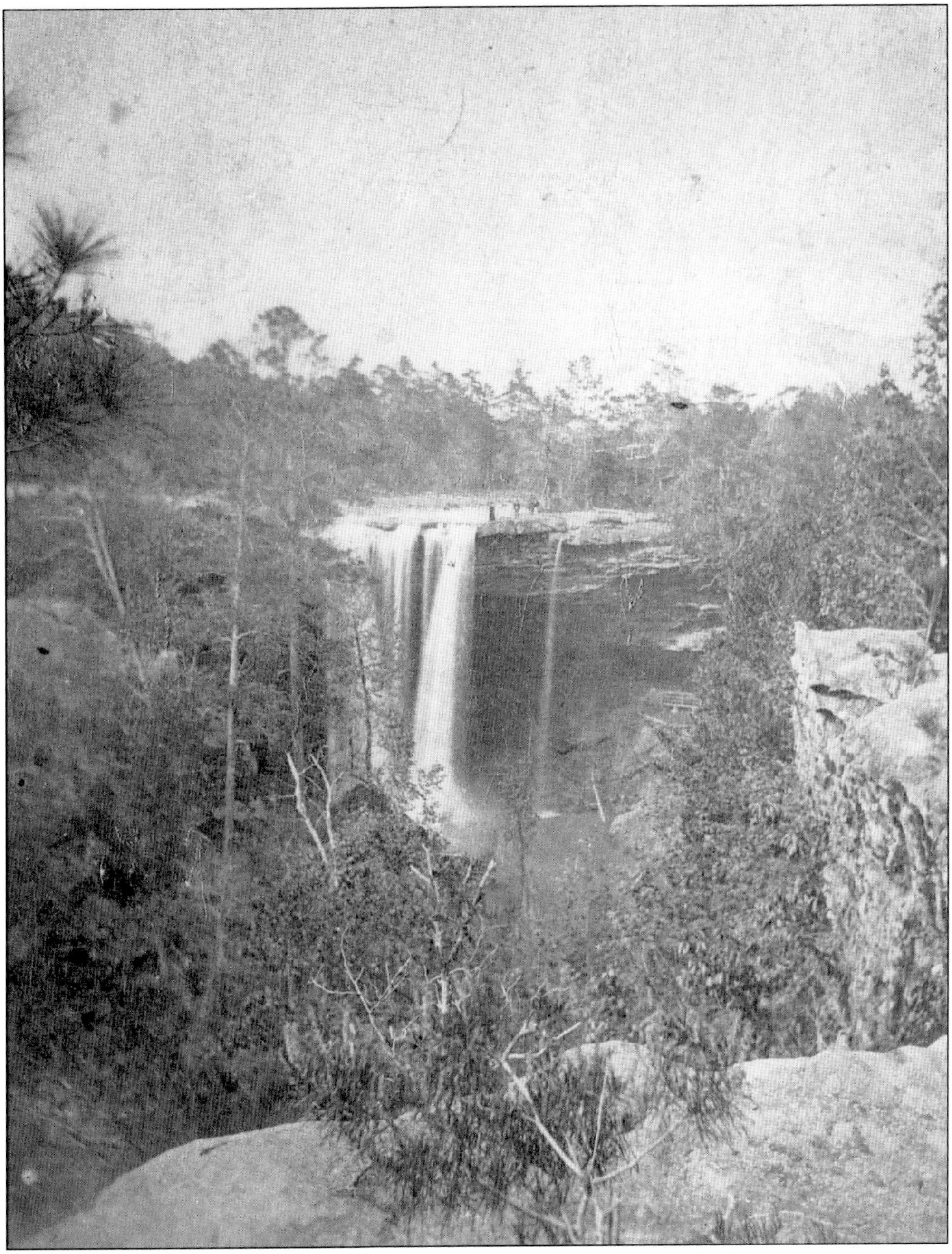

Black Creek Falls, or Noccalula Falls, has long been one of Etowah County's major tourist attractions. This photo from the late 1890s shows many people looking at the waterfall. A large wooden dance pavilion was located below the falls. Many tourists would come by riverboat to take in this breathtaking sight.

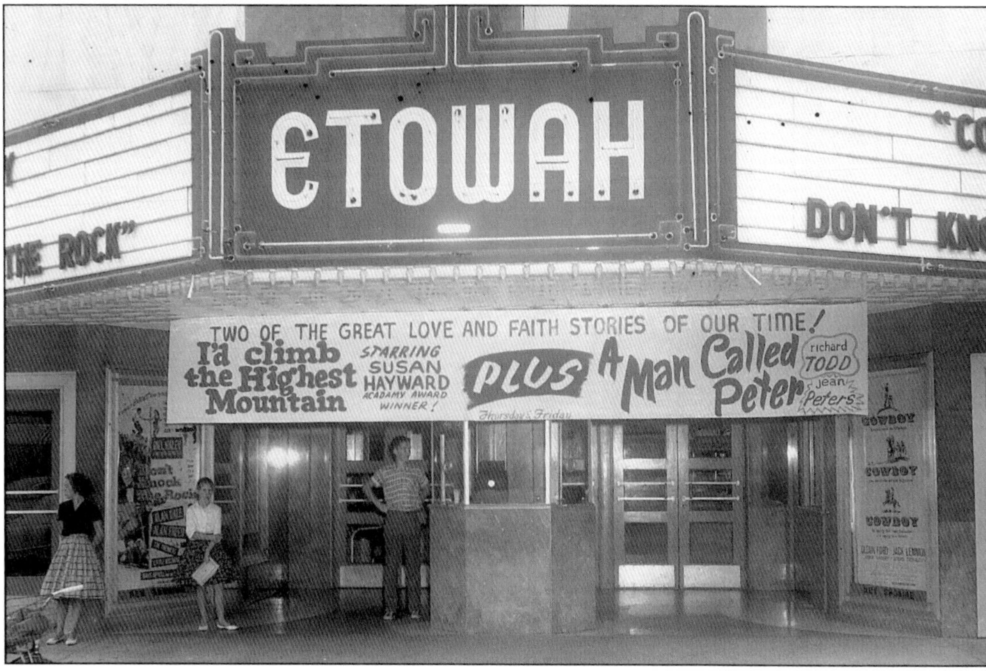

The beautiful Etowah Theatre was located for years in downtown Attalla. It opened in 1948 and was built to replace the smaller and older Liberty Theatre. The Etowah Theatre could seat over a thousand movie patrons and featured a sound-proof room where mothers could take crying babies and continue to watch the movie.

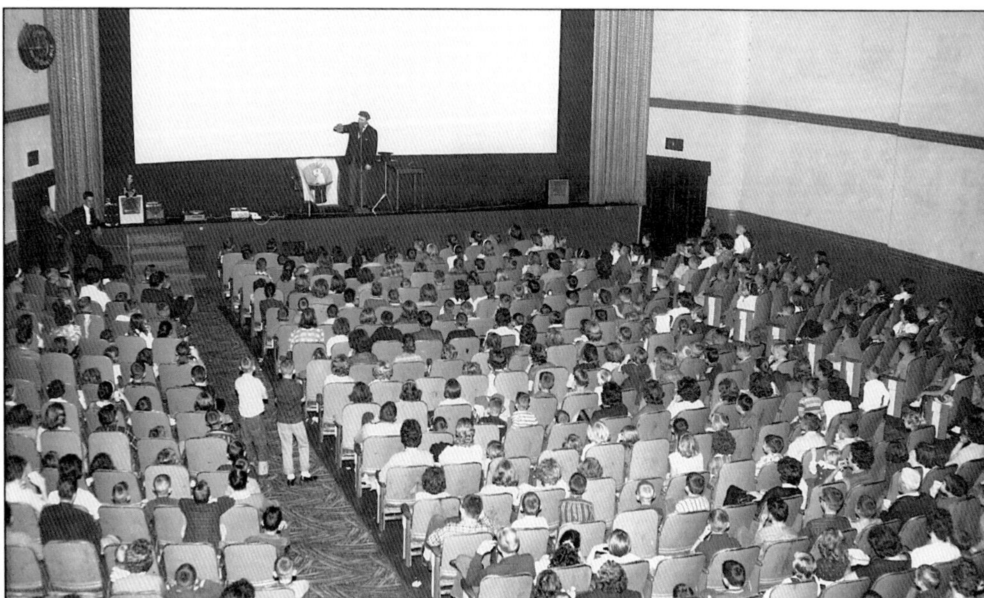

Cousin Cliff Holman is seen entertaining a large audience at the Pitman Theatre during the 1960s. The Royal Crown Bottling Company sponsored a Kiddie Club on Saturdays during the summer months. Young patrons could see a movie, a cartoon, and a live show for the admission price of six R.C. bottle caps. Cousin Cliff hosted the Popeye Show on a Birmingham television station.

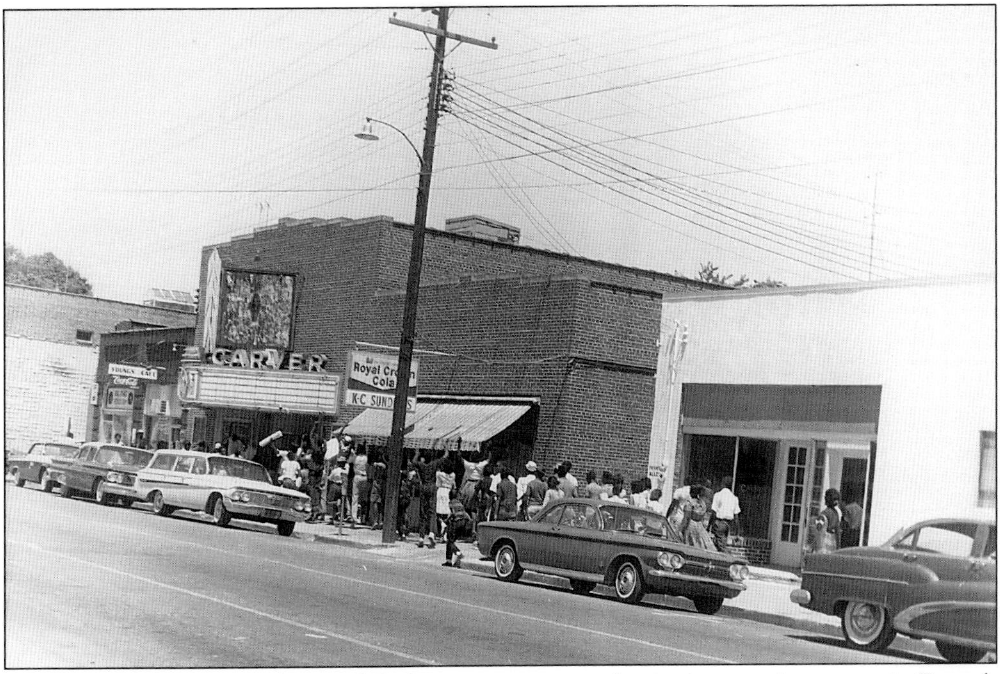

During the days of 1963, the Civil Rights movement was beginning to gain support in Etowah County. The Carver Theatre was the focal point for groups to gather for demonstrations downtown. The North Sixth Street area was the center of the black business district with stores, cafes, and offices, as well as the Carver Theatre.

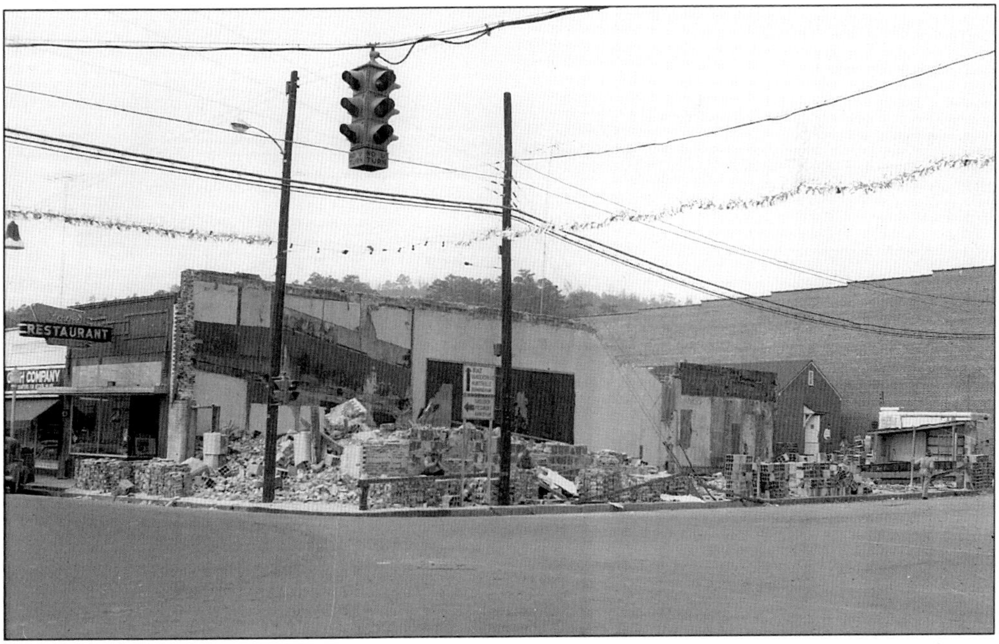

All that remains of the Liberty Theatre is a pile of bricks and rubble. A popular movie house in downtown Attalla during the 1930s and 1940s, the Liberty closed after the Etowah Theatre was constructed during the late 1940s. The Etowah Theatre opened for business on September 5, 1948.

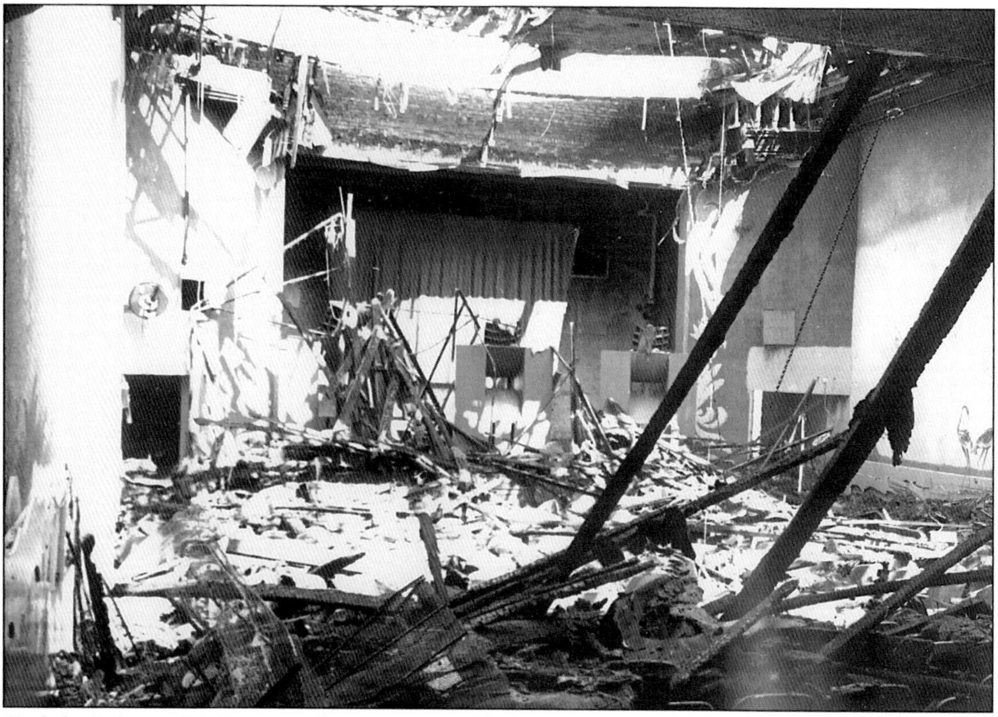

Gadsden's beautiful Princess Theatre was totally destroyed by fire in November of 1963. This downtown landmark was originally known as the Imperial until it was purchased by the Crescent Amusement Company of Nashville in 1925. The theatre was remodeled on two occasions and quickly became the place to go in Gadsden for the finest in movie entertainment. These ruins were all that remained the morning after the fire.

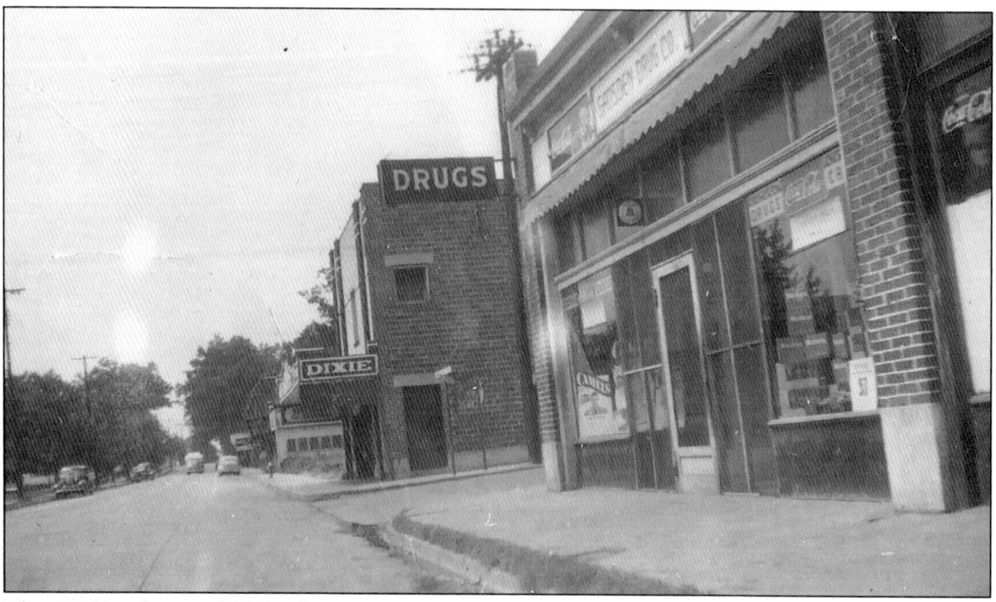

This 1940s photo of Hoke Street in East Gadsden shows the Gadsden Drug Company and the Dixie Theatre located across the street. The Dixie Theatre was one of two walk-in movie houses located in East Gadsden and was a very successful business for many years.

Members of the Central Boys Club are shown here preparing the wooden rails for the twelfth annual Boys Club Horse Show on July 29, 1972. The proceeds from this annual event benefited Etowah County's two Boys Clubs. Pictured clockwise from bottom left are William Sprinkle, Derrick Milliner, Marvin Smith, Mike Goodson, Ronnie Bradford, and Anthony Buggs.

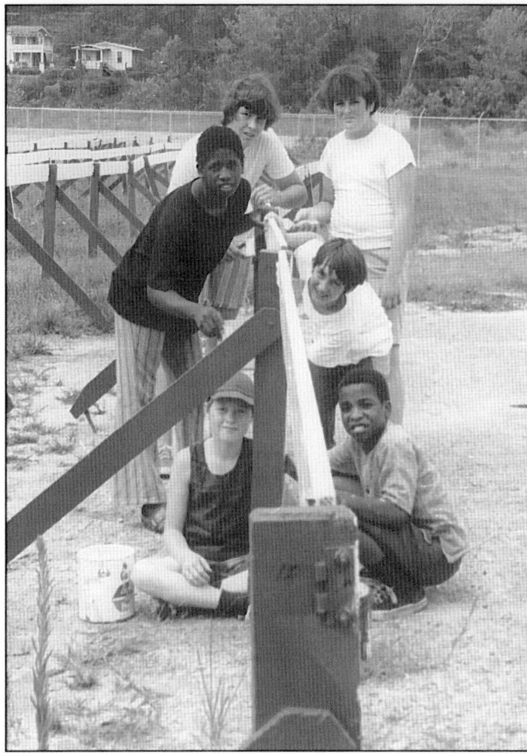

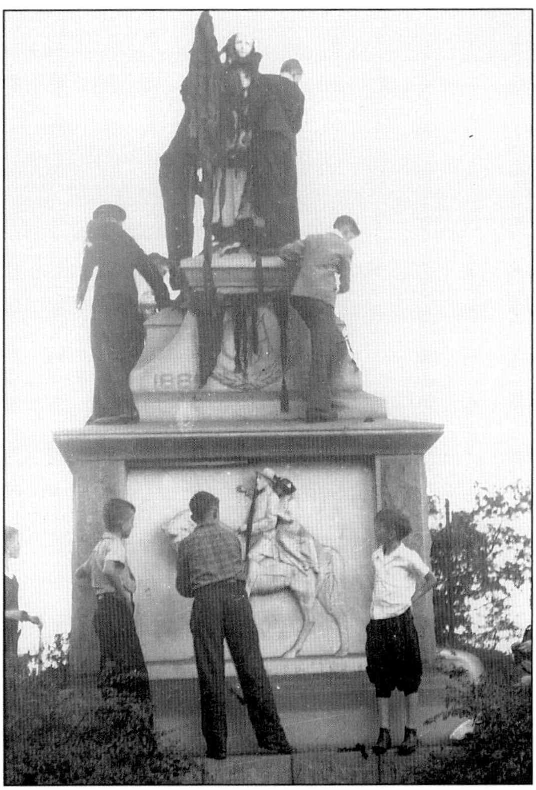

Students are shown here dressing the Emma Sansom monument in orange and black crepe paper. Every year before the football game between Gadsden and Emma Sansom, students from Gadsden High School would "decorate" the statue, and often place a Gadsden jersey on Miss Sansom.

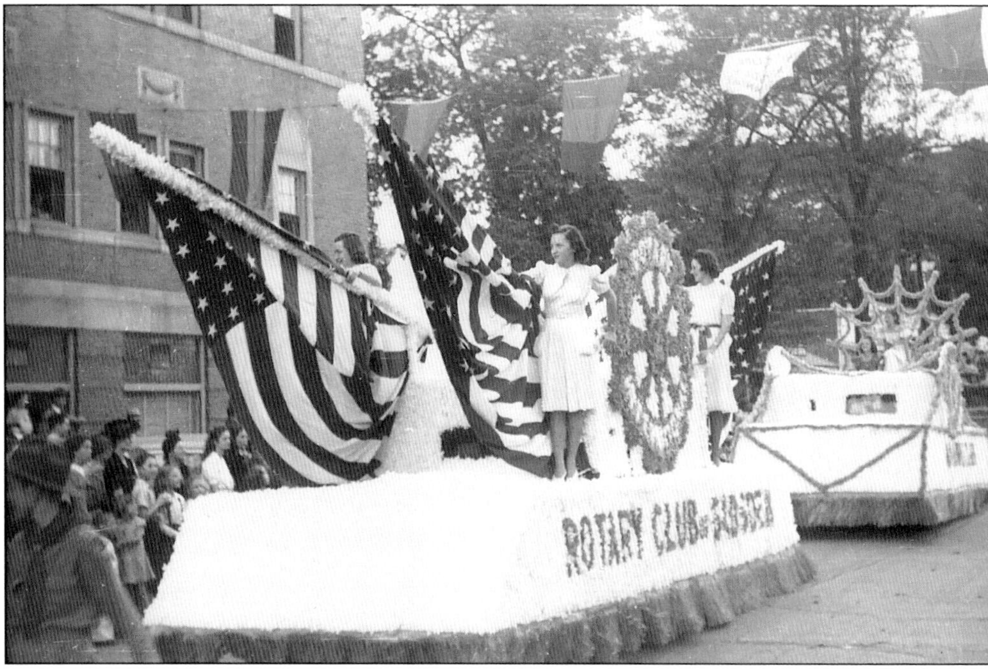

The floats in this photo from 1940 were a part of a parade known as the Calvacade of the Coosa. The parade commemorated the contributions of the Coosa River to the Etowah County area. This waterway brought riverboat trade to Gadsden and was a guiding force in the development of the community.

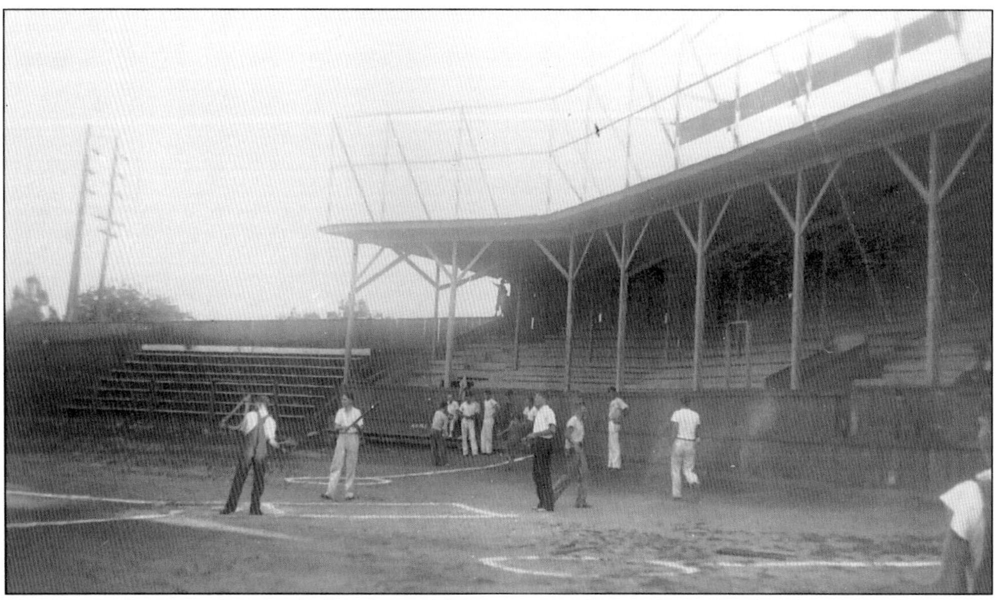

Dwight Park was a famous ballpark in Alabama City located on the banks of Black Creek. Many high school football games were played here over the years, as well as the games of the "Dwights," a local industrial team. The Detroit Tigers played an exhibition game here in the early 1920s. Shown in this photo is an Alabama City softball team warming up before a tournament game.

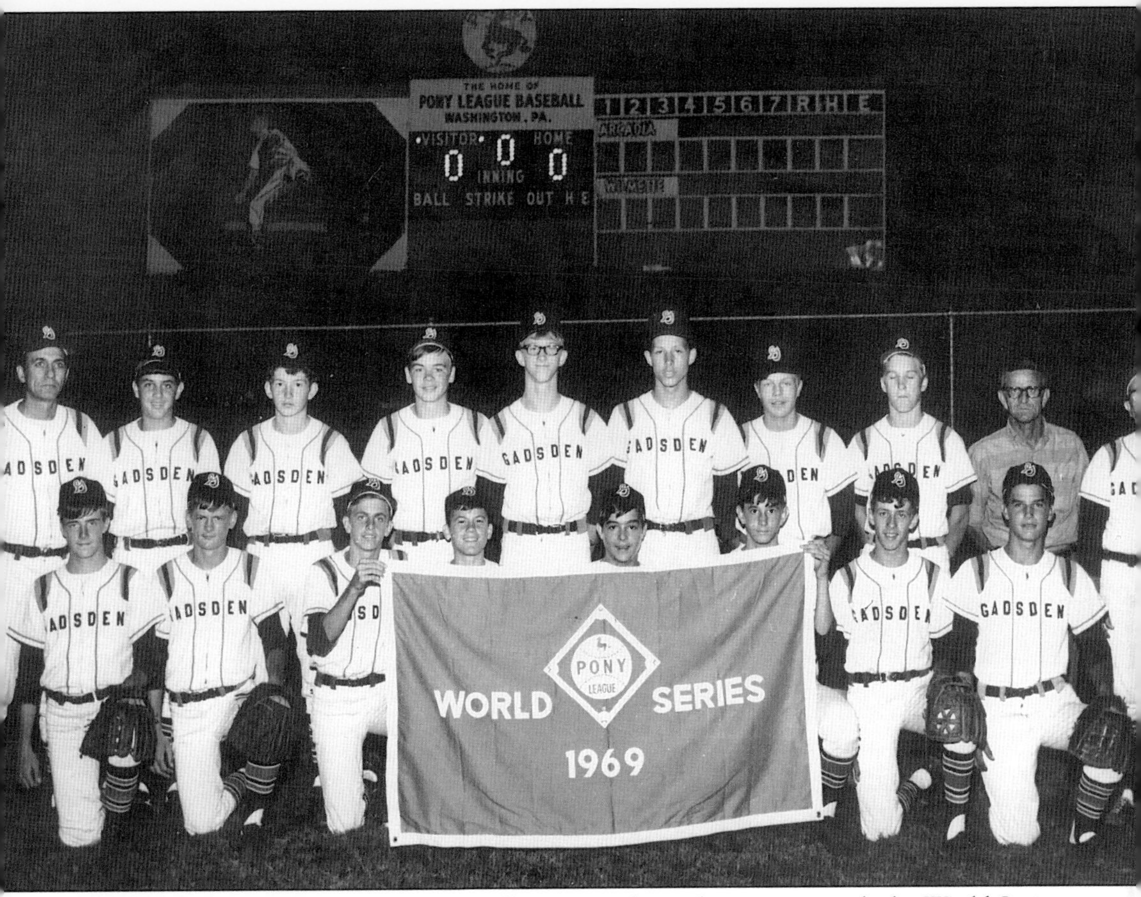

Members of the Gadsden Pony League All-Stars are shown here posing with the World Series banner. The Gadsden team was very successful in the series and finished in the top three in the nation. The World Series was held in Washington, Pennsylvania, and Gadsden's team was eliminated by a team from Arcadia, California. This photo was taken in Washington in 1969.

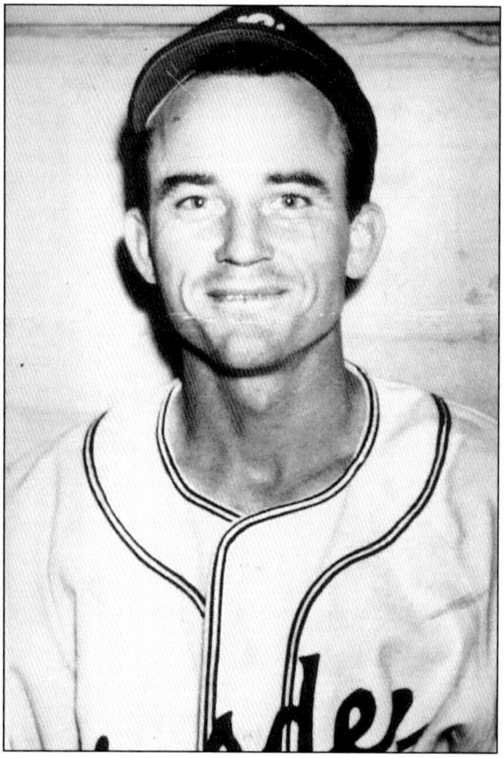

Byron "Barney" Bridgers is shown here in his Gadsden Pilots uniform. A local favorite, Bridgers was a member of the 1946 Gadsden Pilots and played shortstop. He was an original signee of the St. Louis Cardinals, and stayed in the Gadsden area following his baseball days. He held numerous baseball camps over the years and contributed a great deal to the youth baseball programs in the area. (Courtesy of the Bridgers family.)

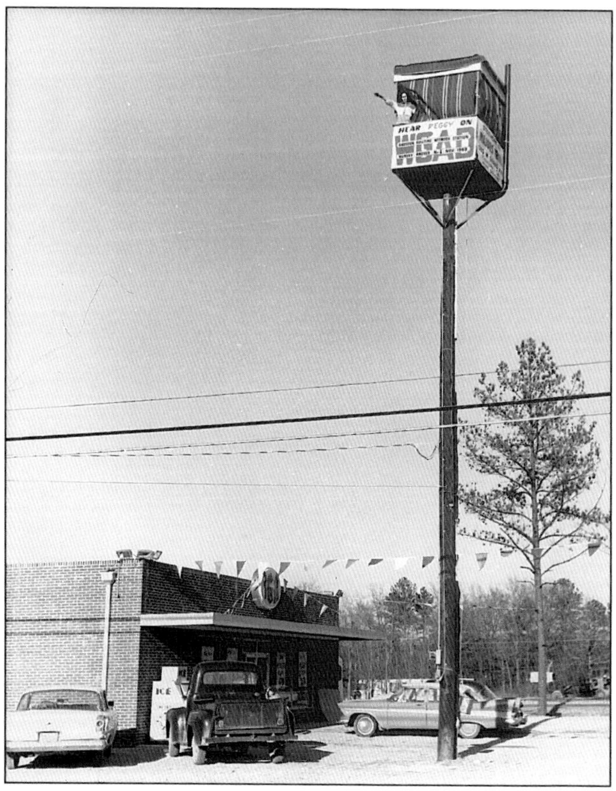

Peggy Townsend is shown here in an attempt to set a new "flagpole sitting" record. The attempt took place in 1964 at the Glencoe Shopping Center where Ms. Townsend entered a 6-by-6-by-7-foot house located atop a 50-foot telephone pole. She was sponsored by WGAD, a local radio station, and set a new record of 217 days atop the pole. The record has since been broken.

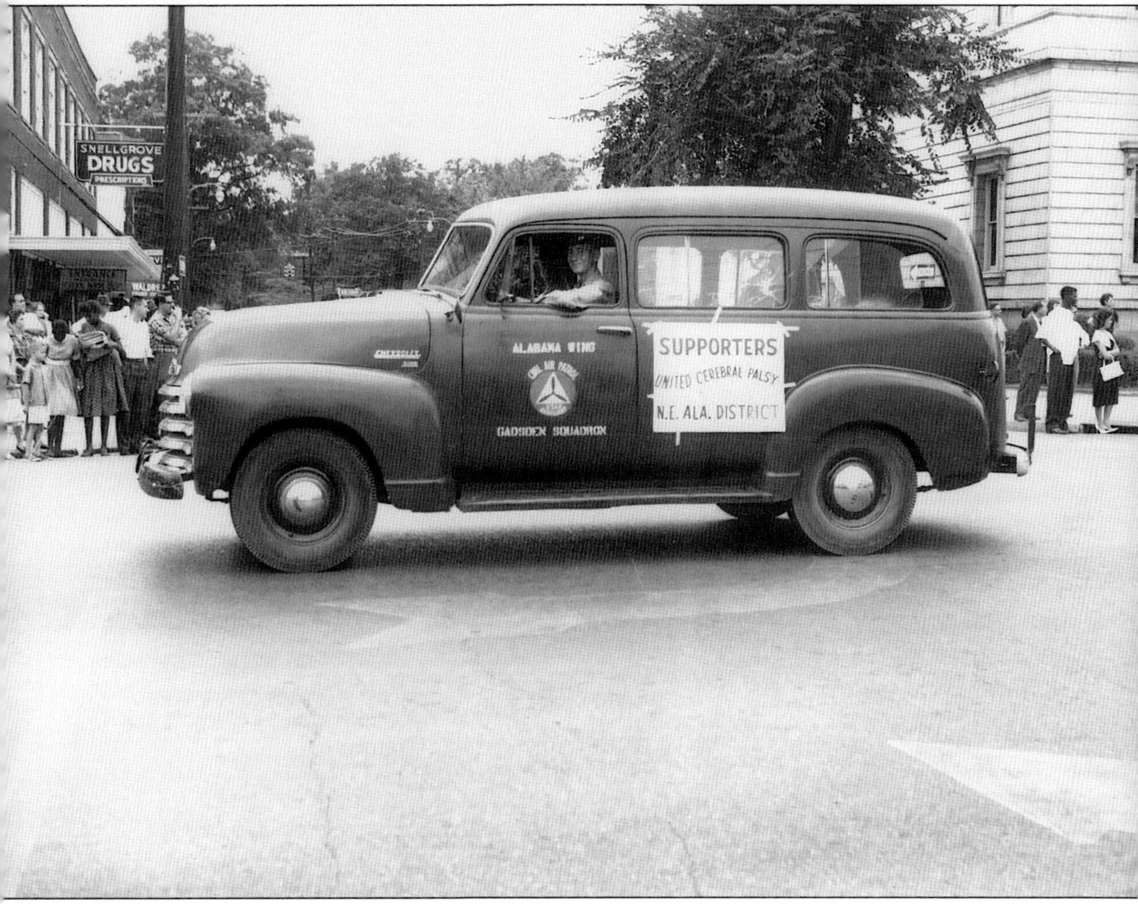

Parades have long been popular in the Etowah County area, and large crowds usually gathered to watch them. This photo from 1960 shows a Civil Air Patrol Vehicle at the intersection of Sixth and Broad Streets. The Snellgrove Drug Company is located on the left and the Federal Building is located on the right.

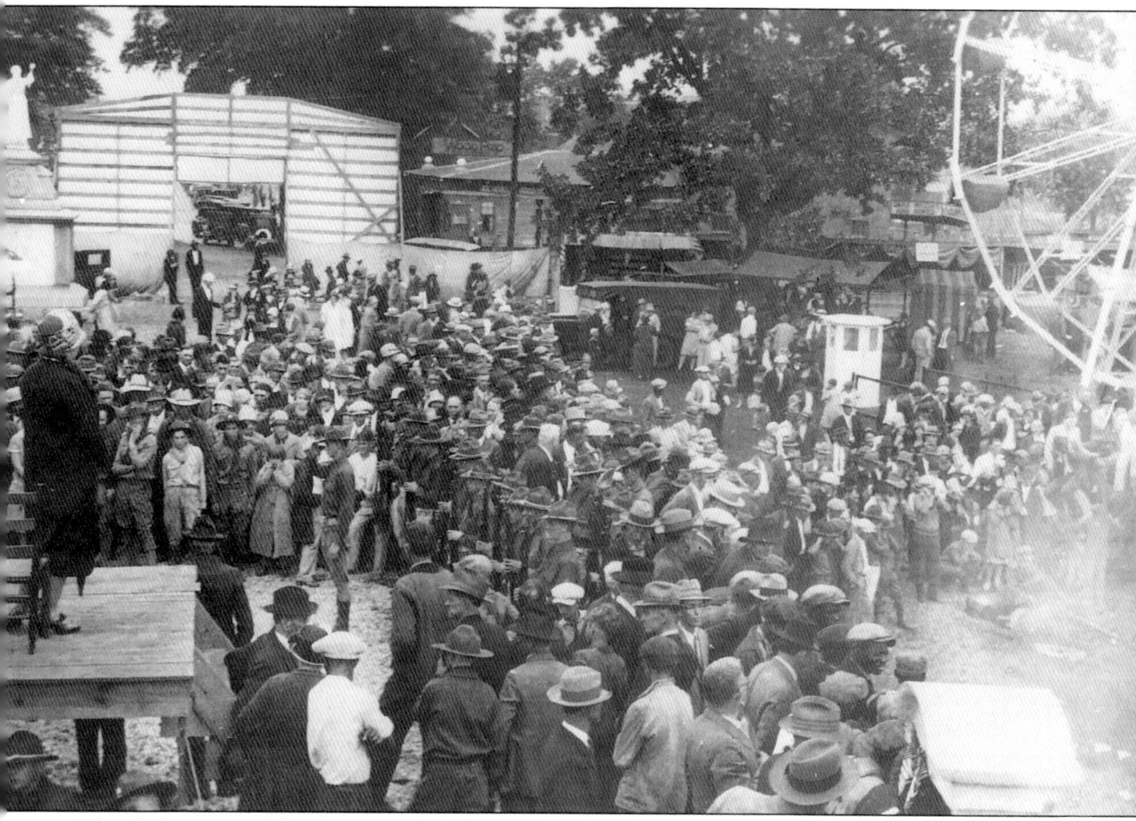

The dedication of the Memorial Bridge across the Coosa River was a four-day celebration in April of 1927. A large gathering of people are shown here near the Emma Sansom monument. Many booths were set up on or near the bridge and housed exhibits or games. National Guardsmen are shown firing machine guns into the river.

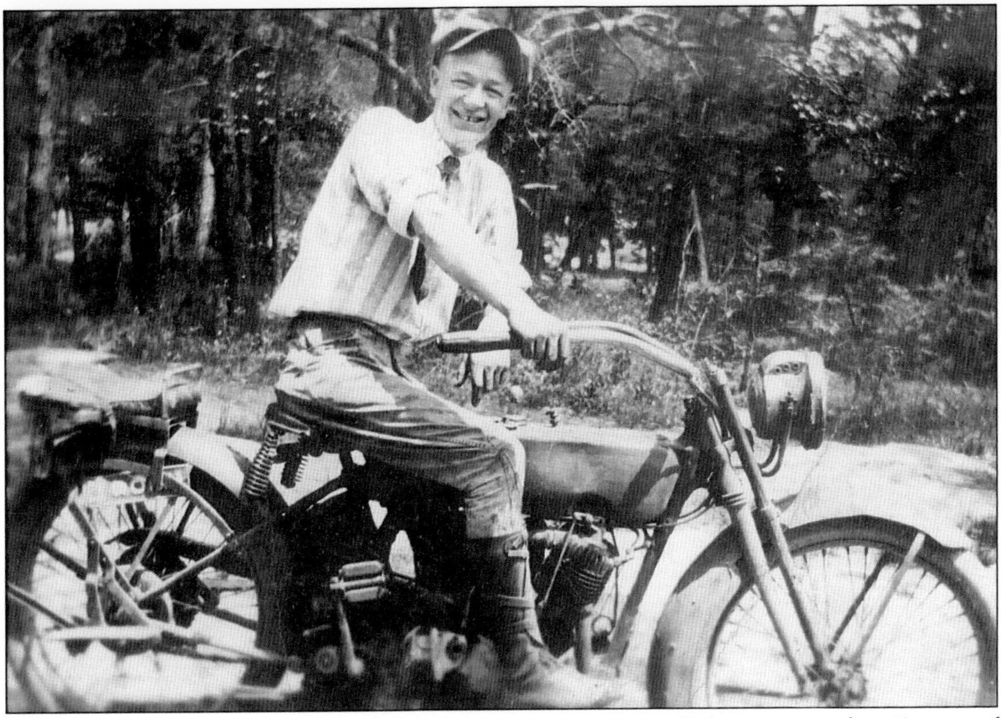

Reid Coleman is shown here sitting atop his motorcycle. A steel plant retiree after 49 years of service, Reid Coleman is one of the many motorcycle enthusiasts in the Etowah County area.

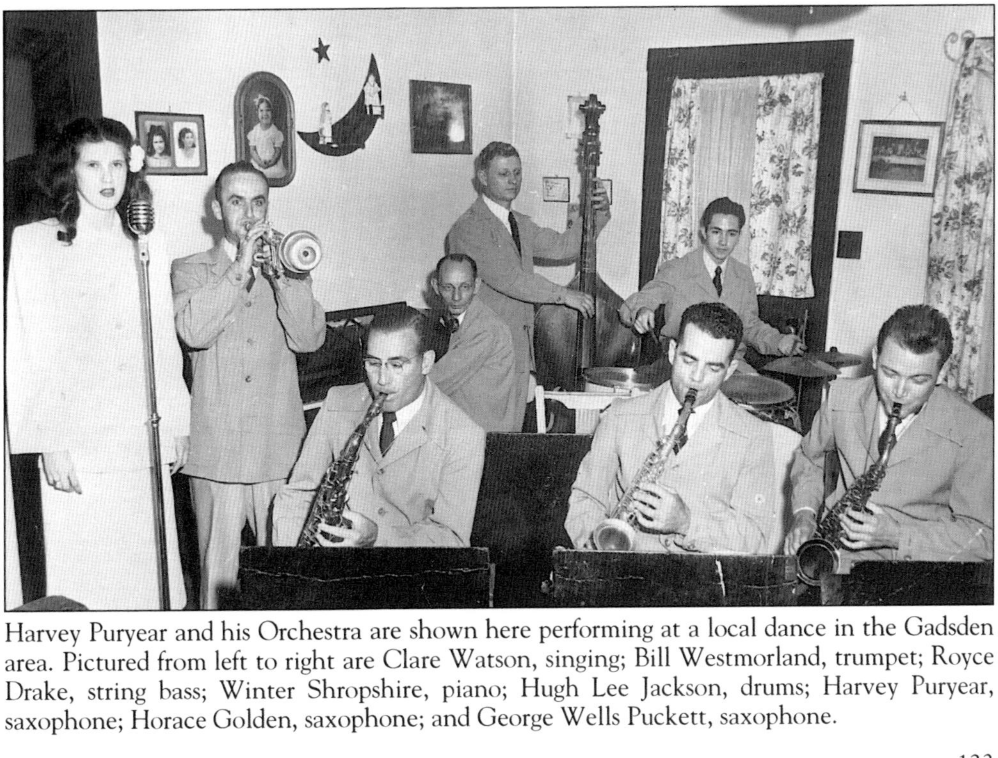

Harvey Puryear and his Orchestra are shown here performing at a local dance in the Gadsden area. Pictured from left to right are Clare Watson, singing; Bill Westmorland, trumpet; Royce Drake, string bass; Winter Shropshire, piano; Hugh Lee Jackson, drums; Harvey Puryear, saxophone; Horace Golden, saxophone; and George Wells Puckett, saxophone.

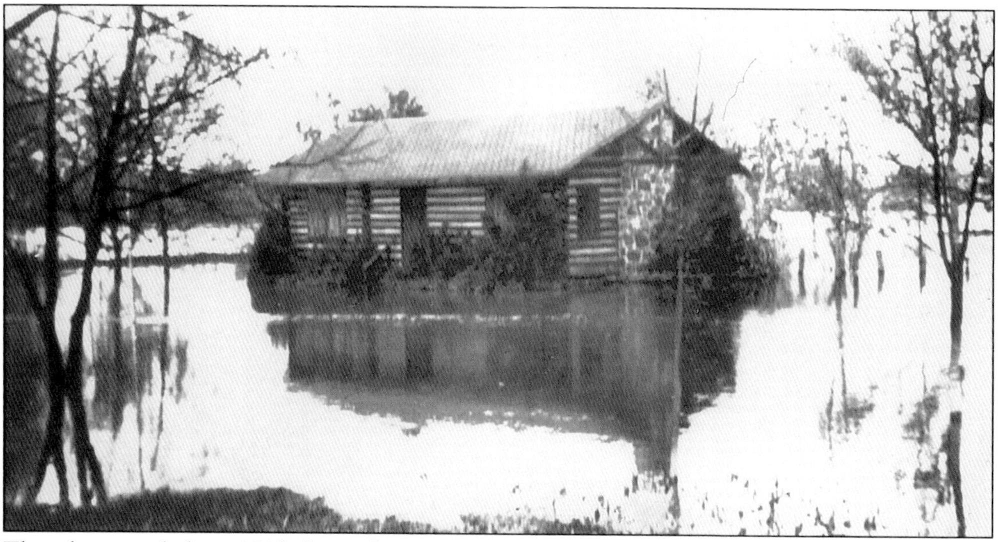

This photograph from 1935 shows the Sea Scout Cabin that was located in Moragne Park near the banks of the Coosa River. The Sea Scouts were very active in the area at the time, but the many cabins located throughout Etowah County have since been torn down.

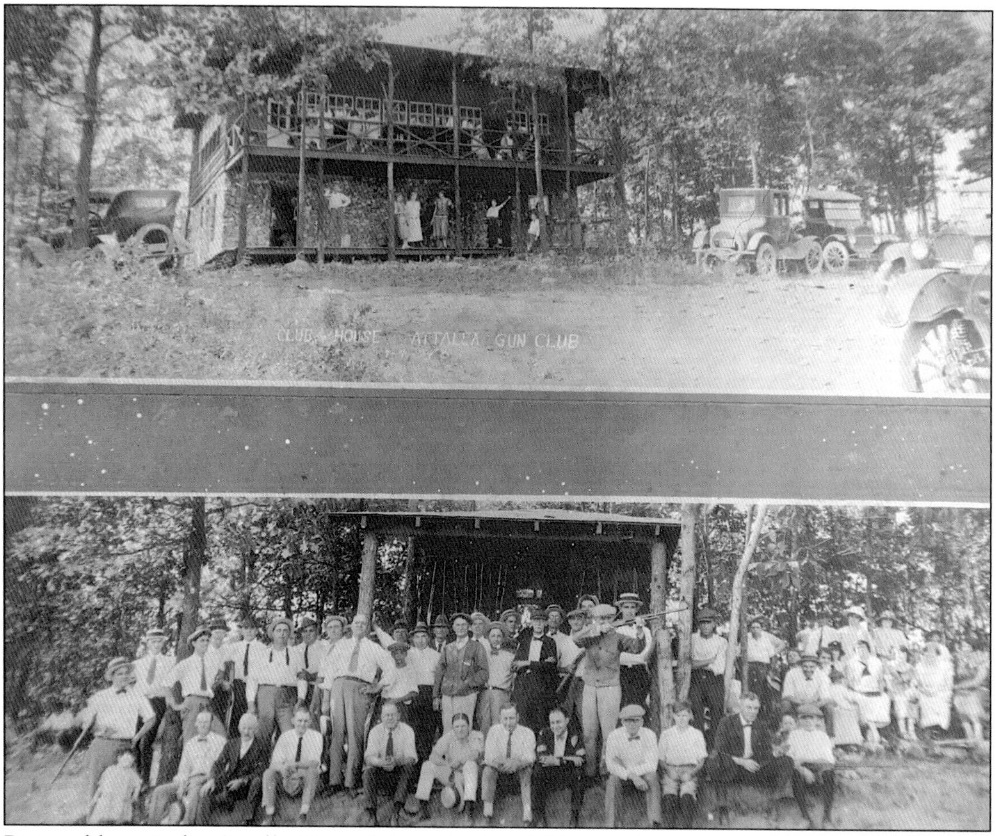

Pictured here is the Attalla Gun Club, with the clubhouse shown in the upper portion of the photo and many of the group's members posing in the lower portion of the photo. Many private clubs such as this one have been formed in Etowah County during the 20th century.

Captured in this scene from the 500 block of Broad Street in downtown Gadsden is Joe Christopher jumping on a pogo stick. This 1922 photo from the north side of Broad Street also shows the Mexican Chili Parlor, and the First Baptist Church at the lower left.

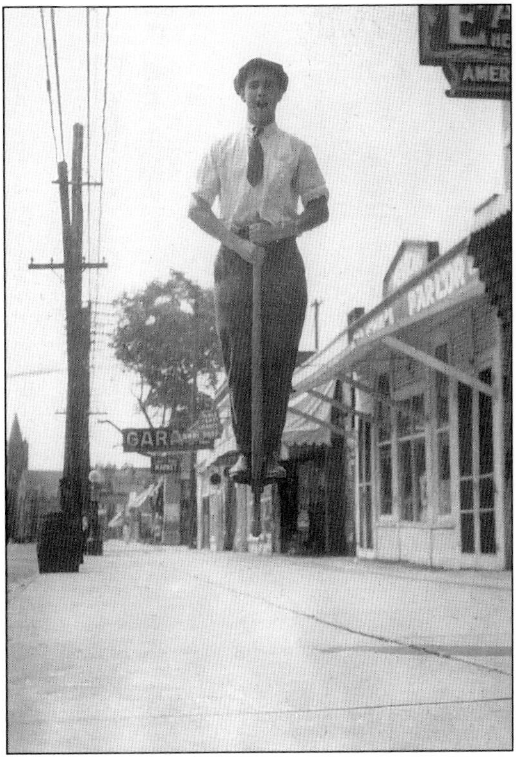

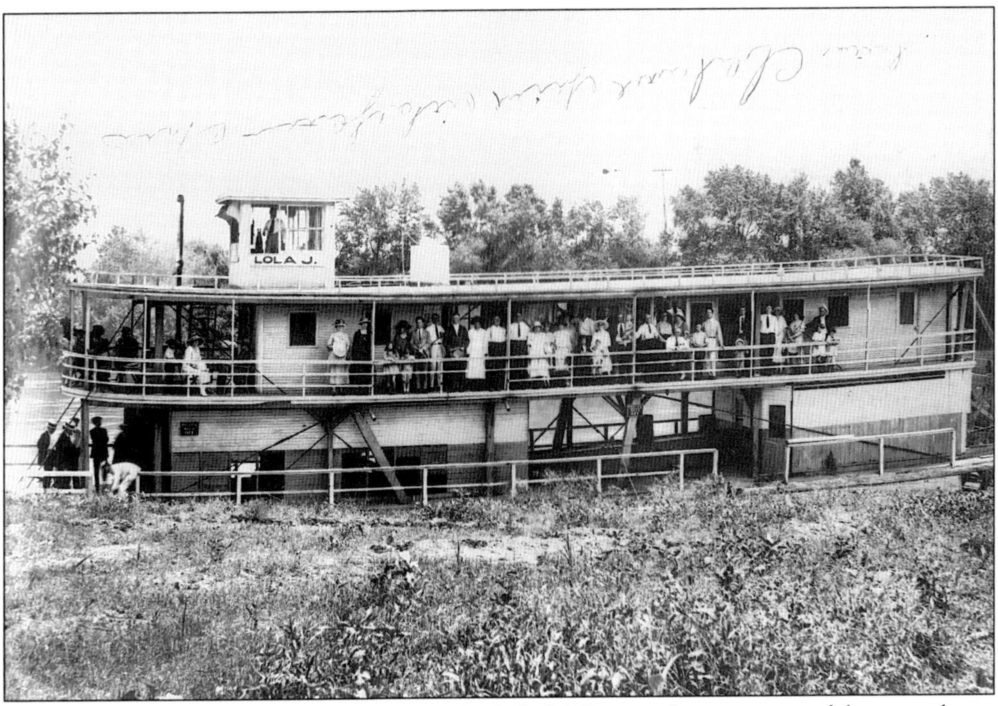

The group pictured here is taking a trip on the *Lola J*. This riverboat was one of the many boats to make the run from Rome, Georgia, to Gadsden on a regular basis. Sightseers came on such boats to view Noccalula Falls, a local tourist attraction.

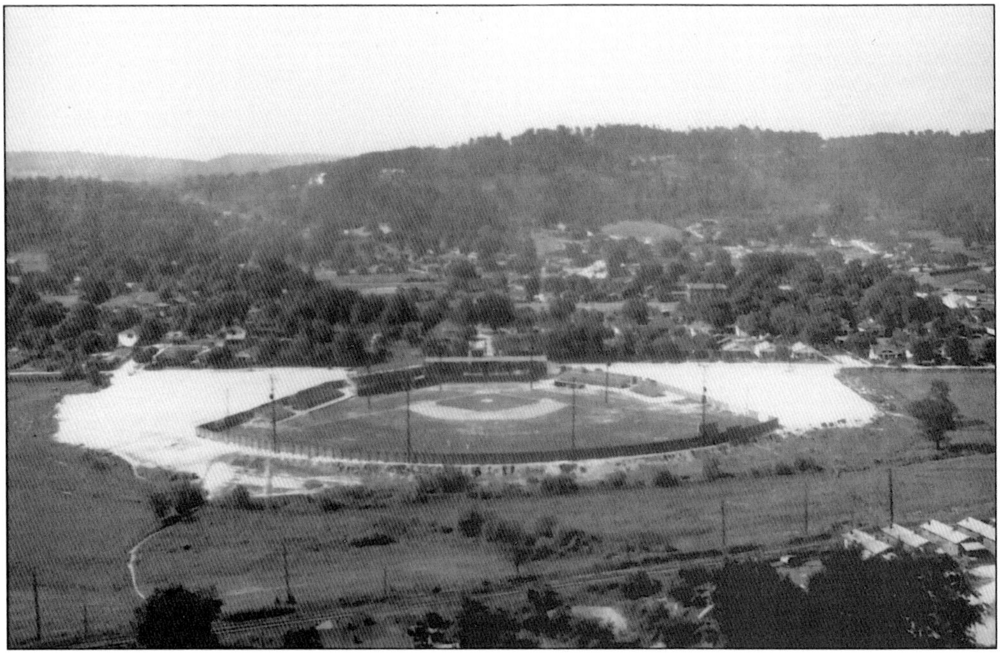

This aerial view shows the baseball park that was located at the present site of the Jack Gaston Sports Complex on Meighan Boulevard. This ballpark was home of the Gadsden Pilots during the 1940s. Presently the site contains a baseball park, a softball complex, and a basketball arena.

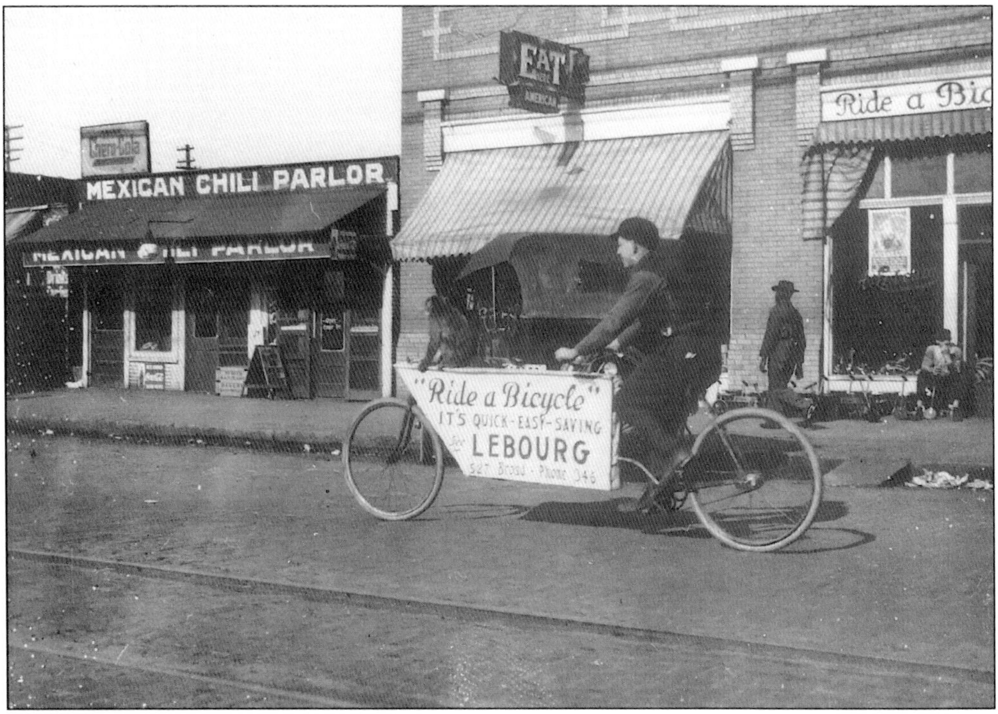

"Ride a bicycle" is the order of the day on this advertisement from the Lebourg Bicycle Shop. Adolph Lebourg would ride through downtown on an extra long bicycle with a monkey to advertise his store. Note the brick pavement and the streetcar tracks.

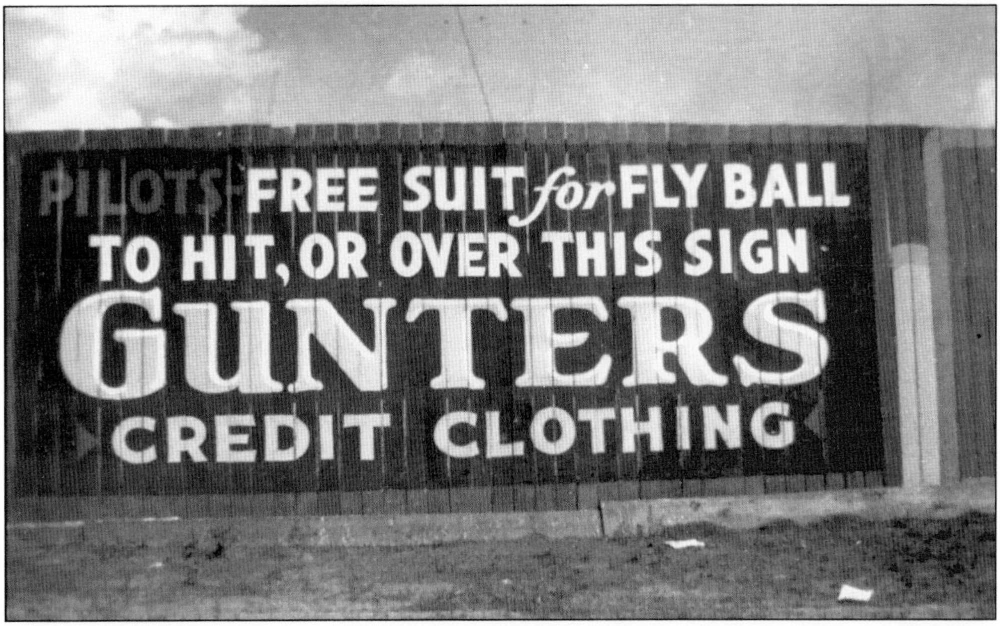

This sign was located in the outfield of the Gadsden ballpark where the Pilots played their home games. If a lucky batter hit the sign with a fly ball or hit a home run over the sign, he would win a free suit from Gunters, a local clothing store.

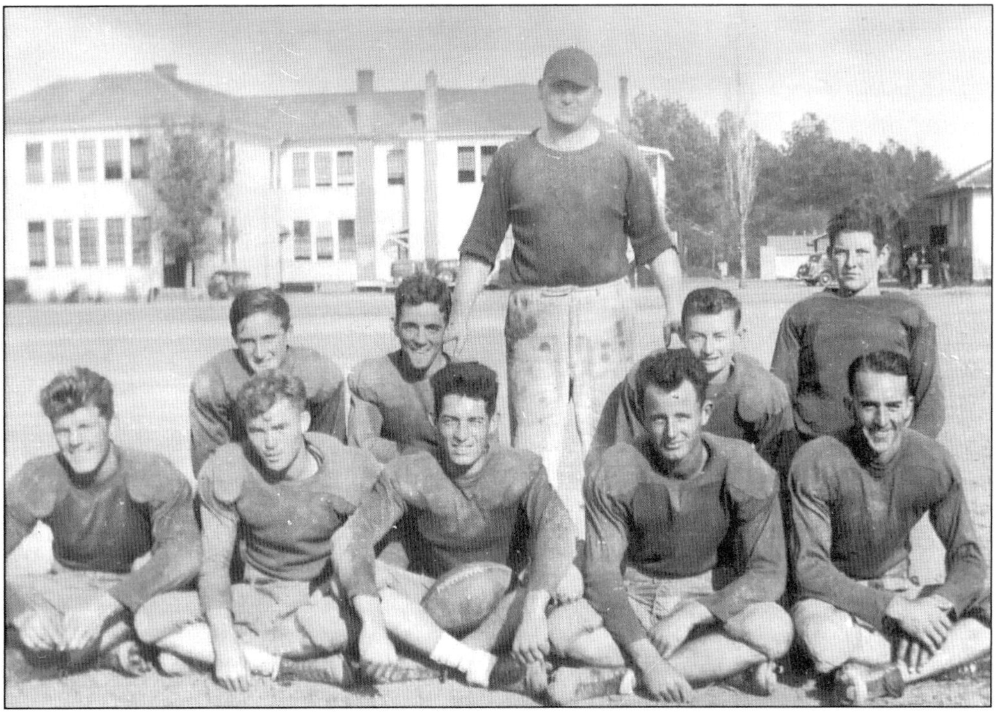

Pictured here are some of the members of the 1936 Glencoe "Yellow Jacket" football team. Seated from left to right are Roy Moore, Eugene McCoy, Robert Miller, Ellis Hulsey, and Loyce Robertson. Kneeling are Louis Joe Barnes, Earl Vowell, Bob Goode, and Sam Yancey. Coach Dewitt Dunn is standing behind the players.

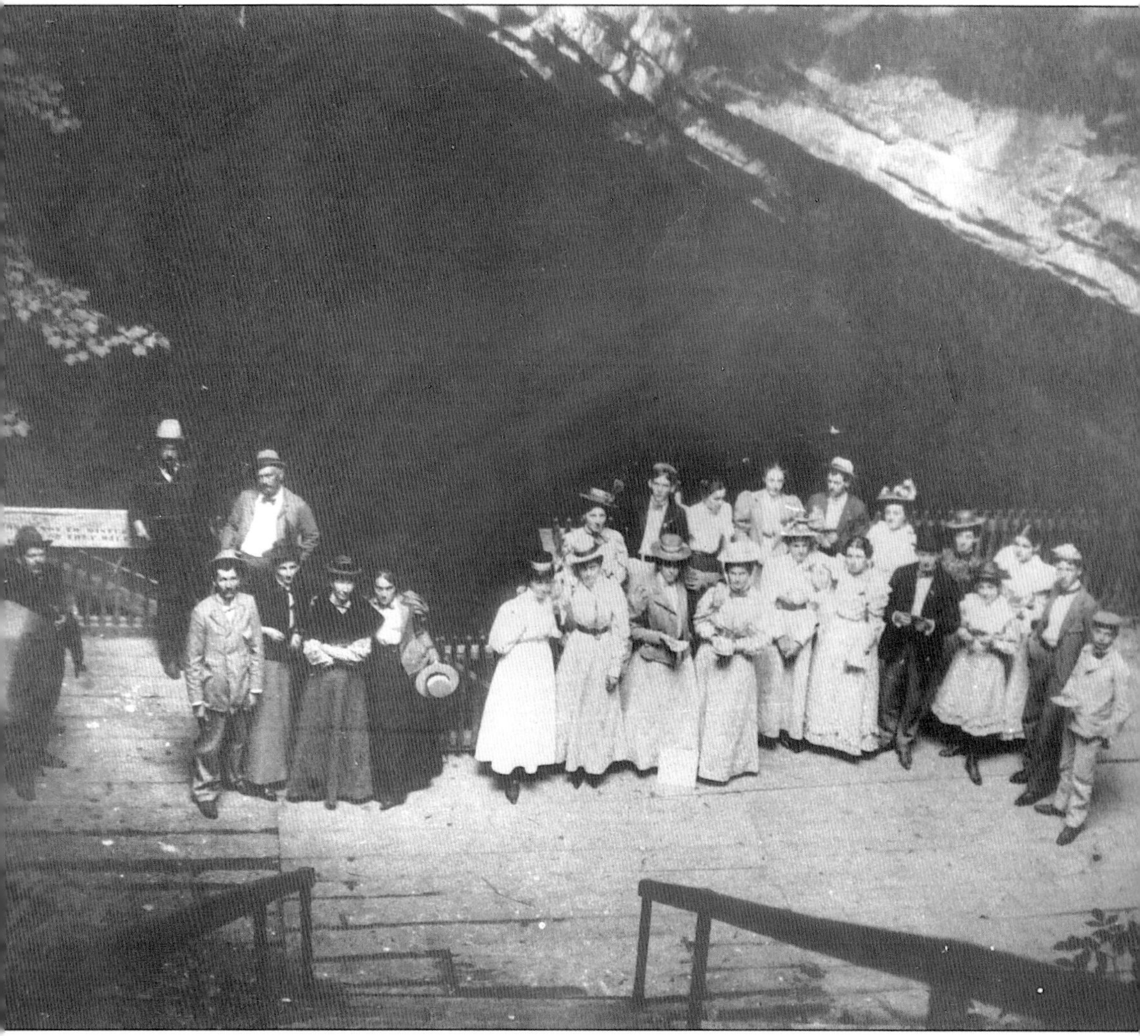

This rare photograph from the turn of the century shows a large group of people at the dance pavilion located at Noccalula Falls. The pavilion was a favorite place for tourists to gather in Etowah County during the early 1900s. Many dances were held beneath the beautiful waterfall. (Courtesy of Don Waite.)